Singing Sappho

Opera Lab: Explorations in History, Technology, and Performance
A series edited by David J. Levin and Mary Ann Smart

ALSO PUBLISHED IN THE SERIES

Music in the Present Tense: Rossini's Italian Operas in Their Time
Emanuele Senici

Singing Sappho

Improvisation and Authority in Nineteenth-Century Italian Opera

MELINA ESSE

The University of Chicago Press
Chicago and London

The University of Chicago Press, Chicago 60637
The University of Chicago Press, Ltd., London

Published 2021
Printed in the United States of America

30 29 28 27 26 25 24 23 22 21 1 2 3 4 5

ISBN-13: 978-0-226-74177-2 (cloth)
ISBN-13: 978-0-226-74180-2 (e-book)
DOI: https://doi.org/10.7208/chicago/9780226741802.001.0001

This book has been supported by the Donna Cardamone Jackson Endowment and Publications Endowment of the American Musicological Society, funded in part by the National Endowment for the Humanities and the Andrew W. Mellon Foundation.

Library of Congress Cataloging-in-Publication Data

Names: Esse, Melina, author.
Title: Singing Sappho : improvisation and authority in nineteenth-century Italian opera / Melina Esse.
Other titles: Opera lab.
Description: Chicago ; London : The University of Chicago Press, 2020. | Series: Opera lab: explorations in history, technology, and performance | Includes bibliographical references and index.
Identifiers: LCCN 2020027458 | ISBN 9780226741772 (cloth) | ISBN 9780226741802 (e-book)
Subjects: LCSH: Opera—Italy—19th century. | Sappho—Influence. | Opera—Greek influences. | Vocal improvisation (Music)—Italy—Philosophy—History—19th century. | Women singers—Italy. | Women singers—France.
Classification: LCC ML1733.4.E77 2020 | DDC 782.10945/09034—dc23
LC record available at https://lccn.loc.gov/2020027458

♾ This paper meets the requirements of ANSI/NISO Z39.48-1992 (Permanence of Paper).

for Julie and Katie—
in all kinds of weather, we stick together

Contents

INTRODUCTION

Before his death in 2014, classicist Stephen Daitz recorded himself reciting Sappho's first fragment, known as the "Ode to Aphrodite."[1] Or rather, he does more than recite. Instead, his voice swoops and skirls, its varied tones tracing the contours of melodies. Emphatic syllables beat out the poem's meter, while fricatives, sibilants, and rolled r's become added percussion. The effect, says Daniel Mendelsohn, is striking: "even without her lyre, Sappho *sings*."[2] Daitz's performance is only one of many attempts over the centuries to recover Sappho's lost music—and to make her newly relevant for contemporary audiences. Writing in the *New Yorker* in 2015, Mendelsohn suggests that Daitz's approach, alive to both poetic meter and the pitch-accented qualities of ancient Greek, is only appropriate, given that Sappho was the most celebrated "singer-songwriter" of her time. "Like Joni Mitchell or Bob Dylan," he explains, Sappho "wrote her music as well as her lyrics, and performed her songs in public. Ancient authors loved to quote lines of her work, but for all we know when they did so readers were [also] hearing certain famous melodies in their heads."[3]

But for eighteenth- and nineteenth-century commentators, it was not simply the melding of words and music that set Sappho apart—it was that she was thought to have composed her songs in the moment.[4] In other words, she was imagined first and foremost as an improviser, an ancient practitioner of an art that continued to be performed all over Italy. From its height in the eighteenth century to its decline in the nineteenth, the act of extemporizing poetry to musical accompaniment combined a Romantic love for the spectacle of impromptu creativity with a neoclassical attention to memory and the past. This "hybrid genre, halfway between poetry and theatre," in Antonella Giordano's words, shared important features with the world of opera.[5] The improvising poet, like the operatic singer, sought to move an audience with a powerful voice unfolding in the moment, sounding in a metrical cadence that could resemble chanting, recitative, or even lyrical song. Whether grappling with divas or star improvisers, however, historians have had trouble not only reconstituting the details of past improvisatory practices, but also, crucially, theorizing the relationship between oral and written in a way that does not merely drape the former in an aura of loss. Accounts of poetic improvisation over the nineteenth century often trace a trajectory of decay, with scholars pointing to both the rise of print culture and increasing criticism of improvisers as mere entertainers as factors in its eventual marginalization. Michael Caesar has explored how the growth of published transcriptions contributed to this decline, while Antonella Giordano places the blame on a seismic shift from a culture of listening to a culture of reading.[6]

The themes of loss and decay are echoed in histories of operatic improvisation. In 1824, the writer Henri Beyle (alias Stendhal) suggested that the composer Gioacchino Rossini, irked by the fact that one of his melodies "had grown completely unrecognizable" thanks to a singer's elaborations, resolved to write out all ornaments himself, insisting in an imagined internal monologue that "in future, no singer of mine shall ever have the slightest pretext for improvising a single *appoggiatura*."[7] Although Rossini's supposed decision to limit singers' ability to display their own improvisatory skills was a product of Stendhal's fancy (the composer continued to work closely with singers, and they continued to improvise on his scores), his assertion that Rossini took to writing down his ornaments in order to protect his scores from intervention continues to shape how nineteenth-century Italian opera is understood today. Improvisatory practices, so the story goes, gradually fell out of favor as operas came to be viewed as works more than events and operatic scores themselves became more immutable.[8] Hilary Poriss, for example, has argued that singers' long-standing habit of inserting their favorite arias into other operas started to "encounter resistance during the first half of the nineteenth century" as "theaters, publishers, and composers began to wrest control from singers." "Although this shift towards a text-based aesthetic took root only slowly in the realm of Italian opera," she writes, "newly blossoming concerns for authorial control and aesthetic purity" began to put pressure on singers to perform works "as written."[9] Susan Rutherford similarly posits a decisive shift around the middle of the nineteenth century, arguing that in addition to the decline of insertion arias, "demands for new arias that better fitted the singers' voices were refused; gradually, the composer gained ascendance and operas were no longer adjusted to display individual talents but became *in themselves* the dominant or fundamental component of the performance process; the composer was . . . refashioned as an Artist."[10] In such accounts, the singer's unique creative power is eclipsed by the rise of the composer's authority.

Singing Sappho explores the connections between operatic and poetic improvisation in order to complicate these narratives and to explore how gender became entwined with both newly emerging ideas of musical authorship and renegotiated relationships between text and performance in nineteenth-century Italy. A focus on improvisation would seem to allow us to recapture some of the lost contingency and frisson of live music and poetry before their concretization into systems organized around the production of texts. As part of a broader scholarly shift toward matters of performance, improvisation in theory and practice has become a topic of consequence in a number of fields, with conferences, journals, and edited volumes multiplying exponentially in the past two decades.[11] Indeed, we could even argue that improvisation has become a field in itself, thanks to the publication of the two-volume *Oxford Handbook of Critical Improvisation Studies* in 2016.[12] Whether in the arts or in everyday life, one of the most attractive aspects of improvisation has been the way it seems to offer a kind of freedom—whether from habit, convention, or oppressive social systems. Dana Gooley has noticed how this embrace of freedom in critical improvisation studies is indebted to nineteenth-century European Romantic rhetorics of improvisation.[13] In addition, scholars have looked to improvisation as a means to escape the hegemony of textual hermeneutics. In musicology, improvisation has seemed to provide a means to break away from the tyranny of the work-as-score, to reintegrate music's sounding, its visceral materiality in performance, into our scholarship. Instead of focusing on the metaphysical qualities of music, improvisation might, as Roger Moseley has argued, allow us to shift away from the literary, the documentary, and the representational and attend to the material, the algorithmic, and the performative.[14] But while Moseley's approach remains sensitive to the imbrication of improvisation with texts—in particular, the "painstaking conceptual, oral, kinesthetic, and material processes by which improvisation could be entextualized"—other scholarly investigations of improvisation tend to maintain a division between improvisatory practices and musical texts. Gooley takes an explicitly documentary approach, preferring to "avoid the limitations of prescriptions (treatise) and stylizations (scores), and maintain a focus on improvisation as performance,"[15] implying that real improvisation can be better accessed through "descriptive sources—press reviews, diaries, letters, archival sketches, and memoirs"—textual traces that seem to have a stronger evidentiary claim than scores and treatises. This book, however, argues that examining the connections between poetic and operatic improvisation, and especially the ways that discourses of improvisatory authorship gendered the creative process, allows a more nuanced story to emerge. Improvisation, as practiced in Italy in the first half of the nineteenth century, was inevitably bound up with a broad spectrum of texts (including scores and treatises) in complex ways. Invention in the moment sparked intense debate about relationships between author, text, and performance, and nowhere was this more evident than in the phenomenon of the *improvvisatrice*, or female poetic improviser, who was almost invariably described as a reincarnation of the divinely inspired Sappho.

In nineteenth-century Italy, the figure of Sappho became a nexus for ideas about gender and inspiration, writing and singing, and a catalyst for aesthetic projects that sought to marry the future with the past. By focusing on how Sappho was reimagined as a poetic improviser, singer, and operatic character, I shed new light on the radical changes taking place in opera and in improvisatory culture more broadly. Rather than uphold the notion that the increasing importance of the work concept did away with oral practices, I maintain that improvisatory values in fact shaped the transition to a more text-centric aesthetic. In other words, the dichotomy between spontaneity and fixity, between text and act, was not so clear as many accounts of this period imply. If improvisation located authority in the moment of performance, those spontaneous acts were imagined as creating poetic and musical authors as well—authors who became both models and foils for poets and composers. By exploring the iconic status of the Sapphic improviser, I offer new ways of understanding the period's shifting notions of operatic authorship. Ultimately, I argue that discourses surrounding the *improvvisatrice* were, paradoxically, used to carve out a new authority for opera composers just as improvisational practices were falling into decline.

Of course, in the decades since Roland Barthes's seminal 1967 essay "The Death of the Author," the view of the author as an individual creative agent whose intentions must be acknowledged has been subjected to thorough critique. But our understanding of authorship in the realm of opera is still incomplete. Matthew Head has argued that musicology, unlike literary studies, has displayed a "relative innocence" about authorship:

> we have no equivalent debate on the historical and theoretical construction of musical authorship. . . . [H]istorical changes in what an author "is" and "does" were long buried within a narrative of musical history emphasizing the development, or simply the changes, in musical style and form. [. . .] The cultural construction of composing, and the composer, makes little claim on the musicological imagination: the composer is, self-evidently, someone who composes, an activity driven, in our dominant accounts, by various proportions of creativity, economic necessity, and politics.[16]

Part of the reason musicology has remained largely untouched by debates about authorship no doubt has to do with crucial differences between literary texts and music, which requires performance to be fully realized and which allows for varying degrees of slippage between text and realization. Recent scholarship has attempted to complicate and broaden our view of operatic authorship by investigating how women composers negotiated and inhabited their positions as well as the ways that singers or performers have played vital roles in fashioning works.[17] I take a different approach: rather than simply broaden the category of "author" to include creative agents other than the composer, I argue that from its inception, the very notion of an operatic author was unstable and contingent, fluid and performative. Because the values of improvisation—spontaneity, brilliance, speed, collaboration, impermanence, and excess—lay at the very foundation of operatic practice, they often seemed to actively undermine the establishment of now-familiar notions of what an author should be. Debates about the status of the improviser in Italian culture were thus, at heart, debates about what an author is—or should be. While certain critics of improvisation rehearsed reasons that improvisers should be excluded from the realm of "true" poetry or literature, others venerated them for embodying quintessential Romantic values. By starting from the perspective that operatic authorship emerged from this concatenation of tensions and contradictions, and was an effect of both practice and discourse, my project illuminates why the notion of composer as primary creative agent became so powerful.

In nineteenth-century Europe, the Sapphic improviser was one of the most important flashpoints for tussles about authorship. From eyewitness descriptions of improvisers to self-fashioning by women writers and composers, Sappho was repeatedly invoked as a model for feminine creativity.[18] In fact, invocations of the famed poet could be thought of as a kind of defensive move designed to appease critics who saw the spontaneous creation of verses as frivolous or questioned women's place in the creative arts. But Sappho was a troublesome model—she was both admired ancestress and cautionary tale. As an icon of feminine authorship, she represented the perfect union of poetry and music and the ideal of creation in the moment. But her works were largely fragmentary or lost, leading to endless rewritings and retellings of her tale. Presented most often as a rebel to her sex and as a suicide (and later, as a sexual deviant for her same-sex affiliations), stories of Sappho display a simultaneous reverence for and discomfort with her agency—and indeed with the agency of creative women in general. Eyewitness accounts of famed eighteenth-century improviser Corilla Olimpica are a case in point. Like other writers who insisted that women were eminently formed for improvisation,

Corilla's critics wondered if her creativity were located in her sex. In a 1777 letter to a friend, Giovanni Cristofano Amaduzzi admitted that

> Whether these virtues be common to all women poets, owing to the greater sensitivity of their nerves, the greater elasticity and delicacy of their constitution and to some bizarre, exceptional relationship between the uterus and the mind, I know not; but I do know well that she has always seemed to me superior in her flights, her ardour, her images and her ideas to all the male poets I have heard in competition with her.[19]

If improvisation was imagined as a quasi-magical practice during which audiences could see and experience inspiration happening in the moment, women improvisers were often extravagantly praised but at the same time characterized as not participating in their own talent, as if their genius were accidental and unthinking. Amaduzzi's account of one of Corilla's performances deploys familiar images of inspiration as a suddenly erupting fire that acts *upon* the improviser:

> After having overcome her usual hesitation, or worry, she began her poem with a low voice, trying out all the ways for lighting the fire, always creating some sparks, but her verses lacked the merit of unity, and an orderly framework. Subsequently she unleashed the hidden fire, gradually towering over others and spread out in feelings, words, voice and gesture up to the point at which she burst into flames, which flared up making her a gigantic figure, disengaging herself, enrapturing her on high, almost uplifting her to face God Himself. Thus the speed of her reciting, the velocity of her expressions, the bliss of her thoughts and all her outward looking activities were the forerunners of that heavenly fire, which had descended upon her and acted on her without any precise, reflective cooperation on her part. Those who accompanied her with instruments had great difficulty in following her and her listeners, electrified by that contagious fire, could not avoid showing signs of such agitation and shock.[20]

Corilla's inspiration is depicted here as unpredictable, spontaneous, and as all-consuming as an inferno, and her improvisation as an admirable melding of all the expressive arts. This creative force does not destroy her—rather, it transfigures her, transporting her to divine heights. She is presented as a phoenixlike figure, or perhaps even as the raw material whose engulfing provides an astounding spectacle. The intensity of the experience for both performer and audience, however, is predicated on a kind of divestment or invited loss of control on the part of the performer herself. Corilla's humility (her "usual hesitation") allows her to achieve her art by giving herself over to a power greater than herself: from her first, tentative efforts to spark a creative flame through intentional action, she is portrayed as unleashing a hidden inner force that rises up to "descend upon her and act on her *without any precise, reflective cooperation on her part* [my emphasis]." Such accounts of improvisers—especially female improvisers—were common in the eighteenth and nineteenth centuries, fashioning a notion of the improvisatory author as one who is curiously divested of control over her own creative process and products.

Whether the force that inhabited the improviser was figured positively (as the holy fire of inspiration) or negatively (the remorseless influence of hoary clichés and poetic conventions), the perceived "emptiness" of the improviser (and her troubling effacement of individuality) has placed her in a difficult position. Even modern scholars have sometimes been hard-pressed to see the appeal and have been ready to take contemporary critiques of improvisation at face value, dismissing any contribution improvisers might have made to Italian culture. Concluding her 2018 study of the *improvvisatrice* in the eighteenth century, Antonella Giordano takes a pessimistic stance:

> Extempore poets had a very ambiguous nature: they presented themselves as the new bards, but were really only entertainers; indeed, in a society grounded in written culture, they could only be able manipulators of literary products made inflexible by tradition, devoid of their original function. It was precisely in this dysfunctional orality that they could play a legitimate role. The improvisers themselves were quite aware of this and never challenged official culture, only aiming to be accepted by it. It may well have been in the ambiguity of the role of the extempore poet, and in these apparent contradictions, that the success of the women improvisers lay. They could be tolerated by the moral prejudices of a society which, nevertheless, and in spite of the Enlightenment, remained deeply male-centred. On the other hand, persons who met considerable difficulties in being considered autonomous individuals could feel comfortable practising a phenomenon which drew upon a way of creating verse empty of individuality.[21]

The "ambiguous nature" of the improvisers that Giordano describes—they were icons of inspired creativity but also vessels for a dead tradition "empty of individuality"—is, of course, not merely a fact but instead the product of a discursive system that continues to value freedom and individuality above all else. Rather than take as a given the opinion of contemporary literary figures who denied improvisers the status of "true poets," I understand such anxieties about truth and falsity, tradition and innovation, as central to the improviser's cachet as nineteenth-century critics sought to define what an author was. Indeed, this feminized version of creativity and inspiration became one of the most potent models for Romantic artists to imitate, to absorb, and to transform.

Writing in 1751, poet and librettist Pietro Metastasio, a failed improviser himself, saw the fundamental problem with improvisation as an imbalance between form and content, an incongruity between inner and outer that inevitably drew it into the realm of theater. "The poet writing at leisure chooses his theme," he wrote, "examines its purpose, orders the chain of ideas that are to lead him naturally to this end, and makes use of meters and rhymes as obedient executors of his plan."[22] But "he who faces the challenge of extempore poetry, enslaved by these tyrannies," must

> make use of the minutes allowed to him to arrange the rhymes to be matched with those of his opponent, into which he slipped carelessly, and then hurriedly accept the first thought that enters his mind, suitable to be expressed by [the rhymes] albeit mostly foreign and on occasion in opposition to his subject. The former searches for clothes for the man at his convenience, while the latter hurriedly and frantically [searches] for the man for the clothes.

Because improvisation requires the ready use of conventional meters and rhymes, Metastasio suggests, there will inevitably be a mismatch between a subject and its expression. What is central (the poem's guiding idea) is unfortunately an afterthought, made to fit into an existing shell. If a good poet is like a skilled tailor—choosing and adapting the garment to fit the person—then an improviser is something like a desperate impresario, hunting for a last-minute understudy of roughly the right build who can be crammed into an empty costume and hustled on stage. This mismatch between form and content can persist, Metastasio argues, precisely because of poetic improvisation's proclivity for theatrical display—a spectacle of seeming inspiration that fools the senses with spontaneous bursts of creative activity. If the verses of these poets were written down and subject to sober judgment, however, they would tell a different story:

> If the extempore poet is barbarously enslaved by this inhuman lack of time, he is admittedly compensated by protection from the severity of his judges, who, blinded by flashes in the moment, have no room for examination . . . But if from the ear they were forced to pass on to examination by the eyes, oh how many Angelicas would show themselves with Orlando's breastplate, and how many Rinaldos with Armida's coif!

Metastasio's description recalls a burlesque parody of classical tragedy, or perhaps the world of eighteenth-century opera, where roles would indeed have been played by singers of a different gender. But his likening of poetic improvisation's incongruity between form and content to the destabilizing spectacle of cross-dressing is not incidental. Metastasio's gender confusion speaks to the problem of the improviser's much-vaunted receptivity. For male improvisers, such receptivity could be configured as effeminacy (perhaps it is no coincidence that Metastasio mentions the tale of Rinaldo, held captive as a love slave by the sorceress Armida) while female improvisers, no matter how much they might have been perceived as "vessels," were still subject to the criticism that they were performing authorship in inappropriate ways. One result of this gendered discourse about creativity is the emergence of a split between performance and creation that affected all performer-creators, men and women alike.

At least one critic saw the emergence of this split as a solution to the problem of improvisation. Writing in the *Biblioteca italiana* in 1816, Pietro Giordani unleashed a harsh critique of poetic improvisation, using the career of Tommaso Sgricci as an object lesson.[23] Throughout the lengthy essay, Giordani is concerned with making a firm distinction between improvisation—characterized by its speed, facility, casualness, and impermanence—and "true" poetic authorship, which is the result of deep study, thought, and time. Improvisation can never aspire to the status of true art because it is impossible, he argues, for something that is produced spontaneously to be anything other than shoddy. Improvisation is more properly understood as a parlor trick, a game for the salon. The very qualities that make it attractive to the public as a spectacle—the ability of improvisers to spontaneously pour forth a torrent of words—are the very characteristics that Giordani finds contemptible:

> To throw out of one's mouth some less than mediocre verses is the kind of habit that anyone can acquire easily . . . an orderly succession of rigorous thoughts . . . can never ever be obtained (no matter what the charlatans say) through *an impromptu fury*, or a spontaneous inspiration. There is no fury other than talent; no inspiration other than hard work.[24]

It is not solely ephemerality that is the problem. After all, other kinds of performance emerge in the moment and then disappear. In a curious sleight of hand, Giordani preserves the dignity of dancing, singing, and acting:

> Those three arts are capable of attaining real perfection, because they all have principles, rules, and exercises that require a long time of study to master . . . Where are the rules, the studies and the exercises of our improvisers? Should something universally denied—that beautiful things can come out of the recklessness of fate—be admitted and believed in just for their sake?[25]

Giordani characterizes improvised poetry as essentially too indebted to chance. It depended upon the arbitrary whims of audiences, who chose themes and subjects, and the very nature of the entertainment allowed no room for revision. Like Metastasio and many of his contemporaries, Giordani suggests that it is only in writing down verses that their true merit becomes evident. Speed of delivery, he argues, prevents the listener from truly judging the value of the verses and places the emphasis on dazzling display rather than thoughtful appreciation: "perhaps it is with prudent artifice that Sgricci falls breathless for going so fast in reciting his verses, so that the ear and the mind can follow him only with great difficulty; he knows that, were he to leave more space for judgment of the concepts and the sentences, he would have less benevolent judges: such a copious and rapid torrent of words, on the other hand, cannot lack a reaction of wonder."[26]

What is the solution to this sorry state of affairs? Giordani ends his essay by proposing that, while it should be permissible to "improvise a little (but shortly and moderately) in the company of a cultured gathering, and even get praised there . . . improvisation should never be the major entertainment of a people, nor the profession of many, nor the pride of our nation." Instead, improvisers should turn their considerable talents not to creating new verses in the moment, but to memorizing and performing existing masterworks, thus nurturing a true national pride:

> In the end, what is this bunch of people—who, not having taken the risk of becoming *tightrope walkers*, preferred becoming improvisers—supposed to do? Exterminate them we surely cannot. To force them to engage in some more useful professions could be right, but it would also be very harsh; isn't it possible to adjust that idle, restless and vagabond genius of the improviser for some practical purpose? We think that is possible. Do they wish to make a living of verses? . . . Let them be similar to the ancient *Rhapsodists* or to some of the *Troubadours* of the Middle Ages. Let them memorize some Dante, some Ariosto, or Tasso, or Metastasio; let them learn to pronounce perfectly, and to recite poetry with charm and decorum . . . these rhapsodists could fill the ears of people, rich and poor, with some Italian sounds; the public spirit would thus begin to house an Italian consciousness, which would nourish the faculty of conceiving—and perhaps even of expressing—some Italian thoughts. This would not be a contemptible part or manner of public education at all.[27]

In other words, improvisers should transform themselves into interpreters of a canon of great works instead of trying to win acclaim with their own feeble efforts. Since, Giordani implies, you cannot be a true author if you create poetry impromptu, improvisers should refashion themselves into vessels for others' ideas.

As the nineteenth century unfolded, the notion that performance and creation could be embodied in one individual gave way to a split between roles. Giordani's insistence that improvisers should dedicate themselves to reciting masterworks from memory thus speaks to a broad and seismic shift in the notion of authorship and indeed creative authority more generally. His critique attempts to limit the improviser's cultural power and curb the authority of spontaneous creation. It speaks to the emergence of the work concept, where art passes the tests of time and judgment only through its solidification into a fixed monument. It also speaks to the emerging division between performer and author. Both the anxiety concerning the over-exalted position of the improviser in Italian culture and Giordani's desire to reserve the title of poet for those who create works of lasting value are clearly linked to the world of opera. If Giordani's solution to improvisation's troubling lack of substance was to turn improvisers into vessels for masterworks, in the operatic world, the association of improvisatory values with authorship was so entrenched as to make this surgical separation impossible. Instead, improvisation had to be integrated, repressed, or subsumed into new ideas of authorship. Excavating these origins, I argue, allows us to see how the emerging ideology of the operatic work and the operatic author owes a surprisingly large debt to the textualization of improvisation and thus paradoxically originates from the very practice commonly pitted against it.

My first chapter, "History's Muse," explores how an aesthetics of reenactment and repetition—in realms of word, sound, and gesture—characterized the Italian improviser's art. Ranging freely from literature to antiquarianism, from *tableau vivant* to musico-poetic performance, I argue that in reenacting both history and memory, the poetic improviser became a living monument to Italy's cultured past and an icon of creative genius. Accounts of the improviser Rosa Taddei by the German poet Wilhelm Waiblinger, for example, tend to recapitulate themes familiar from Madame de Staël's wildly popular novel *Corinne, ou L'Italie* (1807), which dealt with the tragic fate of a poetic improviser who could not reconcile love and fame. Waiblinger, like Staël and so many others, saw the talent for poetic improvisation as quintessentially Italian. It may therefore be tempting to dismiss his portrait of Taddei as another example of what Alessandra Di Ricco has called the persistent "ethnic stereotype" of Italians as more spontaneous and natural. But certain of Waiblinger's preoccupations—his insistence that seeing Taddei improvise was like seeing a "Sappho," his emphasis on the physical suffering she endured for her art, and the way he highlighted both the spontaneity of her talent and her extensive learning—require more subtle attention. In addition, the seven transcriptions Waiblinger appended to his essay on Taddei are surprisingly melodic; to Taddei's nineteenth-century listeners, the link between poetic improvisation and the strophic ballad must have been audible. I show how the music Taddei chose to accompany her poetic effusions in 1820s Rome created a predictable mechanism for producing inspiration by giving the improviser time to recollect. An attention to its musical aspects, then, paints a different picture of poetic improvisation, one that focuses on the *improvvisatrice* as a personification of both personal and cultural memory. This aesthetic of reenactment and repetition means that rather than simply serving as an icon of Romantic genius and spontaneity, the poetic improviser embodied a shifting set of oppositions: spontaneous creation and rote memorization, author and muse, present and past. She is thus perfectly positioned to illuminate the changes in Romantic performance as the roles of composer and performer become more distinct.

The second chapter, "Corinna's Crown," explores the transformation of the poetic improviser into an operatic character. In Rossini's *Il viaggio a Reims* (1825), an occasional work performed in Paris for the coronation of Charles X, the heroine of Madame de Staël's *Corinne* makes a cameo appearance to mark the ephemeral nature of the event. By gesturing across the fourth wall in her hymns of praise to the king, the *improvvisatrice* also draws attention to the evanescent performance of diva Giuditta Pasta, who created the role of Corinne. This is in stark contrast to the character of the Countess, created by Laure Cinti-Damoreau, who exists firmly within the conventional world of florid showpiece arias. It may be tempting to think of these two characters as representing models of "bad" and "good" improvisation as they were defined in much of the critical discourse of the time: self-indulgent and flying free of semantic meaning versus divinely inspired and closely allied with text. Instead, I argue that the tensions between Corinna and the Countess, and between these two kinds of improvisational display, are better understood in the context of debates about the roles of singers and composers in determining what was appropriate improvisational intervention in the operatic text. Though it is common to assume that operas were becoming more and more fixed with the rise of the work concept and the ascendency of the composer's authority, I argue that close attention to the move toward textualization reveals a productive confusion between original and variant. The publication of complete opera scores was accompanied—even prefigured—by an explosion of singing treatises teaching ornamentation and by the publication of single arias that attempted to reproduce the individualities of specific singers' improvisational practices. In the operatic context, creating texts was a way to encourage the proliferation of variants, not hinder it. Finally, as Nicholas Baragwanath has shown, Italian conservatories taught composition via sung improvisation exercises, suggesting that the pedagogy and practices of singers and composers overlapped in crucial ways. Operatic authorship, ultimately, is thus like a game of musical chairs, with the composer, performer, librettist, and so on all circling around an empty seat.

My third chapter, "Divinely Inspired," explores a subtype of the Sapphic *improvvisatrice*—the priestess or sibyl—in Bellini's *Norma*. The paradox of the composer who was both spontaneous and studied reached an apex in a forged letter attributed to Bellini that describes his compositional process as akin to poetic improvisation. As Mary Ann Smart has argued, this account was central to the image of Bellini as a composer with a distinctive music-poetic voice who "worked painstakingly to fit music to words," an image belied, as she has shown, by his extensive self-borrowing.[28] I revisit Bellini's *Norma* through the dual figures of Ossian, the Gaelic bard whose "rediscovered" poetry influenced scores of northern-themed works, and the inspired priestess, embodied in Norma herself. Bellini's translational aesthetic—akin to Italian encounters with the works of Ossian—portrays the truly inspired artist as a medium for other voices. In addition, Bellini's attentiveness to the capabilities of Giuditta Pasta, the first Norma, makes his opera a polyvocal affair despite its reception as a masterful fusing together of influences into a singular compositional voice. In exploring the affinities between images of both composers and operatic priestesses as receptive vessels for divine influence, I complicate the emergence of the notion of the inspired operatic author, arguing that we must continue to hear the other voices these authors channeled.

The fourth chapter, "Saffo's Lyre," investigates the brief vogue for portraying improvising Sapphos on the operatic stage, focusing on Giovanni Pacini's 1840 opera *Saffo*. I show how borrowing the *improvvisatrice*'s cultural cachet to bolster the composer's reputation complicates accepted notions of the emerging ideology of *Werktreue* and the growing gulf between author and interpreter. I begin from the premise explored in the work of Yopie Prins: that creative works based on the Sappho myth were built around an empty center. Sappho was a problematic author, more lacuna than agent: a figure from the ancient past whose works were largely lost or existed in fragments. But nineteenth-century commentators saw Sappho as the mother of contemporary poetic improvisation, as the first *improvvisatrice*. Listening to and transcribing the work of living poetic improvisers created new texts that, like Sappho's, were already fragmented. But this aesthetic of transcription reconfigured the author as essentially a writer/scribe instead of a performer—as someone who tried to capture or record ephemeral performance for posterity. Italian writers, poets, and composers could thus hitch their own authorial wagons to Sappho's star, transforming her from author into muse. Taking Pacini's opera as a starting point, I explore how the figure of the *improvvisatrice* was fast becoming a kind of icon that pointed toward *another's* creativity, genius, and talent for spontaneous creation. Saffo herself became a tragic heroine known mainly for her suicide (attributed to her unrequited love for Phaon) rather than for her poetry. The story is more complicated than simple appropriation, however: Pacini's *Saffo* was composed during a time of transition. Composers and poets touted their ability to write swiftly and spontaneously (in other words, to create like improvisers) while at the same time contradicting these statements. Pacini's autobiography claimed that he "improvised" the final act of *Saffo*, so quickly was it composed. But this claim was followed by the assertion that Pacini was above all a composer of "elaborate works" and "well-thought-out productions." Such ambivalence about operatic authorship suggests that it was in the midst of an identity crisis.

The fifth chapter, "A Sapphic Orpheus," shifts from Italy to France in order to focus on Pauline Viardot, the influential singer, composer, and pedagogue whose career is in many ways a culmination of the themes explored in the previous chapters. Her performance as Sapho in Gounod's opera of the same name prompted Berlioz to cast her in the role of another lyre-toting poet: Orpheus, in Berlioz's revision of Gluck's *Orphée*. Both these projects illuminate the limits and possibilities for women composer-performers in the mid-nineteenth century by highlighting the changing meanings of operatic collaboration. It is in these messy collaborations that the collision of cultural ideas about muses and creators, singers and courtesans, is made apparent. In addition to her skillful melding of Italianate improvisatory values with declamatory delivery in her singing, Viardot's biography overlaps suggestively with the Sappho myth, particularly in the way her life was understood to swing between the twin poles of creative work and romantic love. Gounod's *Sapho* was composed largely at Viardot's country house, and commentators have speculated about how much she contributed to the score. The newly acquired Viardot collection at Harvard's Houghton Library sheds light on the opera's complicated genesis. I explore how an unusual decision about the opera's final scene recasts Sapho as a quasi-domestic figure, whose musical utterances seem to emerge from an intimate parlor setting. Viardot's collaboration with Gounod, however, ended in a tangle of accusations and gossip about the propriety of their relationship. In exploring this biographical drama, I suggest that close working relationships, and with them the notion of the composer's muse, were beginning to be viewed in a different light. As Margaret Reynolds has pointed out, Sappho becomes increasingly sexualized in the latter half of the nineteenth century.[29] The drama of Viardot's precarious reputation thus attests to new, more conflicted instances of the Sapphic trope. No longer the distant, unattainable Beatrice or Laura of the Renaissance, the muse was sliding into the role of courtesan, at the beck and call of the artist who sought to capture her in his chosen medium. Such a shift, I argue, contributed greatly to the ever-widening—and increasingly gendered—gulf between creators and interpreters.

Each of these chapters explores the complicated and gendered relationship between the written and the performed in nineteenth-century Italian opera, engaging broader questions about the usefulness of improvisation and authorship as theoretical frameworks in contemporary musicology. Bound up as it was with tensions between text and performance, fluidity and fixity, and pattern recognition and memory, the reception of Italian improvisers was the birth of critical improvisation studies. At a time when the term "improvisation" has been applied to everything from the actions of emergency response teams to consuming media, it is instructive to revisit improvisation's historical origins.[30] Listening for Sappho in discourses of nineteenth-century improvisation alerts us to a dynamic between gender and authorship that has been unheard in accounts of improvisation that focus on the practice as primarily outside of or in opposition to texts. And understanding the nineteenth-century propensity to portray Sappho as an improviser rather than simply a writer allows us to perceive how nineteenth-century authorship was bound up with notions of performativity, contingency, and reenactment. The Sapphic improvisers that so fascinated critics, composers, listeners, readers, and performers were an occasion for not just admiration or critique, but for song. Sappho was more than a role performed by singers on the operatic stage—she was a spur to poetic creation, a model author, an instrument through which others sounded their own creative individuality. In what follows, then, I add my voice to theirs, singing Sappho in a new era and to a new melody.

1

History's Muse: The Spectacle of Poetic Improvisation

When the German poet Wilhelm Waiblinger first encountered the famous improviser Rosa Taddei (fig. 1.1) in Rome, he described the experience as something like time travel: ". . . we felt transported to an ancient Greek festival of muses, or a Virgilian idyll-world; we believed we had seen a Sappho." His lengthy essay on Taddei, published three years after the 1827 encounter, mixes homage with detailed consideration of the art of poetic improvisation. In breathless prose, he strives to capture the intense, quasi-operatic experience of watching Taddei compose poetry in the moment:

> . . . the first appearance of the *improvvisatrice* is disquieting; one watches her, so to speak, like a sacrifice, and as her deathly pallor points to the powerful effect that such an elevated mental state exerts on the physical part of the inspired one, the entire audience falls silent and listens and watches the pensive, swaying woman, while she lulls the harp into the magic of rhythm; and so every heart pounds when she suddenly steps forward and begins to sing. Now the paleness gradually disappears from her face; fire and inspiration breathe out of it; verse follows verse inexorably, the one calling forth the next, no rhyme without its complement; the eye of the sibyl gazes, wandering, into the infinite; the most violent mime play accompanies the song and its often dramatic content; and when she sometimes—though quite rarely—errs and has to repeat the verse, it only reminds us that she is active, that she is a poet, a creator, and does not merely execute what is no longer living.[1]

By the time Waiblinger witnessed the theatrical display of Taddei's divine possession, improvising poets were weighed down under a mass of literary description—and women improvisers in particular occasioned the most comment. The 1807 novel *Corinne, ou L'Italie* by Madame de Staël made the figure of the female improviser, or *improvvisatrice*, into an icon and spawned

FIGURE 1.1 Rosa Taddei. Engraving, 1836. Muller Collection, Music Division, New York Public Library for the Performing Arts, Lenox and Tilden Foundations. Used by permission.

countless literary imitations. The title of Staël's novel perhaps said it best: to the rest of Europe, the *improvvisatrice* and Italy were simply synonymous.[2] Such an association had a long history. Since the eighteenth century, poetic improvisers—who chanted or sang extemporaneous poetry, often to musical accompaniment—were, along with trips to Pompeii and the opera, one of the main attractions for travelers making the Grand Tour. The men and women who engaged in poetic improvisation performed on the streets and in salons, and their art was depicted as a "foreign curiosity," somehow quintessentially Italian, by tourists and expatriates.[3] Indeed, the word "improvise" made its way into English thanks to tourist encounters with these poets. The *improvvisatrice* thus helped solidify what Alessandro di Ricco has described as an "ethnic stereotype": she personified a cluster of connected qualities that depicted Italians as spontaneous, natural, and rooted in the glorious Greco-Roman past.[4]

The *improvvisatrice*, therefore, poses a methodological challenge because so many of the accounts describing the practice of poetic improvisation were penned by outsiders, especially British and German visitors to Italy. For these commentators, the musicality of the Italian language seemed to melt easily into both poetry and song, and this imagined union between tone and word made the improviser attractive to Romantics of all stripes. Even today, poetic improvisers are remembered chiefly for their influence on foreign poets; Angela Esterhammer, for example, is primarily interested in the Italian practice of poetic improvisation for the way it informed the work of Northern European Romantic poets.[5] But there is more to the story. By the nineteenth century, poetic improvisation had moved from the salon to the stage, becoming a multimedia event that encompassed not only extemporaneous poetry, but also impromptu theatrical scenes, dramatic gesture, and above all, music. In exploring the intersection of all these performative modes, we can complicate the image of the *improvvisatrice* as a kind of divinely touched muse whose primary importance was her effect on other, more lasting artists. To do so, we need to follow a number of threads that converge in improvisational practice, and indeed, converge in Waiblinger's description of Taddei. First, the competing images of creator and muse in the reception of female improvisers highlight inherent tensions in contemporary notions of authorship. Second, the *improvvisatrice*'s dual roles as icon of creativity and midwife to the creativity of others intersected with the widespread notion that Italy was an exotic land where the past could be accessed and that Italy's women were ideally suited to revive it. Finally, I explore how the music used in poetic improvisation, a vital aspect of the art that has received little attention, played a crucial role in the *improvvisatrice*'s performance of embodied memory.[6]

In this chapter, I juxtapose fictional and actual accounts of poetic improvisation—from Madame de Staël's *Corrine, ou L'Italie* to responses to Rosa Taddei—in order to set the stage for this book's exploration of the *improvvisatrice*'s forays into the world of opera. By focusing on both the practice and reception of poetic improvisation, I seek to delineate a series of interrelated shifts in notions of performance and authorship taking place in nineteenth-century opera, as scores and works begin to vie with ephemeral performance for moral weight. Above all, by focusing on poetic improvisation as a theatrical event, I draw out the importance of reenactment and repetition in Romantic performance. While the centrality of spontaneity and inspiration in the art of the *improvvisatrice* appears to make her the perfect object of the Romantics' veneration, I argue that poetic improvisation owed just as much to mechanistic repetition and replication as it did to originality. This is evident in the fact that discourses of improvisation are crucially centered around the problematic role of memory. Contemporary accounts stress the importance of improvisers' prodigious memories but also worry about how memory might work at cross-purposes to spontaneous performance. Improvisers, it seems, were often understood as marvelous technologies of inscription in their own right. Experiences of repetition and reenactment—which, from contemporary accounts, were just as crucial in improvisation as was extemporaneity—helped prepare the way for the textural proliferation that would begin to threaten improvisational practices over the course of the century.

"... she is a poet, a creator, and does not merely execute ..."

Poetic improvisation was practiced by men as well as women, of course, and male improvisers were also models of Romantic creativity.[7] But, owing to the meteoric rise of *improvvisatrici* such as Corilla Olimpica in the late eighteenth century and the widespread popularity of Staël's *Corinne,* the most iconic improvisers were female. Ugo Foscolo claimed in 1826 that "it appears that the sweetness of women's voices, the mobility of their imagination, and the volubility of their tongues, would render extemporaneous poetry better fitted to them than to men."[8] Paola Giuli has noted that "the new mystique of the poet improviser, with its emphasis on divine inspiration, lent itself to a gendered interpretation that favored women's emergence."[9] Women were understood as exemplary improvisers precisely because their supposed receptivity made them more amenable vessels for an inspiring force that originated from outside themselves. Yet it is clear that discourses surrounding the *improvvisatrice* display a certain tension between receptivity and invention, between muse and creator, and are thus perfectly situated to illuminate changing notions of creativity and authorship in both poetic and musical milieux.

Waiblinger's account of Rosa Taddei embraces this seeming contradiction by emphasizing the medium-like aspect of Taddei's performance while also praising her as "a poet, a creator" who "does not merely execute."[10] His account echoes many others that admire the *improvvisatrice* for her own talent while at the same time suggesting that she is a vessel for a higher power. Despite this, or perhaps because of it, the *improvvisatrice* became an attractive model for writers. If the real *improvvisatrice* Corilla Olimpica (Maria Maddalena Morelli, 1727–1800) inspired the fictional Corinne, Corinne herself was, in turn, a source of inspiration for countless women, whose literary efforts transformed Europe, in Patrick Vincent's words, into "a continent of

Corinnes."[11] After the publication of *Corinne*, it would seem impossible to discuss the *improvvisatrice* in terms other than the ones Staël laid down. Indeed, Waiblinger's account of Rosa Taddei bears more than a passing resemblance to passages in Staël's novel.

Corinne, a hybrid of romance and travel narrative, tells of the doomed love affair between the eponymous heroine and Lord Oswald, a melancholy Scotsman. Oswald's northern reserve and conventionality cannot accommodate Corinne's southern exhibitionism, and in the end he marries the docile girl who was his father's choice. From the very first scene that introduces Corinne—her crowning at the Capitol in Rome and improvisation on the subject of Italy's greatness—the problematic nature of female authorship is apparent. While the reader is treated to long passages of speculation about Corinne's character and appearance, Staël chooses not to reproduce the poetess's Italian verses directly. Rather, Corinne's improvisations are, Staël admits, "only imperfectly rendered in prose." They are presented, so to speak, at one remove, which inevitably mutes their immediacy and power.[12] Staël's decision to render Corinne's improvisations in prose summaries is, of course, an eminently practical choice—one that neatly sidesteps the problem of how to integrate long passages of Italian poetry into a novel published in French. But it has both puzzled and distressed scholars. Of Corinne's improvisation at the Capitol, Madelyn Gutwirth complains, "The prosaic quality of the passage is painfully evident. The syntax is flat; passives make the stanzas static; there is a nearly total and murderous absence of imagery."[13] Gutwirth further argues that "Corinne's improvisations are, in terms of craft and of the task she set herself, the poorest part of Mme. de Staël's novel, and the irony of the greatest conversationalist of her age failing to render the pulse of live improvisation is fully realized."[14] The novel ultimately suggests that Corinne's improvisations are inaccessible to the reader, illustrating the problem of representing the improviser's art in a written account. We could see this moment of "failure"—and Staël's admission that even her own prose falls short—as only highlighting the fact that improvisation relies upon live social context for its immediacy and power. Staël does, however, lavish novelistic detail on framing Corinne's improvisation. The drama of the scene lies not in the act of performance per se but in its human relationships—namely, the first meeting of the lovers Corinne and Oswald. The scene at the Capitol depicts Corinne's skill at crafting spontaneous poetry as relational, motivated by her sympathetic engagement with another's plight. Noticing Oswald's melancholy, she alters the form and theme of her improvisation to bring the stranger comfort. Corinne's poetic triumph is thus linked, in Staël's narrative, to her empathetic connection to her listeners.

Such an emphasis on the social relationships that underpin the poetic improviser's art recalls her origins in the academy and the salon.[15] The eighteenth-century practice of improvising poetry in smaller, often domestic, settings helps explain why the reception of nineteenth-century improvisers so often swings between competing images of the *improvvisatrice* as author and as muse. The salon in particular was a site of both feminine accomplishment and feminine receptivity. Women were the honored dedicatees of others' poems, as well as hostesses, listeners, and facilitators of artistic production. But they were also creators in their own right, and the salon helped nurture the reputation of women as gifted poets.

In eighteenth-century Rome, salons emerged partly to serve an ambassadorial function—visiting women tourists needed places to gather and socialize in the evenings—and partly as a secular response to the declining power of the church. They soon became a venue in which genteel Italians and foreign visitors could engage in the business of politics, participate in the arts, and above all, converse. Maria Pia Donato has focused on the salon as a forum for women to exercise influence in the development of a new public sphere. She argues that

> By the end of the eighteenth century, women played a fundamental role in Roman public life in ways that they had not done at the century's beginning: they created a greater space in which secular conversations about culture could occur and, in turn, created opportunities for themselves to become active participants in this new definition of culture. The salon was the primary venue for this transformation.[16]

The growing impact of salon hostesses on culture and politics did not go unnoticed. Alessandro Verri, the author of a popular novel about Sappho, noted that Roman women often used their salons to influence church and court officials; he preferred, however, salons after the French model, where women rarely led the conversation, but instead served as its fulcrum.[17] Perhaps Verri had in mind the salon run by his lover, the Marquise Gentili Boccapaduli (Margherita), who seems to have met his requirements.[18] Boccapaduli is remarkably self-deprecating in describing her role as facilitator. Despite the many learned men she welcomed into her home and the variety of musical and theatrical events she hosted, she discounted her own abilities. "I always remained ignorant," she wrote, "and if some little dusting of knowledge adhered to me, it was the effect of having had the pleasure of frequenting educated and learned persons from whom I was able to take an idea or two."[19] Boccapaduli here lays out one of the central roles for salon hostesses: curious but not savants, their interests ranged widely and they prided themselves on bringing the creative projects of others to maturity. The salon of Maria Cuccovilla Pizzelli is another case in point. Contemporary commentators such as Giovanni Gherardo De Rossi described Pizzelli as an accommodating hostess who adapted herself to the taste of every visitor, while Cesare Stasi emphasized her "profound" and penetrating conversation on literary topics and hailed her as "an oracle of those who aspired to the rank of author."[20] Alfieri's tragedies had their first airing here, and Pizzelli's salon became, Donato notes, a "private testing ground," free of censors or other theatrical bureaucracies, where artists could present their work before an audience—and cultivate a group of sympathetic supporters—before moving into larger spheres.[21] Here we see the *salonnière* imagined as muse, who both inspires and evaluates the works of her circle.

"By means of the salon," Donato observes, "women became the embodiment of a *general* public, very different from the old republic of letters, gifted with judgment without having any specialized competences."[22] Both Boccapaduli and Pizzelli described themselves in receptive terms, "keeping the 'modest' role of listener and placing [themselves] at the service of the authors who frequented" their gatherings.[23] But the networks of social power woven by salon hostesses also helped women enter the ranks of professional artists. The salon was a vital venue for women who made a living from their talents and could become the launching ground for those who wanted to move on to bigger stages. Salon hostesses often facilitated these careers. The improvisers Fortunata Fantastici and Teresa Bandettini, for example, came to Rome and sought out Angelica Kauffmann, who hosted a very important salon for artists of all kinds.[24] As De Rossi noted: "I recall having heard both the one and the other of these able women improvise in Kauffmann's house, and neither sang better than in those moments: and indeed their inspiration had to heat up and catch fire in a place which might almost be called a temple of female glory."[25] While Donato's study clearly seeks to acknowledge the importance of the behind-the-scenes salon hostesses, she seems, at times, to take their self-deprecation at face value, finding more to admire in women who were actual creators.[26] Such a perspective does little justice to the dialogic nature of salon culture, where distinctions between author or performer and audience, listener and speaker, were by nature shifting and fluid. In these domestic settings, participants might alternately recite or improvise, listen, converse, and critique. The later distinction between "auteur" and "reception" studies is thus incompatible with the world of the salon, where boundaries between the roles of creator and muse were often blurred. Especially in the case of poetic improvisation, authorship emerged from this social context of exchange.

Even as the practice of poetic improvisation moved from salon to stage, its roots in the conversational exchanges of the salon remained. Poetic improvisation was above all an event—one that drew spectators into a participatory dialogue with the extemporizing poet. Taddei performed to enthusiastic crowds and, as was typical for improvisers, took her subjects from the audience. Waiblinger tells his readers how a typical evening unfolded. Anyone attending the *accademia* had the right to submit a theme. The themes were then vetted by a priest, who made sure all the subjects were appropriate. Next, Taddei would read aloud the themes—at this point Waiblinger noted that "most people in the theater haven't a refined sense of poetry; normally mythological and historical themes are repeated countless times."[27] He continues: "According to tone and content she'll determine this or that verse form, and, throwing them [the themes] in a box, she presents them to the public to draw, and after the themes are chosen, the *improvvisatrice* begins her performance."[28] Her Italian audience, he notes, is intensely involved in the process: they "seek to find rhymes with her, and when, in a difficult spot, she succeeds in finding a beautiful idea or a fortunate ending, there is universal delight."[29]

Interaction between performer and audience thus remained central as improvisation became a theatrical event, but this change of venue shifted the practice into a more extroverted phase, with superhuman performers enthralling audiences with the spectacle of creative effort. Waiblinger, as we have seen, imagined Taddei as a sort of divinely inspired priestess who offers herself up as a sacrifice to divine inspiration. Angela Esterhammer has maintained that such accounts tend to emphasize the visual and theatrical aspects of improvisation over its poetic content, as if the sight of a pale young woman grappling with words was the primary attraction. Esterhammer has argued that in Waiblinger's description of Taddei as an "Arcadian maiden" at a private *accademia* organized for forty German artists unable to follow the *improvvisatrice*'s Italian, the "visual and even voyeuristic nature of the performance is heightened to the utmost."[30] Such accounts overlap with the idea of the Romantic artist as a victim or slave to art. Waiblinger's insistence that Taddei is admirable because she is an "active . . . creator" and not merely an executant neatly captures the doubleness expressed by the figure of the improvising poet. She is creator and performer, and, in this sense, the *improvvisatrice* is always both the heroine of her own theatrical struggle—complete with the "violent mime play" of her gestures—and the author of it.

". . . we thought we had seen a Sappho . . ."

Poetic improvisation was alluring not only for the spectacle of creative exertion that it staged but also because it seemed to reenact or re-embody a treasured past. In displaying their receptivity to the spark of divine inspiration, improvisers also performed their ability to channel the shades of history. We could say that the *improvvisatrice* embodied memory, and memory of poetry's origins more specifically, as the repeated comparisons between nineteenth-century improvisers and Sappho make clear. Waiblinger's description of Taddei as a reincarnation of Sappho had, not surprisingly, a precedent in Staël's novel. With her lyre, poetic talent, and tragic fate, *Corinne* makes overt reference to the Sappho myth, a story that Staël recapitulated just a few years later in her five-act drama *Sapho* (1811). Indeed, Corinne is laden with the accoutrements of classical antiquity; Staël's chosen name for her heroine not only refers to the *improvvisatrice* Corilla Olimpica but also recalls the ancient Greek poet Corinna.[31]

In what is arguably *Corinne*'s most important scene of improvisation, the spectacle of feminine creativity is played out on ancient terrain. Here, Corinne's sung, extemporized poetry, which she accompanies with her lyre, is explicitly linked both to the picturesque and to southern Italy's classical past. The performance takes place against the backdrop of Vesuvius and the Bay of Naples—famously depicted in François Gérard's 1819 painting (fig. 1.2). Staël sets the scene as meticulously as any travel writer, making the lines of influence between spontaneous performance and antiquity transparent:

> From the top of the little hill which juts out to sea and forms Cape Miseno, there is a perfect view of Vesuvius, the Bay of Naples, the islands scattered about in it, and the countryside extending from Naples to Gaeta. In short, it is the region in the world where volcanoes, history, and poetry have left [the] most traces. So, by common accord, all Corinne's friends asked her to take *the memories aroused by these places* as the subject for the verses she was about to sing. She tuned her lyre and, in a faltering voice, began.[32]

By framing Corinne's improvisation in such a way, Staël suggests that the *improvvisatrice* possesses a special receptivity to the spirits of the past that inhabit the landscape. Corinne is thus a kind of medium who performs her sensitivity and translates "the memories aroused by these places"—in other words, the felt and experienced upwelling of the past—into a display for the assembled company.

Corinne's long poem (the prose description runs several paragraphs) moves from melancholy memories of the famous ancients who walked the region—Tiberius "disarmed by old age," Cicero's death, Agrippina's tomb, and Pliny consumed by Vesuvius—to a series of meditations on mortality.[33] These thoughts lead her inevitably to despair (she senses the imminent demise of her own affair with Oswald), and Corinne breaks off her poem. Here Staël treats the reader to

FIGURE 1.2 François Gérard, *Corinne au Cap Misène*, 1819. Oil on canvas. Musée des Beaux-Arts, Lyon, France. Album / Art Resource, NY.

a tableau-like interlude: "At this point Corinne paused . . . All those gathered together there for the festivities cast branches of myrtle and laurel at her feet. The gentle, pure moonlight made her face more beautiful; the fresh sea wind blew her hair about in a picturesque manner, and nature seemed to enjoy adorning her."[34] As Corinne resumes, extemporizing on lost love, she "no longer divid[es] her song into eight-line stanzas," and instead gives herself "up to an uninterrupted flow."[35] She reaches greater and greater heights of inspiration and agitation, ultimately collapsing in a swoon. Though the Neapolitans in the party are nonplussed by this display of sentiment, the English in the audience

> were filled with admiration. . . . They were delighted to see melancholy feelings expressed in this way with Italian imagination. The beautiful Corinne, whose animated features and lively expression were destined to depict happiness, this daughter of the sun, beset by secret sorrows, was like those flowers which are still fresh and brilliant but which a black spot, caused by a fatal prick, threatens with an early end.[36]

Staël's association between the spectacle of natural beauty and the spectacle of feminine creative excess could be understood as a commentary—or cautionary tale—on the tenuous nature of female authorship. While the scene is certainly a celebration of spontaneous creation, it is also shot through with images of mortality and with an understanding of scenery as reliquary. Fashioning verses on the dead heroes and unlamented heroines of antiquity, Corinne is herself marked for death. The final lines of her outpouring rail against Fate, that "involuntary power which plunges [poets] into misfortune" and predetermines their tragic end.[37]

Here a focus on the unrepeatable event is juxtaposed with the gloomy content of Corinne's improvisation, as if the point of her own performance is to recite herself into history—to become one of the company of tragic ancients and a monument, still and white as she swoons. Though it is Corinne's nature to throw herself wholeheartedly into both love and poetry, she is unable to be both a famous improviser and Oswald's beloved—the two roles cannot be reconciled. Her improvisation at Cape Miseno reveals her to be a frail vessel for the genius that inspires her; the dueling forces of poetry and romantic love undo her. The self-destructive nature of Corinne's creativity recalls depictions of the tragic, Romantic male artist, but the fact that her destruction becomes a pleasurable spectacle for her voyeuristic audience highlights the gendered inflection of Staël's portrayal of the doomed poet.

The elision of the feminine with the antique that characterizes Staël's Corinne was essential, Chloe Chard has argued, to Grand Tourist encounters with Italy's past. She argues that "by selecting objects of commentary that bear the imprint both of the antique and of a version of the feminine, the traveller is able to affirm with double insistence that the topography does offer the allurement of mysterious otherness."[38] Because both women and antiquity seem to resist inquiry, the feminine is employed as a metaphor for difference and inaccessibility.[39] Many travelers' accounts feature mysterious women (often portrayed as uncannily resembling classical statues) who conveniently emerge to lend an air of mystery or embody the antiquity of a place. For example, in Alphonse de Lamartine's 1825 poem "Le Dernier Chant du pèlerinage d'Harold" (inspired by the death of Byron), a note describes the author's visit to Pompeii and his encounter with three young girls who remind him of "three beautiful dreams of life lost in the regions of death."[40] The girls arrive at an excavation and are handed a pick to work the earth. With only gentle taps of the tool, hidden treasure is magically revealed ("art . . . revived by beauty"); their gestures seem to connect the work of excavation to an earlier, ancient rite. "When they lifted their foreheads to shake their hair off," Lamartine writes, "it was as though one saw in this charming exhumation a game or a living allegory, similar to those ingenious allegories invented or deified by antiquity."[41] The material vestiges of antiquity—whether ruins, artifacts, or landscapes—are more easily brought into a private domain of emotional intimacy, Chard argues, if a woman is present to facilitate excavations both literal and metaphorical.[42] In this way, explorers of Italy's past could bring the past into the present and "know" it the way a woman could be known, suggesting that the past is more easily revived when it is embodied anew in the female form.

Lamartine's description of the actions of the three accidental excavators as a "rite" suggests that such elisions between the feminine and the antique worked as spectacle, as both the replication of ancient practices and a present-day theatrical performance. But it was perhaps the attitudes of Emma Hart (1765–1815), later Lady Hamilton, that best exemplified the notion of feminine performance as a spectacle of excavation. Hart, the scandalous mistress (and later wife) of antiquarian and botanist Sir William Hamilton, was famous for her Neapolitan salons, during which she dressed in antique garb, posed in classical attitudes, and sang for guests. It would be difficult to understate the impact of these performances on the European imagination. Rachel Cowgill's recent exploration of soprano Angelica Catalani's imitation of Hart's attitudes on the operatic stage explores the proliferation of images, fictions, and satires of "Lady Hamilton's Attitudes," which, she argued, occupied an uneasy space between "serious aesthetic exhibition" and "voyeuristic domestic entertainment."[43] But, emerging as they did from Hamilton's antiquarian interests and Hart's extensive work as an artist's model, the attitudes also did crucial work in embodying, performing, and translating Italy's ancient past for visitors. According to the Comtesse de Boigne, Emma showed tourists "the poetic imagination of the Italians by a kind of living improvisation."[44] Hart's performances, which she carried out with just a few props—two or three cashmere shawls, an urn, a lyre, and a tambourine—suggest that part of the attraction of southern Italian antiquity for foreigners was as a backdrop for their own imaginative reincarnations of ancient types.[45] As Tommaso Astarita put it, Emma made a living out of being "more ancient and musical than any Neapolitan."[46] Goethe saw her perform several times during his visit to Naples in 1787, and he portrayed the attitudes as a kind of collective fantasy curated by Sir William, embodied by Hart, and "dreamed" by the spectator:

> He has had a Greek gown made for her, which suits her finely, and she looses her hair, takes a pair of shawls, and makes such an alteration of stance, gesture, and countenance that one finally thinks one is dreaming. One sees what so many thousands of artists would gladly have made, here fully formed in

> movement and surprising alteration. Standing, kneeling, sitting, reclining, serious, sad, coy, debauched, repentant, alluring, threatening, fearful, etc., one follows after the other and out of the other. For each expression she knows how to choose—to change—the folds of the veil, and makes herself a hundred kinds of headgear out of the same rags. The old knight holds the light and has abandoned his whole soul to this thing. He finds in her all antiques, all beautiful profiles from Sicilian coins, even the Belvedere Apollo itself.[47]

Goethe emphasizes the vividness of Hart's gestures and her rapid movement between poses, as well as her ability to bring to life lost scenes inaccessible even to an artist's imagination. In performances lasting up to ninety minutes and featuring perhaps 150 individual attitudes, Hart re-created images taken from frescoes and vases and enraptured her observers with her ability to revive the artifacts of a dead culture.[48] Part of the delight for spectators was in recognizing the signs that identified the historical figure she impersonated—rather like a game of charades. The Comtesse de Boigne, who as a child assisted Emma in her performances, recalled that audiences members would call out "Brava, Medea!" and "Viva, la Niobe!"—evidence, Flora Fraser argues, "that each Attitude was intended to recall a particular episode from mythology."[49]

These instances of domestic performance went hand in hand with broader theatrical goals: Hart also cherished operatic ambitions. Her voice was described as clear and strong, if somewhat lacking in flexibility and nuance.[50] Upon her arrival in Naples, Hamilton paid for extensive vocal training (three lessons a day over the space of at least five months) and Hart reported her progress in letters, pleased that she was being courted by impresari.[51] In her familiar, unschooled manner, she wrote, "It is a most extroirdary thing that my voice is totally altered, it is the finest soprano you ever heard, that Sir William shuts his eyes & think one of the Castratos is singing. . . . my shake or tril, what do you call it, is so very good in every note, my mater says that if he did no feil & see & no that I am a substance, he would think I was an angel."[52] Though Hart initially faced several challenges in her voice lessons, she reported that "I have now gone through all difficculties. I solfega at first sight & in reccatative famous." Although Hart's mute, still poses and her brash operatic ambitions may initially seem at odds, she did pair her attitudes with vocal performance: one of her signature pieces was the mad scene from Paisiello's *Nina*.[53]

Despite her confidence, Emma's singing did not garner as much attention as did her poses and her acting. Commentators routinely remarked upon her ability to morph, often puzzlingly or inappropriately, into multiple roles in both life and art. After her arrival in Naples, for example, she reported with some amusement that Neapolitan servants and priests were amazed by her resemblance to the Virgin Mary. She and Hamilton seem to have encouraged such connections; Emma reported in a letter that when two priests came to visit them in Caserta, Sir William told her to place "the shawl over my head and look up," replicating the virtuous pose made iconic in Raphael's paintings.[54] This was convenient, given that she was living as Hamilton's mistress (and was presented as "Mrs. Hart," a widow). The two would not marry until 1791, though rumors of a secret wedding allowed Emma to move about with relative freedom in polite society. Her imitative skill was thus her social currency, and those who encountered her frequently remarked upon it. After witnessing Hart's attitudes ("every one was perfect"), Lady Elizabeth Foster wrote that "she then sung and acted the mad scene in Nina—this was good, but I think chiefly owing to her beautiful action and attitudes—her singing except in the *Buffo* is always in my mind a secondary talent." Horace Walpole also reportedly "admired enormously the acting which accompanied her *Nina*."[55] Despite Emma's liveliness and coquetry, her clear spirit, and her musical and theatrical ambitions, she was most often appreciated as the raw material through which ancient characters and scenes could be made to appear. Cowgill has remarked that "such role-playing was among the essential arts of the courtesan," and it allowed Hart to "transform [. . .] herself into an aesthetic object designed for masculine consumption—a common woman, ennobled by art."[56] Hart's reenactments of antique figures thus spoke to the potential mutability of both class and gender, though this mutability was always limited. Mrs. Trench wrote that "it is remarkable that, though coarse and ungraceful in common life, she becomes highly graceful, and even beautiful, during this performance."[57] As Cowgill notes, "part of the pleasure . . . lay in witnessing the extent of her transformation and the knowledge that the captivating beauty of her attitudes masked a brash and vulgar persona."[58] As Lord Bristol was reported to have said, "Take her as anything but Mrs. Hart and she is a superior being—as herself she is always vulgar."[59]

The attitudes for which Emma Hart gained so much notoriety were a series of vivid scenes meant to bring the past to life—scenes made possible by her ability to change, chameleonlike, into any one of these classical types, using the limited means of two shawls. They were not static or single poses in the style of a *tableau vivant*; in Cowgill's words, their "kinetic energy combined with emotional intensity . . . signaled a new art form."[60] But in artists' renditions, this rapid shifting between different moods could only be represented by the proliferation of multiple images, as if to facilitate wider circulation and repeated viewing. Pietro Antonio Novelli's 1791 drawing, for example, "arranges two rows of diminutive Hamiltons like frames on a roll of film," in Andrei Pop's words (fig. 1.3). As Pop notes, "Time is not evoked by

FIGURE 1.3 Pietro Antonio Novelli, Attitudes of Lady Hamilton, 1791. Pen and brown ink on paper, 19.5 x 32 cm. Washington, DC: National Gallery of Art. Photo: National Gallery of Art.

successive figures but frozen in a multiplicity of bodies . . . There is a sense of succession here, but at the cost of narrative: it is hard to tell if one or many attitudes are represented."[61] Hart's poses were not, of course, a coherent narrative, a retelling of the past as story. Rather, the engravings of her poses capture the collision between antiquarian collecting and performance's power to revivify.[62] The repetition of her figure in a sort of stop motion could be thought of as an effort to capture life and monumentalize it, a strange reversal of the reincarnation of ancient types Goethe and others experienced in her performances. It is as if, in Hart's attitudes, the past is represented in an array of performative accretions. Indeed, the multiplication of her form even bleeds over into more traditional portraiture, as in the painting representing Hart as the three muses Polyhymnia, Terpsichore, and Calliope (fig. 1.4). The multiple Emmas can be placed next to another striking instance of neoclassical replication: Briullov's 1833 painting *The Last Day of Pompeii* (fig. 1.5). A close examination of the female figures in this painting reveals an uncanny resemblance. Not surprisingly, the same model posed for each of them: the Countess Giulia Samoilova, who was Briullov's lover.[63] The numerous Samoilovas have been seen as evidence of Briullov's obsession with her beauty, but set beside the prints and portraits of Lady Hamilton, it is tempting to see the reiteration of Samoilova's face in a variety of attitudes of fear and terror as a series of poses captured in a single canvas. The manifold representations of the same woman in various postures of distress encourage a mode

FIGURE 1.4 Hugh Douglas Hamilton, *Lady Hamilton as Three Muses* [Terpsichore, Polyhymnia, Calliope], 1789–90. The Picture Art Collection / Alamy Stock Photo.

FIGURE 1.5 Karl Briullov, *The Last Day of Pompeii*, 1833. Oil on canvas, 456.5 x 651 cm. Russian State Museum, St. Petersburg. Scala / Art Resource, NY.

of spectatorship that revels in the productive tension between reproduction and reenactment. This mode of performing antiquity relies upon an ideal of the feminine body as eminently pliable and easily transformed—shaped and reshaped into concrete manifestations of ancient types.

The delicate dance between these two modes—bringing the past to life through live performance and the ritual, almost mechanical, reiteration of this past—is central to the work of historical reenactment. Although recent scholarship on the interpenetration of history and theater in historical reenactment tends to focus on sites—such as Plimoth Plantation or Colonial Williamsburg—where American history is reimagined and recast by live "first-person" and "third-person" performer/interpreters, early nineteenth-century Italy was awash with similar practices, from Lady Hamilton's attitudes to poetic improvisation, that reimagined history as spectacle.[64] Giovanni Cesarina's recent work on the role of Greek antiquity in the formation of Italian national identity has emphasized that historians of Magna Graecia who were demoralized by the lack of antiquities in this region often chose to "fill in the void" with theatrical fantasies. Louis-Jean Desprez's initial sketches of Metaponto, for example, include a view of a solitary stand of columns; the published engraving of this same scene, however, "fills the empty space as if it were a stage," with travelers and antiquarians framed by the ruins.[65] I would argue that just as antiquarians attempted to give their discoveries meaning by turning them into spectacle, theatrical culture of the early nineteenth century sought to give performance weight by linking it to the activities of scholarly study and collecting. As we will see, in the case of poetic improvisation, this documentary turn expressed itself in a widespread interest in transcription and, crucially, in portraying the work of improvisers as already textualized. Following the lead of Stephen Gapps, then, we could reimagine the poetic improviser as not only the embodiment of inspired spontaneity, but also a "mobile monument," who was understood by nineteenth-century audiences as a kind of archive of historical and literary knowledge.[66]

". . . she lulls the harp into the magic of rhythm . . ."

The interplay between repetition and reenactment in the visual iconography of antiquity was matched by an analogous balancing act in the realm of poetic improvisation. Through repeating rhymes and meters, as well as strophic musical accompaniments, the sound of poetic improvisation played a crucial role in defining the aesthetics of re-creation, even as it fostered the illusion of an impromptu event. Indeed, for nineteenth-century audiences, one of the most appealing aspects of poetic improvisation was its musicality—whether that meant the sonorous quality of Italian poetry, its instrumental accompaniments, or the improviser's often melodious delivery, described in many cases as simply "singing." Waiblinger argued that music contributed to the total effect of the *improvvisatrice*'s performance by enhancing the impression of spontaneously unfolding poetic creation, despite the fact that the strophic accompaniments he transcribed were obviously repetitive, reusing the same music for each stanza of poetry. Verses that emerged from a divinely inspired mouth with the support of song, he maintained, were not only more moving; they also represented the essence of lyric poetry, which was above all the expression of a momentary feeling.[67] Taddei's improvised poetry, he claimed, is even more affecting than written poetry, and music is the vital indicator of its spontaneity: "the more must we be moved by [the lyric poem], when we see [it] from an inspired mouth, with the support of song, immediately from the creative soul, precisely because this is its true nature, its genuine manner of origination."[68] At the same time, music intensified the physicality of the spectacle of creative effort, as we have seen in Waiblinger's account of Taddei sounding her harp in a hypnotic rhythm in order to create the conditions for inspiration.

But what did poetic improvisers actually sound like? It is difficult to reconstruct the sound of their voices, not least because of differences in performance milieu (street vs. salon) and styles of individual performers. Contemporary critics were typically forthcoming about the poetic gifts of star improvisers and disappointingly vague about matters of vocal delivery. The task is further complicated by the fact that reception of poetic improvisation is dominated by gushing tributes to "Italian" musicality. Both Waiblinger and Staël, for example, recapitulate common and long-standing stereotypes about the lyrical quality of Italian voices and the Italian language. It is as much Corinne's voice that seduces Oswald as her modest manner or inspired words: "The sound of Corinne's moving, sensitive voice, singing in the stately, resonant Italian language, produced an entirely new impression on Oswald . . ."[69] Waiblinger, too, understands the genius for melodious poetry as essentially Italian. Attempting to explain the sound of poetic improvisers to his German-speaking audience, Waiblinger writes:

> Many verse-mongers across the Alps believe that such improvising is wholly charlatanism, that it rests on nothing but fraud and deception, and that a poetess of the art cannot appear without the utmost arrogance. Such a one however knows neither the Italian people nor their language nor their poetry at all. It is well known what a lucky gift, what an inclination to poetry the Roman people alone have. They have an art of *Volkisch* recitative, that is extremely flexible, always varying, extending and drawing together, according to which

> rhymes and thoughts are more or less quickly pushed out of the singers. Every peasant, every street child knows this recitative, and one converses on the street, on a walk, at the gate, in *osterie* for hours at time with a *Wechselgesang* [dialogue song,] which certainly is a happier and richer conversation than the complaints over taxes and tax collectors by which our people spend their sad evenings. "He is a poet," one says, and by that one always understands an improviser, for that is inseparable in its concept—the act of poetizing or improvisation itself however, one simply calls *cantare* [to sing].[70]

Waiblinger suggests that salon improvisers demonstrated a natural inclination toward poetry, one that was shared by the humblest of citizens and practiced on the streets and in wine bars. He paints an idyllic picture of Rome as a sort of nineteenth-century musical stage set, where happy locals call back and forth to one another in southern song.

If such mythic descriptions make it difficult to reconstruct the sound of poetic improvisation, adding to the confusion is the fact that the word "canto" has in Italian a multitude of meanings—song, poem, singing, melody, sound—that slip between closely related realms. At the very least, the notion that an improviser's style of delivery could be located somewhere between speech and song seems to have been widespread.[71] Accounts vary, sometimes describing poetic improvisation as heightened speech, rising and falling in tone, other times as a sort of "half-song" that resembled rhythmically free recitative. Staël, for example, makes oblique mention of these two poles in an early passage describing Corinne's delivery as unique among the *improvvisatori*:

> Most Italians read verse in a kind of monotonous chant called *cantilena* that destroys all feeling. The impression is the same, however different the words, since the tone, which is even more affecting than the words, almost never varies. But Corinne declaimed in a variety of tones which did not destroy the sustained charm of the harmony. It was as if she were playing different airs on a celestial instrument.[72]

Staël's use of the word "cantilena" for what sounds like a species of tuneless chanting may be confusing to contemporary readers; while the term is perhaps most often used in English to signify a lyrical melody, it could also refer (paradoxically) to a style of monotonous, "singsong" recitation.[73] It is clear, however, that she find most practitioners of poetic recitation (aside from the poet Monti, whom she praises in a footnote and, presumably, Corilla Olimpica herself) to be deplorably unmelodic—Corinne's capability for melody marks her as possessing superior creative powers, attuned as she is to celestial realms of sound. For Staël, poetic improvisation's very spontaneity (it is not "read" but created in the moment) allies it with the varied expressive capabilities of melody.

Several "earwitness" attempts to transcribe improvisers' performances suggest that other listeners were just as fascinated by the musical potential of poetic improvisation.[74] Carl Ludwig Fernow, author of a lengthy 1801 essay entitled *Über die Improvisatoren*, included examples in musical notation in his appendix—"probably the first 'ethnomusicological' study conducted on the Italian peninsula," in Ellen Lockhart's words.[75] Fernow does not explain how he came by his transcriptions; they are only given brief mention in the context of his description of the role of music in the improviser's art:

> For every kind of meter, the singer has a unique melody in which he half-sings and half-recites his verses; they [the melodies] are always simple and pleasing, and are all the more easily conformed to any material, since music here, as in the earliest times, is quite subordinate to poetry, and serves merely to decorate the song and to fill in the pauses which arise between the stanzas or individual verses. Most existing melodies of this kind, some of which we will impart at the end of the essay, are invented by famous improvisers themselves.[76]

His attempt to represent the sound of the improvisers was not without its problems, however. As Lockhart discusses, the piece labeled "Corilla" pairs a minuet tune with a text not by the famed *improvvisatrice* but rather by poet and librettist Pietro Metastasio (ex. 1.1).[77] Despite this poem's questionable provenance, Fernow's account makes clear that the improvisations he heard were musical throughout: the accompanist would entertain the audience with a "symphony" while the improviser collected her thoughts on the given subject, there would follow a brief prelude of the vocal melody, and the accompaniment would both support the poet as she sang and fill in the pauses between stanzas and verses.[78] Indeed, the music of Fernow's transcriptions is arresting in its structured melodiousness. While some bear a striking resemblance to recitative, with held chords supporting a speechlike and rhythmically free recitation style, subsequent pieces—such as the "Corilla" minuet and a transcription purportedly recording a performance by Teresa Bandettini—are quite different (ex. 1.2). Not only do we find evidence of vocal ornament, but the melodies themselves, despite Fernow's insistence to the contrary, often seem to conform to musical considerations before poetic ones. The melodic form in the Bandettini example—aabbc—is similar to the lyric prototype later made so popular by Bellini, and its musical "rhymes" do not always chime with the poetry's. "Amica" and "spica," for example, paired as they are with the a and b phrases, respectively, are given different musical material despite their similar sounds. In short, Fernow's transcriptions seem

EXAMPLE 1.1 Transcription of improvisation by "Corilla" (text actually by Pietro Metastasio) in Fernow, *Über die Improvisatoren* (1806).

to offer two very familiar kinds of lyric styles—recitative and aria—and we are left with only his descriptions of the improvisers' delivery as half-sung, half-recited to distinguish the sound of poetic improvisation from other species of vocal performance.

Wilhelm Waiblinger's later attempt to capture the music of poetic improvisation bears several similarities to Fernow's but was presented to his readers with a different purpose in mind—to facilitate amateur attempts to imitate the improviser's art. To his essay on Taddei, Waiblinger appended not only several transcriptions of her poems (which were made at a performance in Foligno and subsequently printed in Spoleto), but also seven examples of her musical accompaniments. These accompaniments, he specified, were "composed for her [*für sie komponiert*]," and he reproduced them in the hope that German-speaking readers who wanted to try their hand at improvising in the Italian style would be able to use them; thus they are stripped of their texts.[79] Here there are no examples of free recitative; Waiblinger presents—as did

Fernow for the "Corilla" and "Bandettini" examples—melodious galant-style pieces, often in rounded binary form. They are nearly folklike in their tuneful simplicity, and when repeated for multiple stanzas of poetry, their links to the strophic ballad must have been audible.

Even without the evidence of Fernow's earlier transcriptions, which attached the words of improvised (or supposedly improvised) verses to melody in the manner of song, it is clear that Waiblinger's transcriptions are meant to be used in the same manner. Each melody is classified according to poetic meter, and in certain cases, idiosyncrasies of the music's phrase structure appear to exist solely to accommodate particular metrical forms. The melody for

EXAMPLE 1.2 Transcription of improvisation by Teresa Bandettini in Fernow, *Über die Improvisatoren* (1806).

Oh! de' partiti
Il genio pera
Che in cruda fiera
Cangia il mortal.

Veggo Ugolino
Co' figli oppresso
Mirar se stesso
Ne' volti lor.

EXAMPLE 1.3 Waiblinger's transcription of Rosa Taddei's *quinario* accompaniment and verses of a separately transcribed poem of the same meter. From "Rosa Taddei, Unter den Arkadiern Licori Partenopea" (1803).

the *quinario flebile*, designed for poems of five-syllable lines, matches quite well the poem in the same meter reproduced by Waiblinger, which treats the tragic fate of Dante's Ugolino (ex. 1.3). Other accompaniments have less typical phrase lengths that seem expressly designed for use with the particular poetic meter. The *settenari* accompaniment, in a pastoral-tinged 6/8 meter, is a case in point: the first half of the binary form is twelve measures long, and is further subdivided into four groups of three measures each, lending an oddly truncated feel to the melody (ex. 1.4). But when the text of Taddei's improvisation in *settenari*, "Il ritorno di Clelia a Roma," is placed beneath it, it becomes clear that each line has three "beats": "Già le Romane giovani / Son tratte a indegno ostaggio . . ."[80] The fact that the first half of the accompaniment contains four three-measure groups means that each line of the stanza can be accommodated. The second section is a different matter, consisting of only ten measures, but here the melody might cue quicker text-setting: the repeated eighth notes of mm. 13–15 replicate a sort of "patter" that fits the first two lines of the stanza. Taddei's verses do not, of course, fit the transcribed melody in a direct syllable-to-note relationship. I would suggest that while the accompaniment and phrase structure remained constant, the small-scale unfolding of the melody itself was perhaps treated more fluidly. In this way, her singing could be at turns syllabic or melismatic, depending on the stress patterns of each line.

In this respect at least, poetic improvisation resembled the parodic practice of making up new words for existing songs. Teresa Bandettini's 1825 autobiographical account of her own development as a self-taught poetic improviser stresses that this childhood game—played with her mother—was one of the very first she engaged in, and was crucial for her development as an *improvvisatrice*:

Già le Romane giovani
  Son tratte a indegno ostaggio,
  Ma sopportar l'oltraggio
  Non può di Clelia il cor;

Quando la notte stende
  Più fosco il denso velo,
  Volto lo sguardo a cielo
  Così favella in se...

EXAMPLE 1.4 Waiblinger's transcription of Rosa Taddei's *settenario* accompaniment and verses of a separately transcribed poem of the same meter. From "Rosa Taddei, Unter den Arkadiern Licori Partenopea" (1803).

> I was not content with the melody of this or that *canzonetta* that I heard sung in the street; to them, I adapted spontaneously verses of my own invention to the great surprise of my mother, who was always the subject of my rhymes. She, lucky for me, knew also how to improvise in *ottava rima*, and she never failed to respond to me when I invited her to sing.[81]

The image of a young child creating new words for old tunes is not an unfamiliar one. The fact that Bandettini insists that her first training as an improviser was had at her mother's knee suggests that part of the mythology of the *improvvisatrice* concerned a natural and unaffected play with words—that poetic improvisation was a kind of original language not unlike the language of children. This emphasis on the mother's voice imparting a natural, aural approach to poetry has been identified by Friedrich Kittler as one of nineteenth-century Romanticism's most powerful "discourse networks."[82] But Bandettini's account also recalls the apprenticeship system that characterized much eighteenth-century training in the arts—from music to drawing. As Robert Gjerdingen has argued, "the focus of this training was on the imitation and reproduction of models and exemplars."[83] Writing about methods of instruction in Neapolitan conservatories, he notes that the acquisition of and familiarity with a web of rules and conventions was gained through sheer repetition. "When an apprentice had internalized all the models," Gjerdingen writes, "he could practice combining them by realizing *partimenti*, which was only a small step away from free improvisation and composition."[84] Bandettini's childhood imitation and transformation of existing songs speaks to the interplay between change and fixity in the poetic improviser's art.

In the end, what is striking about both Taddei's accompaniments and Bandettini's childhood games is how the practice of improvising verses works in tandem with a fixed musical edifice. The decidedly non-atmospheric and highly structured nature of these accompaniments strongly suggests that Taddei sang her poetry to these melodies, instead of reciting or chanting her verses to a musical backdrop in the manner of melodrama. If the transcriptions offered by Waiblinger and Fernow are any indication of general practice, poetic improvisers freely extemporized their poetry, but not necessarily their musical accompaniments. In other words, these modest accompaniments could be described as musical structures upon which the *improvvisatrice* draped her verses.[85] This may seem slightly strange, given the Romantic rhetoric surrounding the practice of improvisation: that it represents the pinnacle of spontaneous creation. But it is not news that poetic improvisers—indeed, improvisers of all sorts—worked within an implicit set of constraints. Indeed, improvisation only makes sense as a free or spontaneous movement either against or within limits; rules of meter and rhyme were well known to poetic improvisers. Still, once we approach Taddei's improvisations as songs—songs with a melodic framework and whose words she could vary as long as she abided by the rules of the poetic form—a more nuanced picture of poetic improvisation emerges. What is striking about these accompaniments is not just that they are fixed, but rather just how slowly the poetry is able to unfold when each stanza of a poem is paired with half of the binary form. As we have seen, Fernow, Waiblinger, and Staël suggest that musical accompaniment played a vital role, whether by setting the audience's mood or by preparing the improviser to receive inspiration. While this could be understood as typical romantic rhetoric about the power of music to unlock the wellsprings of creativity, I would argue that music acted in a much more practical way: it gave the poet time. Time to think of the appropriate rhyme, to find the right word. Time, in other words, to tap into memory.

*

Poetic improvisers were thus storehouses of memory—memories cultural, historical, and literary. And music, of course, is a highly effective mnemonic device. But the very fact that the improviser embodied memory in such a vivid way was quickly becoming a problem in an era when the proliferation of texts could call into question the Romantic rhetoric of divine inspiration. The early nineteenth century saw intense debates surrounding the role of memory in improvised poetry, as critics tried to define the nature of improvisational talent and complained about the ubiquity of a small set of historical or classical subjects drawn from Dante or Tasso. In such accounts, memory is haunted by the specter of memorization, and as the revivification of the past easily tips over to rote repetition.

The very popularity of poetic improvisation made it subject to critical scrutiny; many of Taddei's contemporaries were preoccupied with specifying the differences between premeditated and spontaneously composed poetry. The intrusion of memorized texts into improvised performance—a theme that recurs repeatedly in nineteenth-century discussions—was cited as potentially invalidating an improviser's accomplishment. Waiblinger himself alludes to these debates in his essay, defending improvising poets from charges of charlatanism—from the accusation that they simply memorized stock verses that would be appropriate for any subject proposed:

> It is not to be denied that a certain cleverness is bound up with [improvisation]; that a cultivated improviser has undertaken a full course of study to familiarize himself completely with mythology, history, and the Italian classics;

> that he has even stored away entire speeches, representations of all possible affects, maxims, and adages; but what would be the use of all of that if the quickly associating imagination, the fine feeling, the perfected control of speech, the specially practiced thought were not at hand, other than to perform the learned material correctly and in the right order![86]

Waiblinger proposes that memory is (re)enacted in real time, and that the audience sees and appreciates the spectacle of the performance of memory, poetic skill, and expressive delivery combined. Listening to the simple, structured melodies of the *improvvisatrice* as a gateway to memory offers an alternative to the binary opposition between creators and executants. Improvisers, it is important to remember, had their own set of conventions and constraints: theirs was a structured art, in many ways as predetermined and conventional as an operatic number. Poetic improvisation was thus—in its meter and music—as concerned with fixity as it was with freedom. In fact, the modern notion of improvisation as free play is difficult to find in accounts of eighteenth- and nineteenth-century *improvvisatori*, which tend more often to stress their prodigious memories—their considerable storehouses of knowledge, imagined variously as both crutch and boon.

All this gives us a very different way of thinking about Romantic performance: as dependent upon an aesthetic of repetition and reenactment. Such an aesthetic is manifest both in the discourses surrounding the *improvvisatrice* and in the very practices of poetic improvisation—especially its repeating rhymes and strophic accompaniments. My goal here is not merely to unmask the Romantic ideology of spontaneity, but instead to see this tension (between a spontaneously unfolding event and the dead, memorized, memorialized past) as a productive one. It is the movement between these poles that made the theatrical event of improvisation so compelling and that made the poetic improviser's efforts to craft spontaneous verses on the classical past a living embodiment of memory. Ultimately, then, we might characterize the practice of poetic improvisation as the quintessential nineteenth-century technology: the *improvvisatrice* was both a storage and playback device as well as a fallible, mortal performer wracked by the storms of genius. How this living technology began to be enfolded into the emerging technologies of print culture is the story that follows.

2

Corinna's Crown: Improvisation and Authority in Rossini's *Il viaggio a Reims*

It sounds like the opening of a bad joke: What do an opera singer's improvised ornaments have in common with women's hats? The connection certainly seems tenuous at best. But strangely, one does not have to delve very deeply into the repertory of nineteenth-century Italian opera to find a highly ornamented aria devoted to headgear. The aria sung by the Contessa di Folleville, the frivolous Parisian clotheshorse, in Rossini's *Il viaggio a Reims* (1825) is one of the few operatic numbers sung in praise of a hat.[1] This particular hat is the remnant of a tragic carriage accident that destroyed the bulk of the fashionable Contessa's wardrobe. Rossini makes use of the traditional double-aria form (slow movement followed by fast cabaletta) to stage a tongue-in-cheek scene of loss and restoration. In the slow movement, a lament for her lost luggage, the Countess maintains that "Donne, voi sol comprendere / Potete il mio dolor" (Ladies, you alone can understand my grief). Here the melody is laced with sighs, moans, and other instances of vocal word-painting to ironically convey her misfortune. The Contessa's sorrow, however, is short-lived. Soon her chambermaid emerges with the sole survivor of the "shipwreck" (as Balochi's libretto puts it): a creation imagined in a 2004 Barcelona production as an enormous confection of a hat, festooned with ribbons, bows, and feathers, the whole thing far too large for the Contessa's head. The florid cabaletta of praise she sings to this hat abounds with roulades, figures, and turns and culminates in a sweeping cadenza (ex. 2.1). No matter how comic or frivolous it sounds, however, this is fiendishly difficult music to sing, and it seems expressly designed to display the talents of soprano Laure Cinti-Damoreau, who created the role.

Here is one connection, then, between ladies' headgear and operatic ornamentation: both have been thought to display the taste and perhaps even

Contessa: For this favor my soul will be eternally grateful.

EXAMPLE 2.1 Florid passage from the Contessa's cabaletta ("Che miro! Ah! Quel sorpresa!") in act 1 of Rossini, *Il viaggio a Reims*.

accomplishment of the wearer or singer, and both have been dismissed as frivolous, associated with luxury and decadence rather than utility. Indeed, the denigration of ornamentation in general, whether in fashion, art, or music, has a long history, but began to gain ground in the mid-nineteenth century.[2] The problematic status of musical ornamentation has much to do with the fact that it is improvised and thus brings up questions of freedom and control. But while critics dismissed it as an "added on" effect, like too many ruffles overwhelming a ball gown, ornament's defenders (many of them speaking of instrumental music, in which ornament's interference with text-setting was a non-issue) saw it as an integral aspect of the musical art. C. P. E. Bach called ornaments "indispensable" and argued that they helped "tie the notes together [and] . . . clarify their content."[3] Even Heinrich Schenker, despite his focus on deep structure, ascribed a vital role to ornament as a "manifestation of truth, artistic truth that transcends time."[4] Resorting again to fashion-based metaphors, Stendhal insisted vocal ornament was not an added furbelow but was instead akin to the "delicate tracery" on a costume that reveals the figure of the woman underneath.[5] Despite the initial strangeness of the comparison, then, hats and ornaments do have something in common: a shared discourse that grapples with the essential and the inessential, navigating dichotomies of figure versus ground and depth versus surface. Discussing vocal embellishment's later nineteenth-century association with the superfluous, the decorative, and the exotic, Gurminder Kaur Bhogal has argued that ornament has been understood as a "static, immutable entity that adorns but cannot speak."[6] Despite its subaltern status, however, Bhogal argues that

> at its most intense, a sudden profusion of detail can rupture the musical texture; explore extremes of . . . tessitura; multiply the rate of rhythmic activity; mute, or subjugate, an entire orchestra; and suspend, or momentarily destabilize, the irrevocable periodicity of musical meter.[7]

Noting that "musicologists have yet to engage with coloratura in its capacity as an active dramatic constituent," Bhogal advocates for the "need to analyze ornament in terms of its ontology and behavior."[8] For her, later nineteenth-century vocal ornament is above all expressive and irrevocably tied to the subjectivity of the character who spins it out and is thus amenable to close reading and interpretation. I hear the improvisational ornament of the early *ottocento* slightly differently: as a rhetorical practice and strategy, to be sure, but one that is supremely mutable and capable of floating free of individual authors.

To explain, let me turn to yet another connection between hats and ornaments, one that was put on display in a recent staging of Rossini's *Il viaggio a Reims*—Dario Fo's 2003 production for the Finnish National Opera. Fo decided to magnify the importance of the hat in the Countess's aria, as we can see from one of his preliminary sketches for the scene (fig. 2.1). Here's how Philip Gossett described the staging:

> Fo envisioned not one hat, but a sequence of hats, beginning with one of normal size, then growing larger and larger, out of all proportion. They multiplied like rabbits and began to fly through the air with abandon. Certainly it was that image of flying hats that led Fo to modify the words of the cabaletta to read: "È vivo il mio capell, ha l'ali, è vivo il mio capell" (My hat is alive, it has wings, my hat is alive). The final hat—unveiled as the Countess began the ornamented reprise of the cabaletta theme—was large enough for Folleville to stand on and be lifted into the air by her attendants [fig. 2.2], as she continued to sing her coloratura.[9]

Fo's fantastical and playful staging might remind us of another set of hats: namely, the 500 hats of Bartholomew Cubbins from Dr. Seuss's 1938 book of the same name. The humble Bartholomew, encountering the king passing with his entourage, tries to doff his cap as a gesture of respect. But no matter how many times the poor boy takes off his hat, another magically appears in its place, enraging the king. Seuss's tale imagines the magical transformation of an accessory into a permanent fixture—an object that should be separable from one's person becomes instead quasi-anatomical. Bartholomew's transgression thus touches on two interrelated themes: the apparent "wrongness" of presenting what should be a mere appendage as essential, and how doing so flouts authority.

Perhaps Fo was thinking of Bartholomew when he staged the Countess's aria, for these hats also seem to obey a logic of proliferation. Indeed, the hats in Fo's production multiply like the diminutions and graces of Folleville's melody, swooping through the air on "wings," just as the sound of the Countess's melody flits and flutters through space. I would like to use Fo's staging as a springboard to consider opera as an occasion for material proliferation—not just of hats, but also of musical notes in the form of sung (and later published) ornamentation. Focusing on the proliferation, variation, and dissemination of operatic ornament, I argue, makes possible a new understanding of the sea changes occurring in Italian opera over the course of the nineteenth century. The account normally told of the emergence of the work concept and the growing authority of opera composers in the nineteenth century resonates with the themes of Seuss's fable. The story of Bartholomew's multiplying hats

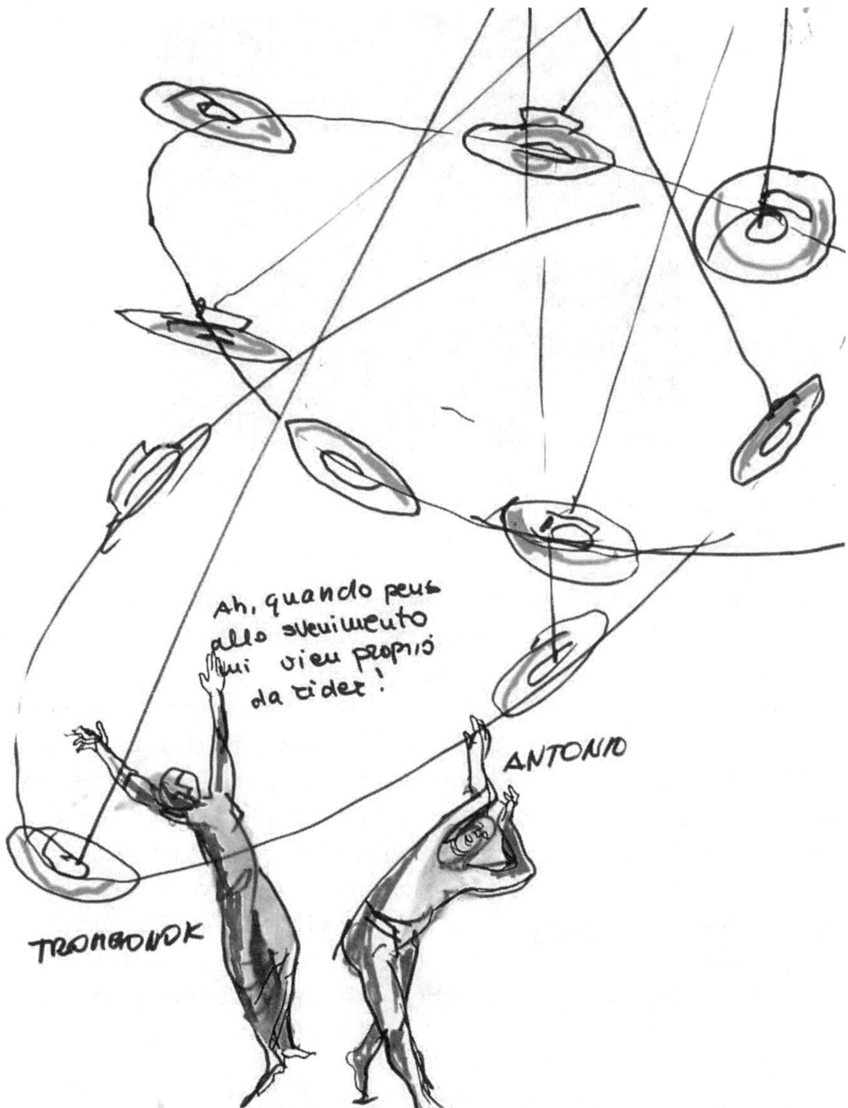

FIGURE 2.1 Dario Fo, storyboard for National Opera of Helsinki production of *Il viaggio a Reims* (2002). © Archivio Franca Rame Dario Fo—C.T.F.R. srl.

is, of course, a story of authority threatened. As I have mentioned in this book's introduction, histories of opera contend that singers had the liberty to sing whatever ornaments they chose (to wear as many and as outrageous hats as possible) until the emerging authority of the composer tamed and curbed their excesses; they then began to doff their hats to the new kings, treating the

FIGURE 2.2 The Contessa held aloft on a hat, Dario Fo production of *Il viaggio a Reims*, National Opera of Helsinki (2003). © Archivio Franca Rame Dario Fo—C.T.F.R. srl.

score with more respect. Susan Rutherford sums up the changes thus: "the composer gained ascendance and operas were no longer adjusted to display individual talents."[10]

This narrative, while capturing the shape of larger changes in the operatic world, obscures quite a bit. It has seemed commonsensical to claim that the ideology of the work arose via textualization—to posit that once things were written down, they were more likely to be thought of as fixed and immutable. Instead, I will argue that the explosion of operatic texts in the 1820s and 1830s—including arias for domestic consumption and vocal treatises and ornamentation notebooks used to teach singers of varying abilities to perform their own cadenzas—was accompanied by a concomitant interest not in fixity but in the dizzying proliferation of possibilities. Authority in this context was associated less with the ability to create a fixed text than it was with the capacity to generate nearly endless textual variants. As in Fo's production, these melodic variants existed to elevate the singer—to bring her talent to the foreground. Rossini's *Il viaggio* makes a particularly good entrée into these issues because it is a work that specifically thematizes improvisation, not only in the melodic language of arias like the Contessa's but also in the presence of the *improvvisatrice* Corinna, loosely based on the heroine of Madame De Staël's *Corinne, ou L'Italie* (1807). Crowned with the classical solemnity of a poet's laurel rather than a frivolous hat, Corinna could not be further from the world of the Countess. Nevertheless, her presence allows us to ask probing questions about the overlapping discourses of improvisation that inform Rossini's opera. Throughout this chapter, I will explore what happens when the literary figure of the improviser collides with the real-world performance space of the opera. In other words, what happens when the poetic improviser is reimagined as a diva? Corinna is contrasted with the Contessa in *Il viaggio* in such a blatant way as to act out nineteenth-century debates about what characterizes good improvisation (divinely inspired, allied to lofty goals, closely allied with text) and bad (self-indulgent, used indiscriminately or inappropriately, flying free of semantic meaning). My discussion will thus circle around these two characters, as well as the women who created them, not to reinscribe such hard-and-fast distinctions, but to tease apart the differences between operatic diva and poetic improviser and in the process to complicate common notions of operatic authority. For, above all, just how the ideal of a stable work created by a single author—the big rabbit of nineteenth-century music history—was pulled, incredibly, from the hat of ornamental proliferation and variation is the story I want to tell here.

Coronation as Theater, Opera as Event

While she was repeatedly invoked in nineteenth-century poems and stories, there is likely only one *improvvisatrice* encountered by operagoers today: Rossini's Corinna from *Il viaggio a Reims.*[11] Performed by the phenomenally successful diva Giuditta Pasta, the *improvvisatrice* plays a vital role in this occasional work, which Rossini composed for the coronation of Charles X in 1825. Set in the present day of its first audience, *Il viaggio* addresses the grand occasion it marks not via heroic allegory, but by comically displacing the coronation of which it was a part. The opera features a group of travelers, each representative of a European nation, who are forced to gather at the Inn of the Golden Lily when their plans to attend the celebrations are thwarted. As a substitute for the coronation festivities, the innkeeper stages an evening's entertainment that features performances by a passing theatrical troupe and national songs performed by each of the guests in turn. Corinna's adulatory improvisation in honor of the king forms the centerpiece of the evening. This final portion of the opera exploits the *mise-en-abyme* effect: she performs for an onstage audience which, at the work's premiere, was itself performing for the audience at the Salle Louvois. Indeed, *Il viaggio* makes many such references to its own status as occasional work, including such real-life intrusions as calling for a character to read a summary of the actual municipal resolution concerning the coronation festivities, which had appeared in the Parisian press.[12]

Benjamin Walton has drawn attention to the way the entire 1825 coronation repeatedly muddled distinctions between stage and life—between the artificial "tinsel and cardboard" of theater and the supposedly powerful effects of the royal presence. Throughout the celebrations of Charles's coronation in Reims and Paris, operatic spectacle and the public display of political power seemed to exist along the same theatrical continuum. Charles X's assumption of the throne seemed like "the performance of a coronation, not a coronation" in Chateaubriand's words; Reims cathedral was overloaded with "ornaments," and Hugo spoke of a "theater . . . constructed of cardboard."[13] What is notable in this case, argues Walton, is not that the coronation itself was understood as theatrical (politics in France was always theatrical), but that it was routinely criticized as bad or failed theater—as patently artificial.

Walton maintains that both the coronation itself and the *pièces de circonstance* commissioned to celebrate it made use of a similar language of spectacle to celebrate the restoration of the monarchy, so much so that they could be treated as "equivalent" pieces of theater in many respects.[14] The town of Reims was made into a stage set, with residents renting out their balconies as boxes for spectators, while officials, worried about a lukewarm reception for the new king, hired a claque to express their enthusiasm during the procession. The cathedral reminded spectators of the opera house—indeed, a stage designer was hired to decorate the door—with boxes for spectators lined up along the nave. The operatic effect might have been the result of a mundane practicality. Walton points out that the props for theatrical productions and state occasions were stored in the same space, and the coronation likely borrowed some of the former for their purposes. Even the peculiar pageantry of the kingly investiture, then, also became a production, a text to be revived: the musical pieces associated with the ceremony were later published with added stage directions.[15]

Il viaggio's emphasis on its own status as event similarly had the effect of blurring the theatrical space of the opera with the theater of the coronation itself. The figure of Corinna was central to this project. The presence of an improviser could only serve to highlight the evening's entertainment as a spontaneously unfolding occasion. Indeed, having an improviser on stage might have been something like having a live television reporter, in that she was associated with unrepeatability, spontaneity, and the audience's involvement in the evening's entertainment. Not only did spectators often provide improvisers with their subjects, but poems of praise or poems marking the occasion were a staple of improvisers. This aspect of the *improvvisatrice*'s performance might recall Philip Auslander's notion of "liveness," a phenomenon he locates in the contemporary imbrication of live performance with the technological media of reproduction—an imbrication that paradoxically serves to emphasize the "live" event's unfolding in the present moment.[16]

Despite the fact that Rossini's opera had its premiere long before the advent of recording technologies, as an occasional work, it too highlighted the immediacy and non-repeatability of the event it celebrated. Paying attention to the *improvvisatrice* in *Il viaggio*, then, highlights a constellation of what we could call "event effects" that cluster around the work, suggesting that its status as an occasional piece, its sense of happening in the here and now, was of crucial importance.

Corinna and the Crown of Laurel

The hallmark of improvisers is their ability to create the impression that they are inventing poetry or composing music on the spot, despite the fact that most improvisation relies upon the deployment and creative recasting of conventional formulae. In this way, improvisation is an acting out of creative authority, a performance of authorship. In *Il viaggio*, however, Corinna is simultaneously granted special status and limited in her access to authorial power. Though Balochi and Rossini were careful to distinguish Poles from Germans, Frenchmen from Englishmen, Corinna is treated differently. She is explicitly identified as a child not just of Italy, but of ancient Italy, the cradle of European civilization; indeed, she is accompanied by a Greek girl, demonstrating her panhellenist sympathies. Such a decision makes a bid for the universality of this iconic Italian figure. Corinna is thus an idealized (indeed, so idealized as to verge on satire) image of Europe; she is able to calm nationalist tensions from the first harp flourishes that accompany her initial improvisation.

Though Corinna is only loosely based on Staël's Corinne, her two improvisations speak in their own ways to the fragility of female authorship thematized in Staël's novel. The first, "Arpa gentil," is performed offstage, a private utterance that is overheard by the other characters (ex. 2.2). Although this is a perfectly conventional operatic device,[17] such eavesdropping is antithetical to the aesthetic of the *improvvisatrice* which, as we have seen, depends on the risky business of composing verses spontaneously in front of an audience that participates in the process. Here, Corinna's alluring, disembodied voice is appreciated as a beautiful object, which, Orpheus-like, can soothe conflict and discord. It is hard not to see this move as a kind of domestication or cordoning off of the spectacle of feminine creativity—a displacement that recalls Staël's decision to summarize Corinne's Italian verses in French prose. Certainly it could be argued that in being made otherworldly, Corinna is placed on a pedestal, elevated above petty concerns and human foibles. Her utterances, perhaps because they seem to emerge from the beyond, are granted more authority than the merely human opinions of the other characters. However,

Corinna: Thou gentle harp, who art my faithful companion ever, join the sounds of joy and love to my songs.

EXAMPLE 2.2 Corinna, "Arpa gentil," act 1 of Rossini, *Il viaggio a Reims.*

in making the improviser an offstage voice, Rossini and the librettist Luigi Balochi turned her into a receptive vessel for divine messages, rather than an individual whose creative power invests her with inherent authority.

It is Corinna's final improvisation, "All'ombra amena," that brings these issues into focus most clearly (ex. 2.3). In lieu of the official coronation, the owner of the Golden Lily offers her guests more modest festivities, the highlight of which is Corinna's performance of a long, improvised poem about Charles X, a subject (unsurprisingly) proposed by her onstage audience. Setting stanzas of *quinari* (five-syllable lines), Rossini's music mixes a naïve and pastoral flavor with extravagant ornaments. As in her first improvisation, the very length of "All'ombra amena" and the regularity of its melody and poetry suggest a link to the practices of poetic improvisers. Artists such as Rosa Taddei would often improvise extremely long poems in regular metric structures such as the *ottava rima*. Such strict conventions of meter and rhyme set expectations for the spectators who waited for extemporizers to complete the line with the required number of syllables and to cap their achievement with a felicitous end rhyme. In "All'ombra amena," this same improvisatory logic is written into Rossini's score. The opening melodic idea, for example, works as a framing device: the gesture is repeated many times in varied form, both beginning and ending the strophe, while each strophe juxtaposes mostly syllabic melodies with highly ornamented flourishes at the end.[18] The very rigidity of Corinna's melodic structure and its internal repetitions seem to provide the platform for soloistic invention.

EXAMPLE 2.3 Corinna's *improvviso* ("All'ombra amena"), act 3, *Il viaggio a Reims*.

EXAMPLE 2.3 (*continued*)

But comparing Corinna's music with that of the Countess reveals that the soloistic invention here associated with the *improvvisatrice* is quite different from established Italianate conventions of vocal improvisation. Indeed, although it may seem that Corinna is the character who most clearly represents the idea of improvisation in *Il viaggio*, I would argue that the unexalted role of the fashion-loving Countess more clearly embodies the living improvisatory traditions of Italian opera. This is partly a result of the different social register of the two characters. Michel Orcel has argued that when Corinne became Corinna, she was transformed into a "statue, a boring divinity, a cold and ridiculous star."[19] Indeed, her music is of a purposely elevated sort, so elevated as to place her outside the realm of human feeling and drama (however petty) shared by the opera's other characters. The Countess is, in contrast, a comic character clearly at home in this realm. To be sure, she ironically mimics an elevated idiom, as when she uses grandiose gestures to mourn her lost clothing (ex. 2.4). Overall, one is struck by the sheer variety of ornamental gestures in the Countess's

Contessa: How can I explain, oh God, the anguish in my heart? Ladies, you alone can understand my grief.

EXAMPLE 2.4 Lamenting gestures in the Countess's "Partir, oh ciel! desio," act 1, *Il viaggio a Reims*.

music. Her vocal line is peppered with imitative gestures such as sighs, sobs, and throbbing heartbeats. Since Corinna does not tend to express individual emotion, she therefore has no need to display it in her public hymns of praise.

The more pertinent distinction between the two characters' music, however, is found in the forms of their numbers and—crucially—the kinds of repetition these forms allow. In effect, each character has a different relationship to repetition, the foundation of improvisation. Corinna's music is relentlessly strophic and accompanied by solo harp, which places it in the realm of self-accompanied, folk-tinged song. Each verse of an unchanging strophic ballad is typically designed to highlight a changing text. This poetic aesthetic, so steeped in Romantic *Volkstümlichkeit*, at times works against Rossini's Italianate aesthetic of vocal improvisation. Each of Corinna's musical repetitions, while they may allow for vocal display, are tied to a rhetorical process more explicitly verbal in nature. Such forms necessarily treat the poetic verses in a more respectful way, and indeed, Rossini very rarely breaks up or reiterates the text in Corinna's numbers. Repeated words are few and confined to the ends of phrases or stanzas. Her final improvisation, "All'ombra amena," contains only one small textual repetition in the body of the piece ("più dolce") and, at the end of the number, a threefold repetition of the king's name (ex. 2.5). This is in stark contrast to the Countess, whose big showpiece is a classic double aria, with many opportunities for the singer to set off vocal fireworks. Her text is marked by many reiterations that create the space and opportunity for improvisatory play. The multiple small-scale duplications of text demand creative reshaping and are thus a kind of "writing in" of melodic improvisatory logic.

Perhaps this is one reason why "All'ombra amena" was received rather coldly: Walton notes that *Le Globe* thought Rossini's music "relied too much on familiar stylistic tricks" and was therefore "unworthy" of the *improvvisatrice*.[20] Listeners encountering Giuditta Pasta as Corinna were, however, struck by the overlap between diva and poetic improviser. The French press gushed over Pasta's uncannily accurate re-creation of Staël's iconic figure, both in her declamation and in her ability to convincingly embody pre-existing visual representations of Corinna. The visual aspects of Pasta's performance no doubt occasioned so much comment because the final improvisation was purposely staged as a *tableau vivant* of Gerard's famous portrait of Corinne improvising at Cape Miseno (fig. 1.2).[21] Dressing Pasta as the central figure in this painting may have only served to highlight the more material conjunctions between the work of the diva and that of the poetic improviser. As Kenneth Stern puts it, "Pasta represented a character of elevated stature that reflected her own dignity and reputation as lyric muse."[22] In embodying the iconic poetess, Pasta could not help but portray herself as well, a performer who envoiced

Corinna: Charles, delight and love of the French! Charles, Charles!

EXAMPLE 2.5 Final measures of Corinna's "All'ombra amena," act 3, *Il viaggio a Reims*.

Rossini's music at the same time that she asserted her own inventive skill through ornamentation. Especially for those familiar with the arts of the *improvvisatrice*, watching Pasta portray Corinna might have been something like watching a cameo performance once removed; just as a famous film actress might play a famous stage actress, a famous improviser of melody here impersonates a famous improviser of poetry.[23] Given the extensive discourse surrounding Pasta as a supremely skilled gestural actor, we might be tempted to speculate that she was perfect for the role of Corinna because of both her reputation and her skill at embodied imitation.[24] But what is striking about Pasta's performance as Corinna is that it appears to have been a kind of citation of the *improvvisatrice* rather than an effort to highlight the connections between practices of operatic and poetic improvisation.

As at all theatrical events attended by the king, however, applause was not permitted: the only sign of approbation allowed was the cry "Vive le Roi!" Thus enthusiasm for Pasta at *Il viaggio*'s premiere had to be redirected, creating a dam in the appreciation that flowed from listeners to performers. Of course, sometimes constructing a dam only generates more power. Stendhal claimed that the audience was in transports of ecstasy during Pasta's performance of Corinna's first improvisation, "Arpa gentil," precisely because their approval could not be expressed openly.[25] Corinna's final improvisation, designed to pierce the fourth wall, harnesses the "here and now" effect so central to occasional works, since Pasta, at least at the premiere, would have addressed her verses of praise to the king himself. Not surprisingly, the text of this number makes pointed reference to the royal presence—that is, not to the (fictionally) distant king of the plot, the one to whom the characters on stage have no access, but to the real Charles X, seated in the audience. "Più dolce aurora / Sorger la Francia / Non vide ancor, / E grata applaude, / Ammira, adora / Di tanto ben / L'Augusto Autor" (A fairer dawn France has never yet seen arise and gratefully applauds, admires, and adores the August Author of so many boons), Corinna intones in her first stanza. This reference to "L'Augusto Autor," however much it is an expected part of the opera's genre as occasional work, also underscores the way that *Il viaggio* locates authority offstage, outside the work, and apart from its realization by singers. Indeed, one could argue that the function of the *improvvisatrice* throughout the opera is paradoxical. She lends a frisson of the "live" to the event, yet she does not fully embody ideals of inspiration or spontaneous invention so much as point to a creative, authorial force outside the opera. Pasta/Corinna, gesturing toward this "author," praises both the actual seat of power in the theater while recalling other, absent authors—librettist and composer—of the words and music she sings.

Ornaments and Authors

Such a move takes on further significance in light of broader debates about the relative status of singers' and composers' creative work. Nineteenth-century writing about opera was rife with discussion about when, where, and how ornamentation was appropriate, and many of these debates espoused improvisatory values while acknowledging the emerging split between creators and executants.[26] Stendhal's *Vie de Rossini* (1824), for example, famously imagined a mythic moment when Rossini began writing down his ornaments in order to protect his music from overzealous singers who might ruin it with injudicious improvisation. In Stendhal's invented internal dialogue, Rossini, supposedly piqued by an 1814 performance by Velluti in which the composer's music "had grown completely unrecognizable," resolves that "in future, no singer of mine shall ever have the slightest pretext for improvising a single appoggiatura."[27] Stendhal maintained that such a decision limited the inventive skill of the performer:

> The revolution inaugurated by Rossini has killed the gift of *originality* in the singer. What incentive can singers have nowadays for taking infinite pains to convey to their audiences, firstly, the *native* and *individual* quality of their voices, and second, the precise expressive quality by which it may be endowed through their own sensibility? In Rossini's operas they are doomed to wait forever in vain for one single opportunity to display to the public those rare qualities, whose acquisition may have cost them literally years of unrelenting labor. But in any case, the mere habit of expecting to find everything already worked out, already written down, in the music from which they have to sing, kills their own inventiveness and makes them lazy.[28]

Philip Gossett has pointed out that "however amusing this story may seem, it is totally without substance."[29] Rossini's vocal lines may have become more florid over time, but he never achieved—or indeed seems to have sought—the iron control Stendhal ascribes to him.[30] Part of Gossett's own project has been to encourage modern performers to adopt some of the freedoms of their nineteenth-century counterparts, arguing that "apart from the improvisational exploits of solo instrumental virtuosos, only in Italian opera was ornamentation integral to the performance of newly composed notated works."[31]

But Stendhal's further claim that "no ornamentation is so sure and so effective as that which springs from the spontaneous invention and emotional response of the singer" may give some contemporary commentators pause.[32] Though scholars maintain that Stendhal's image of Rossinian control was a myth, they are, nevertheless, often at pains to bolster the composer's authority in the face of the many interventions made to his scores. The ornaments of singers thus occupy a particularly uncertain position. Gossett, for instance, has argued that we should treat the collected cadenzas and variants of the Marchisio sisters "with particular respect" because "Rossini deeply admired their art," suggesting that those who are close to the composer may borrow his authority but do not possess their own.[33] What is at issue here is the often uncomfortable clash between the exploration of historical practices and the reconstruction of early texts; the two perspectives obviously inform each other but require different approaches. For example, although Damien Colas notes that "contrary to received opinion. . . . ornamentation of the vocal parts by the singers themselves is completely legitimate in Rossini," he characterizes the published ornaments of nineteenth-century singers as mere imitations of the Rossinian idiom.[34] Colas thus defines Rossini as the "source" of ornament, while performers can only manage lackluster copies:

> The performing material for Rossini's operas preserved in Paris gives a good overall idea of the arsenal of ornaments at his interpreters' disposal, and moreover shows that all their decorative figures descend from the composer's own hand, whether directly or by a kind of family resemblance. Indeed, singers' ornamentation is characterised by less audacity, as is typical of the work of imitators . . .[35]

Even though Stendhal's account has been dismissed as fanciful (Rossini, of course, continued to work closely with singers, and performers continued to alter scores to their own taste), the notion that Rossini's scores should be accorded a certain sanctity or inviolability has persisted. Colas acknowledges that the rich fund of material—ornamentation, cuts, transpositions—passed along from singer to singer created "traditions whose authority ended up supplanting that of the absent composer." But the very multiplicity of these improvisational traces, he argues, precludes "an absolute point of reference," and therefore "only the text left by the composer can be invested with authority."[36] Such explicit claims that improvisation runs counter to authority presuppose that authorship was primarily a matter of creating stable texts, a view that, as we shall see, is not fully compatible with nineteenth-century notions of operatic authorship.

Even a brief exploration of nineteenth-century pedagogy complicates Colas's suggestion that the material authored by singers threatened the authority of the composer. Nicholas Baragwanath has shown, for example, just how closely improvisation and composition were intertwined in the world of nineteenth-century Italian opera.[37] Composers and singers shared the same curriculum, and Baragwanath points out that "musical training was, from

EXAMPLE 2.6 Sung counterpoint exercise from Stanislao Mattei's *Pratica d'accompagnamento e contrappunto del Padre Maestro Stanislao Mattei (Parte Seconda)* (1827).

the earliest lessons, grounded on playing and singing."[38] Harmony and counterpoint were overwhelmingly taught via the use of keyboard partimenti and solfeggi, which required students to sing extempore. Such exercises were the primary way composers gained expertise in constructing melodies. Baragwanath writes, "traditional *solfeggi*—composed by a maestro, using standard contrapuntal formulas and other schemata, for an individual student to sing and embellish—continued to be used throughout the nineteenth century in Italy not only for vocal training but also as *models for melodic composition*."[39] While composers employed solfeggi to learn how to construct melodies, singers used them to learn to "improvise and embellish with a sound understanding of compositional craft."[40] These exercises in the theory of counterpoint were so closely tied to vocal pedagogy that they were typically taught by professors of voice.[41]

How exactly did solfeggi—short compositions for one, two, or three voices plus bass—develop a set of improvisational skills that were crucial for both singers and composers? When looked at on the page, they seem rather static (ex. 2.6).[42] But Baragwanath points out that they were "not so much an exercise to be performed from the page as . . . an idealized version or end-product of a particular learning process, designed to provide the maestro with an exemplar to work toward with his students."[43] In this example, the process would have unfolded in stages of increasing elaboration, from the

> application of the intervals of the sixth and fifth below each note of the soprano's descending scale, followed by the alto's syncopated line in parallel motion. Once this basic pattern has been learned and "sung in," conventional framing devices could be added and the whole could be embellished and elaborated in any number of ways through improvised alterations.[44]

When solfeggi are collected in printed editions, it may be all too easy to see them as graduated exercises designed to instill more complicated vocal techniques in the singer. But Baragwanath contends that the progression from simple to complex was a necessary feature of the improvisatory exercise: "Students were initially given a contrapuntal device in its simplest, most rudimentary form, before embellishing and varying its repetitive outline together, in class, to arrive at something akin to the more polished versions to be found at the end of a course of instruction."[45]

The solfeggio tradition was remarkably persistent, even well into the era of Puccini. Baragwanath argues that while "the singer's contribution began to be subsumed into the work of the composer and incorporated into scores, [. . .] the notated melodies of later nineteenth-century Italian opera nevertheless owe a great debt to the practices of vocal improvisation that continued to be instilled through lessons in practical counterpoint and solfeggio."[46] Certainly, with the specialization that came with the growth of conservatories, composition and performance—and their pedagogies—began to diverge. But even as singing treatises began to be more narrowly focused on issues of vocal technique, they continued to follow the progressive curriculum designed to build improvisational skill: "Countless editions of vocal exercises (*esercizi*), *vocalizzi* and *solfeggi* published during the nineteenth century continued nevertheless to remain dependent upon a progressive division into scales, leaps, suspensions, and embellishments, rounded off with short didactic compositions."[47] Rossini's own published *gorgheggi* and *solfeggi* followed this format, and Baragwanath notes the similarity between his treatise and traditional counterpoint pedagogy.

A consideration of the unified pedagogy of composer and singers—and how it relied on improvisational performance as a foundation—complicates the direction of influence assumed by scholars such as Gossett and Colas. It is not so much that composers wrote melodies that singers then varied, imitating the original, but that both composers and singers were trained to construct melodies by practicing a range of improvisational solutions to certain schemata. Instead of attempting to tease out the issue of whose ornaments are "better"—more sophisticated, more innovative—I would like to suggest that we understand Rossini's ornamented style as participating in the same creative, improvisational practices that were used to train singers. One result of this shift in perspective is that the notion of an "original" and a "variant" becomes virtually meaningless, something that Carl Dahlhaus hinted at long ago:

> When we try to extract an underlying melody from the coloratura, we sometimes arrive at nothing even remotely resembling a musical idea. We should not view this as a technical or artistic shortcoming on Rossini's part so much as an indication that, in Rossini's case, the premise that the substance of music resides in its melodic contour, with coloratura a mere adjunct or paraphrase, will often lead us nowhere.[48]

Though he is speaking only of music authored by Rossini, and not of singers' ornaments, the point still holds: rather than place Rossini's scores at the origin point of improvisational intervention, we can better understand them as stages in a process of musical invention—a process that involves more than one authoritative participant. This is an aesthetic of potentially endless variation and repetition: when a musician arrives at a particularly successful realization, he or she may rely upon that formula again and again.

The Contessa's Hat, Cinti-Damoreau's Cadenzas

We can see this aesthetic at work in the pedagogy of Laure Cinti-Damoreau, the creator of the role of the Countess di Folleville, who was acknowledged as a master of Rossinian ornamentation. Born Laure-Cinthie Montalant in Paris in 1801, she came, in Austin Caswell's words, "to personify the practice of virtuosic extemporized vocalization, a practice always held by the French to be quintessentially Italian."[49] Italianizing her name at the suggestion of prima donna Angelica Catalani, Cinti-Damoreau made her reputation as a Rossinian soprano; her voice was praised for its lightness and delicacy, with a range from c1 to b2, and she was noted for her agility and creativity in embellishing melodic lines.[50] One critic wrote that "She performs, in a marvelous and prodigious fashion, the most extraordinary difficulties that modern vocalisation can invent, and sang cadenzas which resembled true concertos."[51] All of these qualities are evident in her treatise, the *Méthode de Chant* (1849), which is a rich source of insight on ornamentation practices, especially as they apply to Rossini's operas.

As Austin Caswell has skillfully demonstrated, Cinti-Damoreau's treatise provides us with a fascinating glimpse into the many contradictions that marked improvisational practice. Framed by rhetoric that seems to subsume it under the composer's authority, the exercises and method itself seem to tell a different story, one worth revisiting here. The style of ornamentation Cinti-Damoreau's treatise teaches is firmly rooted in a past golden age: the Rossinian style that took Paris by storm in the mid-1820s. But Cinti-Damoreau's treatise first appeared in 1849, at a time when improvised ornament had been subject to strident critique from a number of quarters. Cinti-Damoreau's prefatory essay, "Advice to my students at the Conservatoire on the art of singing," is clearly a product of this later period and therefore treads carefully, reassuring her readers that her method is respectful of the composer's work and urging singers to fit their cadenzas to the spirit of the composition—admonitions that set the preface at odds with the content of the method.

But Cinti-Damoreau is not simply practicing a kind of "spin"—her advice is more than respectful lip service. Rather, faithfulness to the "spirit" of the work emerged in performance, and it was necessarily more than a matter of fidelity to notes on the page. The distance between the rhetoric that frames Cinti-Damoreau's treatise and the content of the treatise itself is often quite striking. Despite the fact that it prefaces a collection of mostly wordless cadenzas, roulades, and vocalises, the "Advice to my students" repeatedly stresses that singing should be understood as a kind of speaking. And, perhaps surprisingly for a treatise that purports to teach singers how to embellish and ornament in a florid style, Cinti-Damoreau stresses the values of simplicity and of relating music to text. Indeed, placing words above melody is consistently spoken of as the high road, whereas merely indulging in ornament represents the easy and fame-seeking way. She speaks of learning to sing the canzonet, because it is more difficult—"difficult beyond belief, because it demands to be spoken rather than sung."[52] Cinti-Damoreau also cautions young singers to resist the temptation to indulge in ornament for the sake of audience acclaim:

> this facility in varying virtuoso passages, although it provokes applause, should not be pushed to an extreme; it is important that the ornaments be rhythmic, appropriate to the genre and the tempo of the piece, and always subordinate to the words. Beware always of that torrent of notes, lacking in intelligence, in character, and in color, with which mediocre singers try so hard to charm the public and do not forget, I repeat, that the embellishments must ever be subordinated to the words, because varying a musical phrase should not involve distorting it or rendering it unrecognizable.[53]

Her final exhortation does not scruple to restate the theme: "Above all, one must, in effect, 'speak' when singing; accent, expression, these are the things that should concern you continually; I have said this to you before in the strongest terms, and I dare to say again."[54]

Cinti-Damoreau's wariness and words of caution are not unique; they could stand in for countless other such pieces of advice and critique. Her relentless reiteration of the importance of textual clarity and the meaning of the words over and above mere flurries of notes owes much, no doubt, to long-standing debates surrounding the importance of text-setting in French melody versus Italian melody. Certainly, by 1849, Cinti-Damoreau had likely absorbed the transformation in operatic style—the decline of elaborate Rossinian melody—and it thus made sense to frame her method as relevant to contemporary concerns. But her "Advice to my students" also speaks to a competing set of values—values that have little to do with textual clarity. Cinti-Damoreau suggests that the point of improvising ornamentation is for the singer to be recognized as a creative force of her own. This idea is elaborated in two reminiscences. First, she relates that "some true opera lovers attended each and every one of my performances, and I could not add even an unexpected appoggiatura to one of their favorite pieces without it being immediately noticed and enthusiastically applauded." This suggests a core constituency of regular operagoers who knew the works she performed and could tell precisely how she was altering them. For her part, she claims to have aimed her "musical coquetry" at the orchestra, hoping to gain signs of approval from her fellow musicians and the conductor, in particular.

A second memory is even more telling: Cinti-Damoreau describes how she and another singer prepared a duet together, agreeing in advance on the ornaments they would perform. She does not name the piece, but describes it as a "question and answer" duet; her role was to respond. Unexpectedly, however, during the performance "an evil thought seized hold" of the other singer and she changed all the agreed-upon ornaments. Cinti-Damoreau writes, "Greatly disconcerted at first, I did not falter, and through one of those flashes of inspiration that defy explanation, I answered her phrase for phrase without missing a fraction of a beat, improvising other passages where, I must admit, one could sense some of the vexation I felt at the unexpected turn of events." The lesson is that you must vary all the time—as she says, "playing with any and every musical phrase."[55] Here there is no mention of the importance of the words or the spirit of the piece, because this virtuosic performance is all about demonstrating Cinti-Damoreau's skill, her depth of study, and her inspiration—which is clearly de-mythologized here, and connected to hard work. The story of Cinti-Damoreau's own improvisatory triumph rubs up uncomfortably against her admonition to always keep the text in mind and to never overwhelm either it or the composer's melodies with one's own improvisations.

If Cinti-Damoreau's repeated cautions concerning the dangers of excessive or tasteless ornament seem to melt away in the face of this moment of triumph, even a cursory glance at the method itself reveals other cracks in the dutiful façade. Despite Cinti-Damoreau's protestations that ornament must be restrained, appropriate, and rooted in speechlike aesthetics, Caswell notes that they are not an "accurate reflection of her own vocal practice."[56] Above all, Cinti-Damoreau's insistence that cadenzas should bear the stamp of the piece is not carried out in the exercises themselves. As Caswell puts it, "It is hard to find evidence of this advice among her own cadenzas and variants. Upon studying them, one is struck by the similarities of structure and the stereotyped melodic technique which make any of them resemble the others."[57] Cinti-Damoreau's prefatory remarks and her method seem to be working at cross-purposes, and the fact that her exercises so stubbornly resist the ideology of subordinating music to words seems to call for explanation. And yet, the sheer number and apparent sameness of Cinti-Damoreau's cadenzas—and of ornamental variants in general—can easily engulf the scholar trained to deal with musical texts. The impulse may be to try to discern individuality in the face of their reliance on certain formulae, perhaps by following Caswell's lead and cataloguing their gestures and strategies—and noticing when she departs from her norm. Surely, one thinks, we could make something of the substitution, in this or that instance, of fast arpeggios for the soprano's normally favored descending chromatic scales? But these cadenzas adamantly resist close reading. Instead, I would like to let go of the desire to dissect and categorize to focus instead on the sheer abundance of Cinti-Damoreau's cadenzas. The very multiplicity of ornamentation—and its proliferation in and as texts—spurs us to reconsider the story we normally tell about the role scores played in the emergence of the operatic work and the decline of improvisatory vocal traditions. I maintain that the explosion of vocal treatises and piano-vocal scores in the early decades of the nineteenth century can be understood as an outgrowth and facilitation of—rather than a challenge to—improvisatory values.[58] Since improvisation depended on the repetition and variation of existing models, the proliferation of texts is something akin to the proliferation of improvised variants themselves, and an expression of older performative values carried over into a new medium.

Vary the Repeat

It seems a given that writing something down reflects an urge to fix and standardize, to make an authoritative copy from which other copies hopefully do not deviate. In the intersection between written and oral traditions, the former often emerges as the victor: once you write something down, so the story goes, you reduce variability, improvisation suffers, and standardization follows close behind.[59] Scholars maintain that as more and more copies of the same cadenza became available, the less variety was heard in operatic performances. Conformity and consistency become the watchwords, rather than individuality and spontaneity. This is the argument put forth by Naomi Matsumoto, for example, who claims that the late nineteenth-century dissemination of the famous cadenza with flute used in the mad scene of Donizetti's *Lucia di Lammermoor*—composed by Mathilde Marchesi for her student Nelly Melba—stemmed from a "patriarchal" apprenticeship system that led to greater uniformity in moments of supposed spontaneity.[60] This interpretation accords with what Susan Rutherford has called the standardization of vocal pedagogy in mid-century: as greater numbers of teachers began to publish their methods, she claims, the notion of the unique character of individual voices began to decline. Rutherford has linked the growth of published treatises to increasing standardization in approaches to cultivating an operatic voice. Vocal treatises, which became more common as the century unfolded, conveyed to their users the confidence of learning a particular star singer's method. Instead of working with an instructor who sought to tease out an individual's unique sound, students flocked to gurus to learn the "Lablache method," or whichever star singer's method was thought to carry the imprimatur of authority.[61] In this view, treatises like Cinti-Damoreau's played an important role in the formation of singer-focused operatic authority, but at the cost of individuality. The many exercises Cinti-Damoreau provides also seem designed not to help the individual student find their own particular strengths, but to replicate Cinti-Damoreau's successes. Her treatise takes an approach that is obviously suited to an individual voice and attempts to generalize it, instructing the student in supposedly objective principles.

The publication of complete opera scores—and the rise of publishing giant Casa Ricordi—has been similarly understood as crucial to the development of the work concept and to the consolidation of the composer's authority. During the 1840s, Ricordi's deepening relationship with Verdi, who insisted on greater control over the fate of his operas, and the launching of the *Gazetta Musicale di Milano*, the publisher's house organ, both reflected and contributed to this broader ideological shift.[62] But remaining attuned to the historical infiltration of improvisational values into the early *ottocento* publishing process reveals detours and switchbacks in the trend toward concretizing both works and practices. As Stefano Baia Curioni has discussed, in the early decades of the nineteenth century, it was often impresari who commissioned works and who then had "responsibility" (as notions of intellectual property were still very hazy) for the scores. The continued life of the operatic work—either in domestic settings or in new productions—necessitated the services of a copyist (it is no coincidence that Giovanni Ricordi began his career as a copyist), which introduced the potential for more changes and variants.[63]

One other result of the copyist system was the potential for piracy, as Philip Gossett's meticulous detective work on the publishing history of Rossini's *Semiramide* demonstrates. Although the Viennese publisher Artaria bought the rights to Rossini's autograph from La Fenice with the intention of releasing the complete score, pirated extracts published by Ricordi—and shamelessly advertised in the press—began to appear in Italy before Artaria could publish their own edition. Angered at the potential loss of income, Artaria appealed to La Fenice to "take steps with the police there, so that the named Ricordi [could] explain from whence he received the manuscripts," force him to withdraw his scores, and pay damages.[64] All threats of reprisal were for naught. Ricordi, in defending his actions to the head of the provincial delegation in charge of theaters, argued that each version of an opera is a new work, and (disingenuously for someone who vehemently defended his own rights in other situations) that operas given in public performance are public property:

> The law determines the rights and obligations of an author and of the editor of an opera, including musical compositions; but it neither mentions nor prohibits anyone from making variations and modifications on the work of others, which constitute the subject of a completely separate and new work in and of itself. When for public pleasure *Semiramide* was performed, that music with its poetry was offered to the public and became in this sense public property.

As for the matter of how he obtained the material upon which he based his published extracts, Ricordi went on to claim that "whoever then owned the score knew, and must have known, that with an extraordinarily fine memory it is possible to retain all or most of a heard discourse," arguing that someone with a good memory could "set down on music paper, even with no differences, the motives and notes of the score, solidly fixed in the mind and remembered with precision."[65] Clearly Ricordi is trying to weasel out of the question of how he was able to acquire any written sources, since he had no legal access to either the autograph or parts prepared for rehearsals. Gossett notes that while in some cases Ricordi did appear to have acquired material in less than legal ways ("a copyist might have provided him with musical manuscripts surreptitiously; a singer might have shared with Ricordi's agents a vocal part"), it is clear that several of the extracts were generated by "a musician with a prodigious memory" who was likely sent to the theater to "spy" for Ricordi.[66] Gossett analyzes several passages that seem to have been "overheard"—for example, cases in which vocal lines are largely accurate but accompaniments are not, or where Ricordi's vocal parts differ substantially from the autograph, suggesting that the score records changes singers introduced in performance. Noticing several telling details in Ricordi's version of the duet for Arsace and Assur, Gossett maintains, "This is not merely a careless copy of a written score; it cannot have been based on a written score but instead must have been surreptitiously and inaccurately transcribed from the actual performance. We are here faced with oral transmission, not copying."[67] These new "works" are thus generated from and are records of the performance. Even when Ricordi eventually secured the rights to issue his own complete score, he simply collected his previously published extracts (despite their "inaccuracies") and filled in the gaps by consulting the autograph manuscript.

The publication of complete operas—and the creation of physical representations of "works"—thus went hand in hand with the practice of generating multiple copies of operatic extracts for use in different contexts, both domestic and professional. In the case of extracted arias, their authority relied in part upon the attempt to reproduce the individualities of specific singers. Aria scores often prominently displayed the names of singers, along with the claim that the music followed the changes introduced by the singer in performance; in this sense, they were more likely to be considered transcriptions of successful performances than idealized works (fig. 2.3). In the hierarchy of operatic fetishism, the moment composer put pen to page was of little interest to nineteenth-century audiences and domestic music-makers. Rather, the supposedly spontaneous outpouring of the star singer was the moment of creation worth capturing and preserving. This is of course at odds with the idea of the source or original that we now tend to focus on in text editing—the closest thing to the authorial hand.

Operatic scores and vocal treatises thus had a very different textual status than that granted to musical scores in the post-Urtext era. They can be seen not primarily as an attempt to fix and control but as a manifestation of an aesthetic of variation. Laura Moeckli, writing on variants for "Una voce poco fa," notes that the practice of ornamentation relies on what pedagogue Manuel Garcia Jr. called "progressive variation," a principle that we have already encountered: the singer begins simply and spins more and more complex figures.[68] What makes this variation possible is repetition. Speaking of "Una voce," she writes, "As the textual and musical repetitions increase, they are progressively varied, again demonstrating the structural and rhetorical function of ornamentation. Obviously if this had been his aesthetic aim, Rossini could have composed arias which fit the exact number of words in the text and thus avoided the numerous repetitions so typical of this repertoire. If interpreted correctly, these repetitions are not redundant, but create vast improvisational spaces for singers to insert their variations."[69]

This "variation principle" was so widespread that it inflects even those moments when musical notation was used to establish a stable ground for improvisational alteration. Will Crutchfield writes of Garcia's multiple citations of a

FIGURE 2.3 Rubini (singer) listed above composer (Donizetti) in the score for the aria "Da quel di, che lei perduta" from *Anna Bolena*. Sibley Music Library Special Collections, M1508.D683 A61 D1 1860.

particular phrase from the first number of Rossini's *Il barbiere di Siviglia* in four different discussions of the passage in the second part of his 1847 *École de Garcia: Traité complet de l'art du chant.*[70] "Clearly working from memory and not seeking any consistency of notation," he writes, Garcia's four variants display a remarkably casual attitude to time signature, rhythm, and textual emphasis (ex. 2.7). Crutchfield uses this example to caution modern scholars to take the seemingly precise notation of ornamentation notebooks with a grain of salt; not every variant is an intentional interpretive decision. But I would add that each of these versions has its own validity in Garcia's world. Although we might think of ornament as a kind of filigree applied to an unchanging melodic structure, that framework itself was likely much more flexible than we have imagined. It seems to have remained so; Crutchfield has discussed how early recordings show that, even in the early twentieth century, a considerable amount of individual variation persisted. He suggests that it was the advent of recording, not necessarily of printed texts, that led to the standardization of operatic performance that we find today.[71]

If, as I am arguing, the notion of an "original" in our modern sense is somewhat foreign to the context of early ottocento Italian opera, what then do we make of the drive to textualization represented by vocal treatises, singers' ornamental notebooks, and published versions of arias "as sung by" famous vocalists? We only have to recall Garcia's "mistakes" in transcribing Rossini to realize that textualization allows for the introduction of multiple variants, changes, mistakes, and alterations. Jeffrey Kallberg, for example, has teased apart the "problem" of Chopin's variants, showing that every time he prepared a manuscript for printing, he apparently thought of it as an opportunity to introduce improvisatory alterations to his scores.[72] For many musicians of the early nineteenth century, scores were a way to facilitate the process of generating multiple variants rather than a system by which they could

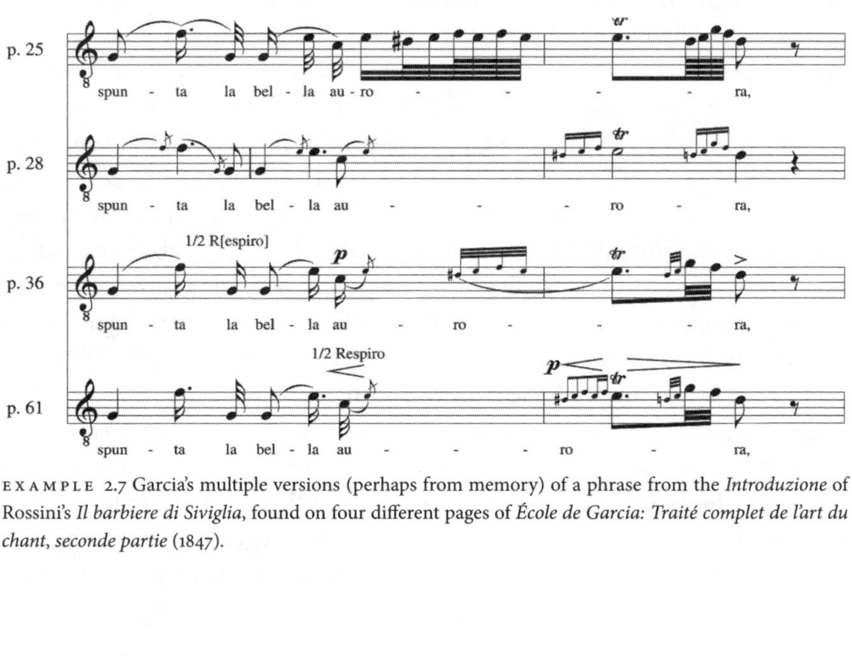

EXAMPLE 2.7 Garcia's multiple versions (perhaps from memory) of a phrase from the *Introduzione* of Rossini's *Il barbiere di Siviglia*, found on four different pages of *École de Garcia: Traité complet de l'art du chant, seconde partie* (1847).

introduce consistency—much the same way that the superior ability of today's data-capturing technology allows us to save every single revision made in a document, for example. I propose that at least in this Italian context, the "technology" of the easily printed piano-vocal score was used to similar ends: to capture and preserve (but more importantly to disseminate) the multiple variants of singerly performance, including improvised ornament. This is an important historical circumstance that cannot simply be either lamented or glossed over. While the making of a critical edition may require the ferreting out of an original, authoritative manuscript and may require the hierarchical ranking of variants in order of closeness to the authorial "hand" of the composer, we must guard against letting the values of text editing obscure historical practice. We might think of scores not as an endpoint or the goal of a creative process, but as both contributing to and documenting the endless stream of operatic performances, each of them slightly different.[73]

Increasing textualization goes hand in hand with changes in both the production and consumption of opera. Just as changes in the notation of the appoggiatura accompanied shifts in the transmission of performance practices, the proliferation of treatises and scores similarly speaks to the growth of music publishing and a burgeoning audience for scores.[74] The increasing specificity of the notational practices surrounding the simple appoggiatura is not evidence of a growing concern with honoring a composer's intentions, but rather a sign that scores were traveling into new territories, beyond the boundaries where knowledge of conventional practices was a given. As more people sought to study voice, often with the help of treatises and methods, and as they bought individual arias to perform in domestic settings, specifying "proper" performance practices became more vital. The increasing textualization of opera was in part an attempt to codify and explain practices for new audiences or potential new performers.[75] Like Waiblinger's transcriptions of Rosa Taddei's musical accompaniments, they become necessary only because others might be attempting the practice. If we construct authoritative texts based on values that, even while acknowledging the collaborative nature of operatic composition, privilege the composer's decisions above all others, we fail to grasp that, for audiences, it was the singer's charisma that was of primary importance. As we have seen, the split between "creator" and "interpreter" was by no means as clear as we assume.

If an operatic performance was the venue, then, in which a singer asserted his or her own authority, nineteenth-century operatic authorship was something like a game of musical chairs. The "author" in this scenario is not any one individual, but is rather a space one briefly occupies—until the music starts up again. While the music is playing, the participants (composer, performer, librettist) circle the authorial chair. We are quite happy to hear now the singer, now the composer, now the librettist or conductor or stage director or costume designer, all as potential authors of the event; while the tune plays on, they are all performing their authority in various ways and to different extents. But when the music stops, there is only one place remaining, and it has tended to accommodate only one person—the composer. We might well ask whether the chair could be large enough to accommodate several bodies. Or whether we might attend to this game of musical chairs itself as it unfolds, even long after the music has stopped.

*

In *The Man Who Mistook His Wife for a Hat*, neurologist Oliver Sacks describes the case of a patient who came to him with a puzzling set of symptoms. The man, identified only by the initial P., is a music teacher who seems to be experiencing difficulty identifying and relating to visual data: he notices the rose in Sacks's lapel, for example, but can only describe it as a "convoluted red form with a linear green attachment."[76] When the patient gets up to leave Sacks's office, he firmly grasps his wife's head and attempts to lift it off and put it on his own head: as Sacks describes it, "He had mistaken his wife for a hat!"[77] Despite these seemingly debilitating symptoms, P. has found a way to compensate—he sings. As long as he is able to make up songs about the activities of his daily life, he can function, but when the song is interrupted, he does not know how to proceed.

We might imagine that Rossini, like Oliver Sacks's patient, is in need of someone to distinguish his work from a hat. The work of the scholar, it would seem, is to separate the real and essential from what is layered over it: the accretion, the accessory. But Rossini, too, was a singer—not precisely like our patient P., but one whose compositional aesthetic was steeped in the improvisatory and performative values of his time. If we remain attuned to Rossini's operas as, in one sense, an assemblage of performed songs—songs that were made to showcase the skill, taste, and improvisatory prowess of the singers who performed them—suddenly the distinction between hats and heads, between ornaments and melodies, seems less important.

I have returned at last to the question of Fo's hats, flying through the air, multiplying like rabbits, growing large enough to support a soprano. What are we to make of them? One thing that is clear in this scene is that Fo has turned the normal order of things literally upside down. This hat supports the Contessa—it elevates her (fig. 2.2). She stands upon it rather than it upon her head. I find it almost impossible not to think of this moment as a giant visual pun on the notion of the masterpiece: the "capo-lavoro" (head-work) in

Italian. Here the capolavoro is revealed as the "piedilavoro": the masterwork is really the fancy footwork of the singer. What was figure is made ground, accessory becomes foundation, and the real work is not simply what is written down but instead what flies through the air: the sounds that emerge from the singer's throat.

3

Divinely Inspired: Incantation and the Making of Melody in Bellini's *Norma*

> As an aesthetic experience, improvisation foregrounds time in its passing and its presence; it is an art of occasion that privileges the experience shared between performer and audience here and now. There is, therefore, a crucial distinction to be made between *inspiration* as a private, cognitive aspect of the act of composition, one that traditionally has religious or spiritual connotations, and *improvisation* as a performative, public, normally secular phenomenon.
>
> ANGELA ESTERHAMMER, *Romanticism and Improvisation*, 4

Nineteenth-century composers of Italian opera were at pains to show that they were both spontaneous and studied, that they combined the best of improvisation's performative flair with the solitary inspiration of written composition. Bellini famously embodied this paradox. His compositional process was described in an oft-quoted letter, purportedly sent to Agostino Gallo in 1829:

> Shut up in my room, I begin by declaiming each character's lines with all the heat of passion, and I closely observe the inflections of my voice, the speeding up and slowing down of the declamation in each situation, the overall accent and the expressive tone that characterizes a man in the grip of passion, and I find the motives and the general rhythmic character best suited to demonstrate them and infuse them with new life by means of harmony. Then I throw them onto paper, try them out on the piano, and when I myself feel the corresponding emotion, I judge that I have succeeded.[1]

The fact that this letter was forged, probably in 1843 and likely by Francesco Florimo, Bellini's close confidant, has done little to dim its power; its appeal lies in how it presents the moment of creation in a flattering Romantic light.[2] It was a popular trope. Giuseppe Giacosa's memory of meeting Verdi during the composition of *Otello* in 1884 draws on the same themes, with the exception that here the composer's recitation is witnessed by both Giacoso and the opera's librettist:

> Verdi would sometimes clutch the libretto and read several pieces aloud. Boito and I looked at each other, our gazes expressing our great admiration: the

> voice, the accent, the cadences, the force, the anger expressed in that reading betrayed such an ardent kindling of the soul, magnified so immeasurably by the sense of the words, that the source of the musical idea was clearly revealed to us. With our own eyes we saw, as it were, the flower of melody blossom.[3]

Both these accounts claim to pull back the curtain on the normally hidden moment of inspiration, giving us a glimpse of the birth of operatic melody. Though the Verdian tale, like the Bellinian, also has the "all the hallmarks of a manufactured myth," in Nicholas Baragwanath's words, the crucial element shared by the two is not that the account they present is fictionalized. Rather, it is notable that in both scenes, a perfectly conventional facet of operatic composition—speaking the poetry aloud to determine the verses' rhythm and affect—becomes invested with a new significance. In Bellini's case, as Mary Ann Smart has pointed out, the forged letter became central to the composer's image as "a composer who worked painstakingly to fit music to words, often going through numerous drafts of a single aria."[4] Bellini's speech-oriented melodies were both applauded and decried, depending on his contemporaries' own aesthetic prejudices—and modern scholars often point to his *filosofico* style as a definitive break from the improvisatory, ornamental excess represented by Rossini.[5]

But these (perhaps mythical, perhaps merely exaggerated) scenes of inspired composition are striking for the way they depict the making of operatic melody as a reverse engineering of poetic improvisation. Bellini and Verdi are portrayed as declaiming poets, but instead of producing verses in the heat of the moment, it is melody itself that emerges from poetry spoken aloud. The performative aspect of recitation—the speeding up and slowing down of speech, investing spoken discourse with the accents of passion—is what yields music. Bellini displays more than an admirable attention to text, then; operatic composition is rendered performative, as the composer uses technologies of writing and keyboard to capture and assess his own performances. Each composer is, of course, reciting someone else's words in these scenes: he is possessed by them, inspired by them. The imaginative act of embodying the spirit of another artist (here, the librettist) ties the opera composer even more firmly both to the world of the poetic improviser and to the figure of the divinely inspired sibyl, who is a vessel for an unseen creative force. The imbrication of the act of poetic declamation with melodic composition in these accounts suggests that one nineteenth-century model of operatic authorship was that of the medium, who has the ability to become a vessel for, and translator of, other voices.

This chapter explores how mythic accounts of the origins of Bellinian melody intertwine with his actual compositional practices (inasmuch as they are

FIGURE 3.1 Ossian and Malvina, Pelagius Palagi (1775–1860). Italy, 18th century. © DeA Picture Library / Art Resource, NY.

accessible to us) by focusing on a pair of figures iconic of nineteenth-century ideals of creative inspiration—the bard and the priestess—and their echoes in Bellini's *Norma* (figs. 3.1 and 3.2). Although Bellini's opera and the Italian craze for the third-century Scottish bard Ossian have both been understood as part of the burgeoning desire for archaic, northern subjects, they have much more in common.[6] Tracing the connections between the northern poet that critics hoped would revitalize Italian letters and Bellini's Druidic priestess, I point to the new centrality of poetic voice in the making of operatic melody. Translators and adaptors of Ossian looked to him for a new model of creativity, one that seemed free of restricting conventions and combined poetic authenticity with theatrical immediacy. Bellini's Druidic priestess, on the other hand, was a crystallization of contemporary notions of creativity that emphasized oracular speech and portrayed the artist as a vessel for a message from beyond. As James Q. Davies has shown, it is in the reception of *Norma* that we find the first reference to an operatic soprano as a diva.[7] "Casta Diva," its most famous aria, thus became the number to most vividly embody the overlapping Romantic values of divinity, inspiration, incantation, and mediumship.

To be sure, if the image of Bellini as a composer who "declaim[ed] each character's lines with all the heat of passion . . . closely observ[ing] the inflections

FIGURE 3.2 Giuditta Pasta as Norma, 1831. Art Collection 3 / Alamy Stock Photo.

of [his] voice" recalls the poetic improviser, the composer's extensive self-borrowing presents a challenge to this image of a creator blessed with a ready fount of inspiration. The debates surrounding Bellini's reuse of his own material and its challenge to Romantic authorship, however, were foreshadowed by Ossianism, with its concerns about authenticity and the appropriate relationship to both the past and the voices of others. By examining the Romantic tendency to hear melodic composition as similar to the act of poetic declamation, we can attune our ears to the many different voices—including those of the librettist and singer—involved in the creative process. As I explore how the figures of the bard and the chanting priestess open up to broader questions about the origins of creativity, I argue that Bellini's *Norma* blurs traditional distinctions between inspiration and improvisation, privileging heightened receptivity as a precondition for artistic creation. As we will see, this model of the artist as an oracular sibyl was not confined to performers—indeed, both poets and composers were just as bound up in this new Romantic fantasy of creation. That such a fantasy was often directly at odds with the realities of operatic production created an intriguing set of frictions and compensations.

Ossianic Inspiration

When Felice Romani encountered the 1831 play by Alexandre Soumet that served as the source for *Norma*'s libretto, it must have seemed doubly attractive: replete with theatrical situations suitable for soprano Giuditta Pasta's abilities and set in a mythical-historical Celtic world with which he was already intimately familiar. Romani was no dabbler—he coauthored a six-volume dictionary of ancient mythologies and antiquities—and his scholarly immersion in the ancient Northern world was part of a larger trend that went back to at least the eighteenth century, when the works of Ossian first arrived in Italy.[8] He certainly would have been intimately familiar with the translations of Ossian by Melchiorre Cesarotti.[9]

James Macpherson's original English volume of the bard's poetry, verses, and epics was first translated into Italian by Cesarotti in 1763, and subsequent editions helped Ossianism spread throughout Italian literary and theatrical culture.[10] Influenced by both his style and themes, Italian artists saw in Ossian a bridge to a new aesthetic—the Scottish bard offered a fresh model of creativity in the midst of a debate between ancients (who believed poets should continue to look to tradition for inspiration, and preserve metrical and verse conventions) and moderns. Those who espoused the "modern" position, arguing for the importance of direct inspiration from nature, were in dire need of a figure to place up against Homer, who dominated Italian literary discussions. Cesarotti saw in Ossian support for his own agenda regarding ancient poetry: he provided, in Enrico Mattioda's words, "the very instrument that could undo the canon from within, an ancient text devoid of the rules that had been rigorously followed up to that time."[11] From the beginning, Ossian was such an appealing figure because, in his supposed wildness and barbarism, there lay the proof that poetic inspiration did not emerge solely from knowledge of the classics. His genius lay in his connection to nature and thus his freedom from civilization's strictures.

One of the most vexing problems facing any translator of Ossian was how (or even whether) to versify Ossian's poems. Macpherson's prose offered few clues as to how to transform the poetry for audiences used to the regular verse forms of Petrarch or Dante. Cesarotti's image of the bard as outside of tradition no doubt guided his decision to use blank verse (*versi sciolti*), non-rhyming groups of mostly eleven-syllable lines, rather than the *ottava rima* or other traditional rhyme schemes.[12] Cesarotti chose to render verses in rhyme only where Macpherson noted that the original Gaelic text shifted in meter.[13] But whether in the long passages of blank verse or in the briefer rhymed and versified interludes, Cesarotti always looked for ways to introduce rhythmic variety by breaking speeches in the middle of lines, altering accents within each line, or mixing lines of different lengths.[14] Such strategies sought to replace the smooth uniformity of classical poetry with a more blunt and varied—and therefore more "authentic" and ancient—style.

The *poema drammatico* "Comala" is a case in point. Macpherson's note accompanying the English text claims that "the variety of the measure shews that the poem was originally set to music, and perhaps presented before the chiefs upon solemn occasions."[15] As is clear from the poem's layout on the page, Cesarotti thus made his translation into a libretto:

Comala
Poema drammatico

Scena Prima
Dersagrena e Melilcoma
Dersagrena:

Già la caccia è compita;
Altro in Arven non s'ode
Che 'l rumor del torrente.
Vieni o figlia di Morni,
Dalle rive del Crona.
Lascia l'arco,
Prendi l'arpa;
La notte avansizi
Tra dolci cantici,
Tra feste e giubili;
E larga spandisi
Per Arven tutto la letizia nostra.[16]

Cesarotti departs from convention, however, by varying the length of his lines in both recitative passages and arias.[17] The tale of the beautiful Comala, who waits for her beloved Fingal to return from battle, features many operatic touches—including a scorned lover who causes Comala's death from shock and distress when he (falsely) reports that Fingal has been slain, and a lamenting chorus of bards who sing Comala's praises to the heavens. The poem also begins with explicit musical performances by Comala's companions, the daughters of Morni. The first, Dersagrena, opens the action with an apparently operatic utterance: a recitative-like section in unrhymed seven-syllable lines (*settenari*), followed by several five-syllable lines (*quinari*) all ending similarly—*avanzisi, cantici, giubili, spandasi*—suggesting an aria. But before that rhyming passage of *quinari*, Cesarotti inserts a single line of *ottonari*, broken into two four-syllable fragments: "Lascia l'arco, prendi l'arpa (Lay down the bow, take up the harp)." This fragmentation was certainly characteristic of Cesarotti's "striving to create a broken rhythm in the rhyming verses so as to move beyond that melodious Metastasian style," as Mattioda argues.[18] Here, however, the fragmentary utterance also works to frame this vocal performance as both foreign and ancient, the remnant or echo of a song excavated from the past.

But precisely because of the "broken and varied" nature of Cesarotti's translations, critics grappled with the translation's suitability for musical setting. In Italy, poetry was, quite simply, an occasion for performance—and musical performance in particular. Unrhymed and unversified poetry was not very good fodder for musico-theatrical productions. Therefore, many readers focused a disproportionate amount of attention on the small portions in Cesarotti's translation that were rendered in rhymed verse—and were disappointed that they did not conform to existing theatrical conventions. The scholar Saverio Mattei, for example, corresponded with Cesarotti in 1779, sending him a detailed, lengthy critique entitled "Comments on the lyrical and dramatic parts in Ossian." In it, he praised Cesarotti's innovations while (somewhat obtusely) taking him to task for breaking with the Metastasian model.[19] Mattei would have much preferred it had Cesarotti housed these exciting new subjects and situations within traditional poetic forms:

> Comala would be much more beautiful if it were more Metastasian in style. The recitative parts are hardly distinguishable from the arias, and this seems to create some confusion. The entrance and everything that makes up the dialogue should be in full verses of eleven and seven syllables or begin with the controlled aria. . . . Melilcoma's aria has a very irregular metre. In contrast, the last 4 lines are sensibly irregular and convey passion in an innovative manner; however, the first 4 are irregular for no reason whatsoever.[20]

For Mattei this was not merely an intellectual exercise. He urged Cesarotti to think about the suitability of his translation for music and reconsider his abandonment of convention: "I assure you that if your great Ossianic poem, interrupted as it is by lyrical moments (an innovation completely unknown to all other ancient poets), were tempered by the fluidity of the regular metre of Metastasian lyrics, your work will be one hundred times more worthy, it would be popular, and you would have the pleasure of hearing so much of your beautiful poetry sung."[21]

Perhaps Mattei needn't have worried—from Calzabigi and Morandi's 1780 *Comala* to Rossini and Tottola's chorus of bards in *La donna del lago* (1819) to Cammarano and Pacini's *Malvina di Scozia* in 1851, the world of Italian opera was fascinated by Ossian.[22] Mattioda, perusing the libretti of these operas for traces of Cesarotti's poetic innovations, inevitably finds himself disappointed: "The popularity of Ossian in melodrama continued without really developing the innovations proposed by Cesarotti . . . Ossian offered a mannered primitivism that could serve as the backdrop for plots based on contested loves and damsels in distress, familiar themes that would live up to the expectations of the melodrama audience."[23] What is missing in particular, except for brief and notable exceptions, is any departure from the ubiquity of isometric verse forms and the conventional distinction between recitative and aria. Surveying this trove of *melodrammi*, Mattioda is forced to conclude that often, operas invoke Ossianic themes simply to provide "a stylized exotic setting."[24] Mattioda's critique is not new: the fact that many Ossianic adaptations diverged from the epic nature of their model annoyed contemporary critics as well. A review of *Oitona*, an Ossianic tragedy, complained that "The turgid and boisterous style could not be more anti-tragic. The aim was to imitate Ossian, but Ossian did not declaim from the stage; his harp was born amid warfare and would waken to the clamour of victories."[25] The fact that Ossian was a participant in the dramas he narrated (and that performing bards appear in epic scenes of action) lent the poems an air of authenticity but also made them susceptible to stage portrayals, with all the clichés and artificiality critics ascribed to them. The Ossianic ideal, then, was often in conflict with Italian theatrical reality.

An Aesthetics of Transcription

Moreover, Ossian embodied the problem with Romantic authorship because he was both an archetype of and a threat to poetic authenticity.[26] The very fact that the "original Ossian" was held up as a model of a new, more authentic creativity was in itself an irony—for the bard himself would eventually be revealed as an imaginary (or composite) author, the poetry stemming from a variety of popular and oral sources not nearly as old as Macpherson claimed. But, as Francesca Broggi-Wüthrich has argued, for his supporters "the Ossianic poems . . . become the legitimate *occasion* for authentic lyrics. They offer a variety of expression that provided proof of originality since they were far from any inferior and blind imitation . . . This was the only true form of originality for the modern mind: the inspired *canto* that is retrieved from an ancient past and manifested in the specificity of historical form."[27]

Cesarotti strove to find a middle path between credulous acceptance of the fidelity of Macpherson's "translations" on the one hand and the dismissal of Ossian as an elaborate hoax on the other. Instead, as Paola Gambarota has noticed, he "reframe[d] the whole discussion by shifting the question of authenticity from the texts themselves to the poetical voice."[28] Though Cesarotti does affirm the existence of the bard named Ossian, he does not seem to have believed, she argues, that Macpherson had offered a "literal translation of ancient manuscript texts that had been preserved in their integrity." In an early letter to Macpherson, Cesarotti casually suggested (perhaps to encourage an admission of creative invention) that "people of *esprit*, to whom the whole dispute is utterly indifferent . . . would find much more power of spirit in a *moderne* who had been able to transform himself in Ossian than in Ossian himself."[29] Later on, he would be even more blatant: "[Macpherson] did not possess the legitimate Ossian, which could not be found in any single version of the retrieved songs, though he was scattered in all of them. The true Ossian was only in the compilation made by him and transcribed by his hand."[30]

Cesarotti's insistence that the "true Ossian" emerges only in compilation is crucial, for it articulates a notion of authentic authorship that is based both on a sounding poetic voice (with all its performative connotations) *and* on an aesthetic of transcription. Indeed, this is poetry that is both envoiced and written down, as if the work of improviser and stenographer were melded into one. Authorship emerges through a process of imaginative empathy with a singing voice and the act of capturing it in writing. As Gambarotta puts it, "In Cesarotti's interpretation of the Ossianic question, two individuals are involved in the process of handing down popular tradition: the bard, with his unique voice, who establishes tradition by defining it in songs, and the transcriber, who reproduces it by empathizing with it."[31] Certainly there is an interesting tension in this formulation: the voice is the locus of authenticity, but it only truly emerges in writing, not in ephemeral performance, whether recitation or song. It is the synthesis of the two—of transcription and song—that transcends any surviving fragments from a historical source.

Ossianic authorship is thus a transformative, almost mystical process whereby authorial identity emerges through an act of mediumship. This model of authorship as imaginative transcription of a remembered singing voice would seem to hold some promise for opera studies at a time of increased interest in both performance and decentering the composer's authority. Perhaps we could think of the composer functioning as a kind of scribe, setting down on paper the unique qualities of the singers with whom he worked and making himself a receptive medium for inspiration from both singer and poet. Bellini's creative process, for example, could be understood as an imaginative internalization of multiple voices, both singerly and poetic.[32] And yet, in a genre where the singing voice reigned supreme, Bellini, perhaps more than any other composer, has been praised for the way his own characteristic authorial voice was "sung" through the voices of his performers. As Pierluigi Petrobelli argued: "Bellini is unique and striking: Almost constantly, the total attention of the listener is directed to the melodic line: Bellini expresses himself principally through the singing of the soloists, and above all through the melodies entrusted to them."[33] If Bellini's compositional process depended on channeling many voices, the real mystery is how he was able to flip that process on its head, creating instead the impression of a singular authorial voice. Equally mysterious is how his melodies themselves became the medium through which this newly "poetic"—and timelessly authentic—authorial voice could be heard.

Opera's "Chaste Goddess"

Collaborating with Giuditta Pasta, the singer who created the title role of *Norma*, was perhaps ideal for such a purpose, in part because she already embodied a polyvocal ideal. Pasta was widely acclaimed for her consummate acting skills, her "spellbinding" timbre, and her impeccable musical understanding. Stendhal praised everything from her *portamento* to her sheer variety of tone and inflection.[34] But above all, the most unique aspect of Pasta's voice, which might have been a defect in any other singer, was the fact that she seemed to have (at least) two distinct voices, head voice (which Stendhal also called falsetto) and chest voice, that were produced, he posited, with entirely different mechanical means.[35] Susan Rutherford notes that Pasta's "long, multicoloured voice" never "match[ed] the ideals then set for *bel canto*—the registers remained forever unequal, joined by a middle, 'veiled' section that at times had a dark tone described as 'suffocated.' "[36] For her listeners, this was anything but a flaw: Pasta's voices were so "diametrically opposed" that the shift between their timbres was, Stendhal asserted, akin to the fascinating play of shadow and light.[37]

Writing in 1824, seven years before *Norma*, Stendhal lamented that as of yet no composer had produced music specifically suited to Pasta. He marveled at how she was able to hypnotize her audiences even when forced to contort her voice to accommodate melodies entirely unsuited to her skills.[38] The broader problem for Stendhal, however, was the absolute necessity of allowing singers the freedom to improvise. Pasta, he argues, is a consummate improviser—and composers should give her the scope to shine. "Between a singer struggling as best she can with music composed for someone else," he complains,

> with a score which denies her any freedom and any chance to come up with inspirations of her own; and the same [singer] performing *cantilenas* written expressly for her own voice, i.e., not only within her particular compass, but also within the range of her own [individual palette of] colours and the general shape [*physionomie*] of her talent, the difference is . . . striking![39]

It was not only that Pasta, as a restrained and tasteful improviser, could be trusted with such independence. Stendhal argues vehemently that the most inspired ornament only happens in the moment. After waxing rhapsodic about the myriad subtle variations in inflection, from bravery to sweet irony, to surprise and resentment, that Pasta was able to bring to the single phrase "Tremar Tancredi?"—different, he claims, in each of the thirty performances of Rossini's opera that he attended—Stendhal argues that such momentary inspiration can never be captured in a score:

> In the case of Madame Pasta, the subtleties . . . which change from one performance of *Tancredi* to the next, are [what Pascal might call] "infinitely small" things, so small indeed that no composer would possibly succeed in notating them. And if he were to try to write it out . . . it is obvious that this mordent or that embellishment—though perfectly fine in itself—may not suit the voice and mood of the actress on, say, the evening of September 30. This being so, she could not possibly have stirred the passions of the audience if she had performed that [particular] ornament at that [particular] performance on the evening of September 30.[40]

To showcase the fleeting, momentary inspiration of the singer is, for Stendhal, opera's primary reason for existence. Although he raises the possibility of the operatic score as transcription of performance (and thus of the composer as transcriber), he dismisses this possibility in the same breath. Truly expressive ornament *must* be improvised in the moment, and its extemporaneous nature is the key to its effectiveness. Because the singer has no idea what inspiration will find her at any given time—"say, the evening of September 30"—it is folly to attempt to fix her ornaments in advance. What Pasta needs above all, he continues, is a composer who will give the singer an appropriate canvas to display her expressive and improvisatory gifts. Stendhal insists that if Rossini could perceive the "intelligence, moderation, and good taste" of Pasta's own *fioriture*, he would "recover the passion with which he burned at the beginning of his career, and those delicious and simple melodies that first made his fame." He continues: "Fully convinced of the wisdom and good taste that Madame Pasta shows in her *fioriture*, and knowing how the effect of ornamentation is more reliable when it is born of the spontaneous emotion and invention of the singer, Rossini would no doubt entrust the ornaments to the inspiration of this great *cantatrice*."[41] He predicts that Pasta will make the fortune of the composer who studies her voice; any rival who would eclipse Rossini would do so by focusing on the "*genre simple* [simple manner]," in which she excels.[42]

Vincenzo Bellini would seem to be the answer to Stendhal's prayers. Not only were his early operas lauded by reviewers for abandoning elaborate Rossinian ornamentation in favor of syllabic melodies, but he worked closely with Pasta, tailoring his music and operatic subjects to her strengths. The first role he composed for her was that of Amina in *La sonnambula*, and while working on *Norma*, he wrote to Pasta's husband: "As far as *Norma* is concerned I shall alter anything that the good Giuditta wishes to have changed; but I shan't write a note for any of the other singers . . ."[43] Rutherford has explored the ways that Bellini shaped the score of Norma to showcase Pasta's talents. "Pasta's particular vocal qualities," she writes, "are invoked not only in Norma's long spinning melodies and *canto sillabico*, but in Bellini's markings on the autograph score: 'con voce soffocata', 'con passione crescente', 'con voce repressa' and so on."[44] But for Rutherford, it is mainly Pasta's unparalleled mastery of physical gesture that can be discerned in Bellini's score. Pasta's skill as a singing actress (*attrice cantante*), she maintains, led critics to accord her performances the status of an artwork, with an authority equal to the composer's. As debates arose about whether or not Pasta's performance as Norma was so authoritative as to allow no other interpreters (especially Maria Malibran), Rutherford maintains that

> The conjunction of these separate and yet profoundly related anxieties about issues of ownership and authenticity are suggestive of an important shift in the perception of the function of operatic performance. The concept of *Norma* as the embodiment of Pasta as much as Bellini, as an artwork of *both* composition *and* performance, was clearly unsustainable, because it made the work essentially unrepeatable, a position fundamentally at odds with the thrust of the nineteenth-century commercial ethos.[45]

Rutherford paints a picture of an opera so closely tailored to an individual singer that it represents a kind of end of the line, one of the last of its kind before composers started to compose for not actual singers but instead "imaginary voices."[46] Stendhal's call for a composer to study closely Pasta's unique voice and provide her with a score that allowed her talents to shine would seem to have been met in *Norma*. But I would argue that Bellini's score also displays a tendency to idealize the diva's voice, to make it speak new, apparently universal truths about creative process. This is true especially in Pasta's entrance aria, the famous "Casta Diva."

"Casta Diva" has long been at the center of the Bellinian mythos, put to work to attest to the perfection of the composer's union of words and music. David Kimbell claimed that "Bellini's most astonishing achievement in *Norma* is, amid all the more obvious excitements of musical Romanticism, to have asserted his belief that the true magic of opera depended on a kind of incantation in which dramatic poetry and song are perfectly fused."[47] His use of the word "incantation" suggests that he had this aria, in which Norma intones a prayer to the moon as incarnation of the goddess Diana, in mind. "Casta Diva" stands as exemplar of Bellini's style in textbooks and television commercials, despite the fact that the number is idiosyncratic, markedly different from Bellini's other arias for solo voice. Perhaps it achieved this mythic status because it does not so much showcase Pasta's improvisatory skills as it transfigures her unique timbral qualities into a theatrical staging of inspiration, that mysterious force normally unseen and unheard. The aria achieves this in two ways; first, by exploiting the peculiarities of Pasta's two "diametrically opposed" voices, and second, through Bellini's approach to *ritmo* and *accento musicale*, the performative conventions of text-setting.

Silvery Sounds

It is fitting that Pasta should sing a hymn of praise to the moon as her entrance aria, given Stendhal's earlier prescient comparison of her voice to shifting moonlight. Seven years before Bellini's opera, Stendhal engaged in his own act of ventriloquism to portray Pasta's varying vocal timbres as evocative of the moon's magical light. A Neapolitan admirer of the soprano, he wrote, "spoke to me in a tone of such burning enthusiasm that I would give everything that I possess in the world to be able to reproduce it here in cold print." Stendhal attempted to capture that enthusiasm in a long passage channeling the speech of his Neapolitan friend:

> *The changes of timbre in this sublime voice remind me of a sensation of tender happiness that I felt sometimes during those perfectly clear nights in our*

> *unhappy country, when twinkling stars stand out so well against a dark blue sky; it was when the moon lit up that enchanting landscape [i.e., the Isle of Capri], which one can see from the shore of the Mergellina [a seaside quarter of Naples], and which I shall see no more . . . Imperceptibly, a light cloud comes to veil the moon, and its light seems for a few moments softer and more tender, nature's presence is more touching, the soul is attentive. Soon the moon will show itself again, purer and more brilliant than ever, flooding our shores with its bright and pure light, and the landscape reappears in all the clarity of its lively beauty. Eh bien! The voice of Madame Pasta, in its changes of register, gives me the feeling of that [moon]light, more touching and tender when veiled one instant, only to reappear soon after a thousand times brighter.*[48]

Pasta's dual voice is imagined as a natural phenomenon, synaesthetically transformed from sound into flickering moonlight. Not only is the passage shot through with nostalgia and longing for Italy's landscape—this voice has the power to transport. Like the changeable heavenly body that alternately obscures and transfigures the distant landscape of Capri, Pasta's voice both reveals and conceals. Its shifting timbres cause shifting emotional responses in the listener, from tender softness that speaks to the soul to a lively clarity that illuminates places normally out of reach. Stendhal makes a virtue, then, of the ever-changing and manifold nature of Pasta's voice.

Even taking into account his habitual verbosity, Stendhal is remarkably prolix about Pasta's skill in manipulating and employing these different vocal timbres: "this fundamental variety of tone produced by a single voice," he writes, "affords one of the richest veins of musical expression which the artistry of a great *cantatrice* is able to exploit."[49] Pasta's different registers are not simply rough or unequal; instead, she demonstrated the important point—true of many great singers, he says—that "defects might be transformed into beauties, and effects of fascinating originality drawn from them." Stendhal argues for the Romantic beauty of this flawed but original voice: "it is *not* the uniformly silvery voice, impeccably accurate in tone throughout every note of its compass, that lends itself to the greatest achievements in impassioned singing. No voice whose *timbre* is completely incapable of variation can ever produce those *opaque,* or as it were, *suffocated* sounds, that can portray, with such power and truthfulness, certain moments of violent emotion or passionate anguish."[50] Pasta's expressive power is apparent especially at the margins of her voice, where she possesses many notes that are "not only . . . very beautiful, but . . . produce a certain vibration—at once sonic and magnetic—that, I believe, captures the soul of the spectator at lighting speed through some still unexplained combination of physical effects."[51]

"Casta Diva" seems expressly designed to highlight the shift between

Pasta's two voices—and, in particular, to theatricalize the revelation of her head voice (ex. 3.1).[52] Reading the aria's text, we might be tempted to speculate that Bellini or Romani had read Stendhal's account of Pasta's moonlit voice.

> Casta Diva, che inargenti
> queste sacre antiche pianti
> a noi volgi il bel sembiante
> senza nube e senza vel.
>
> [Chaste goddess, who bathes in silver / these sacred, ancient trees /
> turn upon us your fair face / cloudless and unveiled.]

EXAMPLE 3.1 "Casta Diva," from act 1 of Bellini's *Norma*.

EXAMPLE 3.1 (*continued*)

Although the cavatina is in G major in Bellini's autograph, subsequent printed editions (including the piano-vocal score published by Ricordi on the occasion of *Norma*'s premiere at La Scala in 1831) present it in F major. Most scholars agree that Bellini himself approved the change either during rehearsals or soon after the first performance in order to accommodate Pasta, which suggests that achieving certain timbral effects was important to him.[53] The melody begins in the middle of Pasta's voice (A4), most likely a more veiled or dark register, and unfolds slowly. Starting in shadow would have made Pasta's ascent into the brilliance of her upper voice all the more striking. The first ten measures explore the half-step A4 to B-flat4, while measures 27–28 dramatize the same upward half-step motion in a more compressed way an octave higher. After a leisurely opening, two short, fragmentary statements ("a noi volgi" and "il bel sembiante") voice the half-step movement more urgently. A subsequent shift up to C5 launches the dramatic ascent to syncopated, sobbing A5's that gain in force and volume until an ecstatic B-flat5 on the phrase "beautiful face." The voice then floats down by thirds decorated by three-note figures to rest on F4 at the word "veil." Certainly, these choices could be simple word-painting—the melody ascends to the upper register when the text speaks of the moon goddess revealing her face and descends into the shadows at the words "cloud" and "veil." But this effect, crucially, relies upon the distinctive timbral qualities of Pasta's voice—in particular, its polyvocality, the sense that she could marshal multiple unique voices for expressive effect. In drawing down the moon, as it were, it is as if Pasta calls down a different voice into her body; as her vocal line climbs to that climactic B-flat5, her upper register is mysteriously unveiled and her head voice is allowed to shine upon all who hear her, perhaps achieving the hypnotic effect Stendhal described.

This melodic enactment of divine inspiration was hard won: the autograph manuscript of "Casta Diva" is made up of mostly single folios, rather than bifolios, which suggests much revision.[54] Perhaps the biggest problem, surprising for a composer so assured in his long melodic statements, was one of proportion. Two places in particular occasioned much crossing out and rewriting. Bellini had initially intended the second stanza ("Tempra, o Diva") to unfold like the first, with Norma singing the entirety of the theme before the chorus entered. However, he ultimately compressed these two events so that the chorus entered to support Norma in her second ascent. The final cadence figure was initially longer, as well. The several measures canceled out in folio 63 verso contained an ornamental embellishment built on a familiar additive logic, with the second iteration leaping up to an expressive double appoggiatura figure (1-6-5-7-6) before climbing down and ending rather prosaically with a 5-1 motion (ex. 3.2a). Bellini ultimately compressed this ending, substituting just two measures (on the words "tu fai"), with the second held note blossoming into a short cadenza (ex. 3.2b).

Although it is unclear what motivated such changes, they do indicate a concern with how the aria unfolds through time, the relative roles of soprano and chorus, and, in the last example, perhaps a desire to avoid the end-weighted emphasis on ornamental embellishment that characterized many entrance arias. Indeed, "Casta Diva" is unusual in that the very opening melodic gesture sounds something like a decorated cadence, with turns and passing notes filling out the descent from the third scale degree to the tonic. Damien Colas has shown that most of Bellini's melodic revisions to his autographs tended to follow a singerly model; figures were added or changed in the "segmentation zones" of the melodies, such as the ends of lines or stanzas.[55] But instead of following this well-established convention for conveying rhetorical emphasis,

EXAMPLE 3.2A Crossed-out ornamental passage at the end of "Casta Diva" in Bellini's autograph (folio 63v).

EXAMPLE 3.2B Short cadenza substituted for crossed-out passage.

"Casta Diva" comes from a different world, one where ornament is front-loaded, as it were. Comparing "Casta Diva" to another Bellini aria, Beatrice's "Ma la sola, ohimè! son io," that at least some contemporary listeners heard as similar, we find that they take radically different approaches to the rhetorical deployment of ornament.[56] Despite the fact that the two numbers both feature descending lines juxtaposing sustained notes with decorative flourishes (set up by repeated choral exhortations that launch the singer upward), Beatrice's cavatina, another entrance aria written for Pasta, begins and ends as we might expect. Short, speechlike gestures that blossom into tiny ornamental desinences open the aria; Beatrice's abrupt exhortations could not be further from Norma's intoxicated melismas. An extended cadenza caps off Beatrice's final filigreed descent, while the excision of the cadential measures in folio 63v of "Casta Diva," in contrast, shows a desire to simplify and shorten the end of the aria (typically a place for ornamental display), rather than introduce any further variation.

One other change to the manuscript is intriguing. The aria's long orchestral introduction, during which the flute foreshadows Norma's melody, was initially canceled out. The folio itself was folded in half, and replaced with only two measures of music for strings that served as a transition to the aria proper. Philip Gossett suggests that the decision to excise the introduction may have something to do with the later decision to transpose the aria to F major to accommodate Pasta.[57] At what point the longer introduction with flute was reinstated is unclear. Though orchestral introductions to arias are perfectly conventional, this one is notable for its length; it runs the risk of stealing Pasta's thunder even though the flute stops just short of the ascent.

Certainly the flute is another kind of "silvery sound," and on a practical level, the long introduction allows time for the stage action (the ritual cutting of the mistletoe). But it also suggests a kind of inevitability, as it is difficult to hear Norma's melody as emerging spontaneously once it has been so thoroughly foreshadowed. It contributes to an impression of dreamlike inexorability and highlights the sense that the aria's melody emerges not in the moment but thanks to Norma's ability to open herself up to divine inspiration, to access realms of both memory and ritual. In this way, "Casta Diva" does double work: the aria's slow, pensive pace and intricate ornamental flourishes evoke improvisatory utterance, but perhaps only the memory of an improvisation, one long divested of its spontaneity. Rather, this is a kind of recasting of improvisation as primarily about making oneself a vessel for inspiration by means of trance. The incantation that results echoes with the multiple voices that speak through the singerly medium.

Ritmo, Accento Musicale, and Reading Aloud

One of those voices, of course, was that of the librettist, Felice Romani, with whom Bellini worked quite closely on the aria's text. In setting a text, opera composers had recourse to a haphazardly theorized but still incredibly powerful set of conventions. Perhaps the most pertinent of these conventions in this case are the notions of *ritmo* (rhythm) and of *accento musicale* (musical accent, or the "speech accent" of music). Friedrich Lippmann has identified a group of conventional rhythmic gestures—*ritmi*—that were used for setting poetic verse. Each characteristic rhythm provided a framework for different poetic meters, mirroring syllable counts and stress patterns (ex. 3.3).[58] Composers were expected to alter these conventions. "During the nineteenth century," writes Baragwanath,

> the method . . . for setting verses to music—involving the selection and application of more or less standard phrase rhythms (*ritmi*) and accompanying melodic and harmonic designs—appears to have been so generally known by those in the profession that any composer who adhered too closely to its pedagogical models or allowed its workings to show too obviously at the surface of a score ran the risk of being branded a "hack."[59]

Creative alteration of the conventions of *ritmo* was one of the primary ways a composer could demonstrate his originality, his own unique authorial voice.

Bellini's idiosyncratic approach to *ritmo* in "Casta Diva" causes the text to unfold quite slowly, as if intoned by a celebrant in a trance. Romani's opening

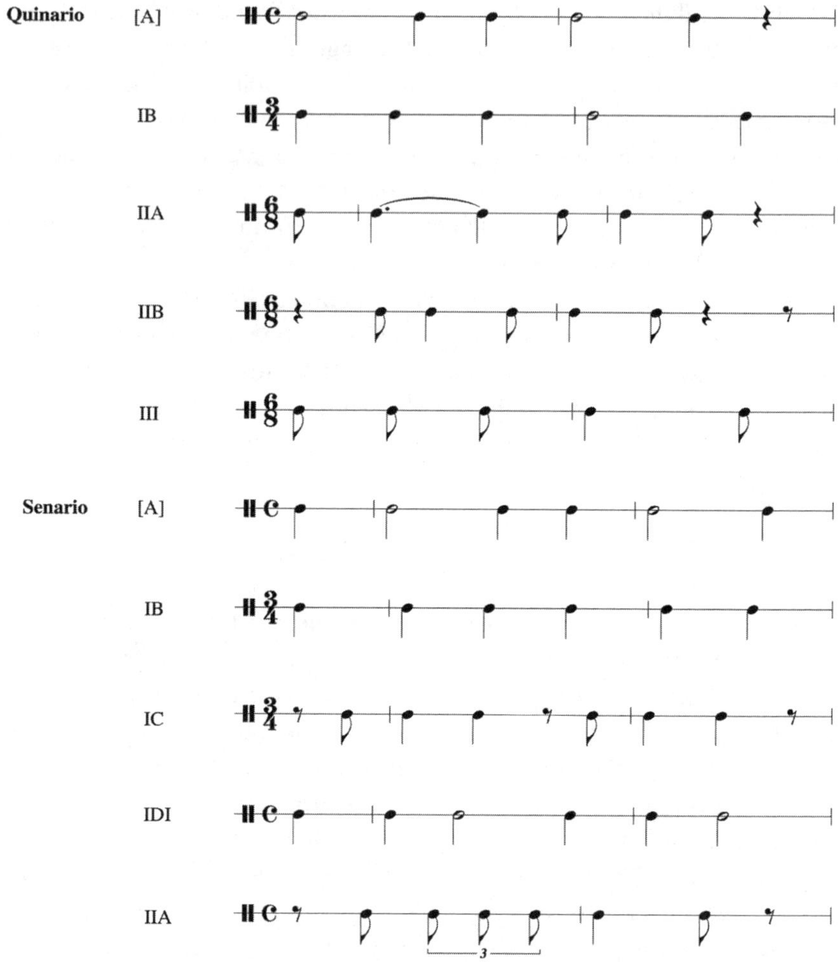

EXAMPLE 3.3 Some of Lippmann's "rhythmic musical types" from his *Versificazione italiana e ritmo musicale* (1986).

eight-syllable line—"Casta diva, che inargenti"—is broken in half, with the first four syllables of text voiced over two slow measures of 12/8 time in the tonic key. That half line is then repeated and continued ("Casta diva, casta diva, che inargenti"). Kimbell argues that "the repetitions and ceremonial flourishes suggest some audible equivalent of the solemn gestures and fervent ritual genuflections of a priestly celebrant," while Baragwanath hears a reference to the call and response of liturgy.[60] Both of these commentators understand "Casta Diva" through the lens of religious ritual—helped along by their generic identification of this moment as a prayer (or *preghiera*)—and thus characterize the number as more preordained than spontaneous. But broader poetic contexts help illuminate other possible meanings. First, the simple repetition of text, called epizeuxis or pallilogia, was extremely common in Italian opera and was often a platform for improvisatory embellishment. Because this repetition is not built into the metric structure of the ottonari itself, and because it happens at the very beginning of the aria, it recalls a poet searching for ideas: uttering a few words, stopping, and beginning again. Second, the fact that Bellini combines two different *ritmi*—a quarternario followed by an ottonario—conveys an impression of poetic variety akin to the mixture of meters Cesarotti favored in translating Ossian. More specifically, opening with a four-syllable fragment evokes the beginning of "Comala," where Cesarotti broke an eight-syllable line in half to signal the initiation of an ancient song. Baragwanath, as we have seen, hears this "short-long" structure of the melody's opening *ritmi* as a call and response. Crucially, however, this call and response takes place within a single voice. Norma, the supplicant, calls out to the divine goddess of the text and is subsequently filled with inspiration in the form of new words: she is now able to spin out a complete eight-syllable line. Both the four-syllable and the eight-syllable statement are the same length, so we hear a melismatic phrase followed by an increasingly syllabic one, as if a sonic vessel woven of vocal figuration is subsequently filled with more text.

Ritmo provided a foundational rhythmic motive distinct from any notion of beat, bar lines, and time signature, but it could be altered through the unique delivery of the text. This *accento musicale*, or "speech accent" of melody, was a concept that, as Baragwanath notes, encompassed all those variables of textual delivery that characterized a vocal phrase.[61] While *ritmo* in Lippmann's studies can be deduced from the assemblage of a lexicon of typical gestures, Italian treatises are often more ambiguous about *accento*—particularly the questions of whether it was more properly the business of the composer or the singer. In 1830 Luigi De Macchi asked, "What is meant by *Accento musicale*? It refers to the phrase rhythm that regulates the entire phrase or period; the several parts of a period controlled by the strong and weak beats of the measure; the increase and decrease of force; the smoothness or jaggedness; the slowing down and speeding up; the loud and soft; in sum all that can give color to a phrase."[62] As Baragwanath points out, it is not clear whether De Macchi is speaking of the composer's text-setting strategies or of performance choices such as rhythmic variation, rubato, articulation, and dynamics that were at the discretion of a singer.

It is this confusion—exactly whose *accento* speaks through operatic melody?—that Bellini was so skilled at fostering. His melodies were consistently praised for their close connection to the "natural" rhythms of speech, and were therefore thought to represent a model, "singerly" approach toward declamation and expression. As Simon Maguire has noted, like many of his nineteenth-century counterparts, Bellini more often used the verb *dire* (to speak) to refer to an individual singer's performance and *cantare* (to sing) to singing in general.[63] Indeed, the broader Italian culture of reciting poetry aloud dramatized an individual's encounter with the words of another and connects operatic composition and performance with dramatic recitation. As Michael Caesar has argued, the overemphatic rhetoric, percussive language, and vivid (thus memorizable) imagery that characterized published transcriptions of improvised poetry were meant to be read aloud. Transcription did not take a poem out of the oral realm, but instead granted it continued life in performance: "The transcriptions, though they may have been intended just to get the words on paper, expected and required an active reading."[64] Skilled poetic recitation was demonstrated in part by the ability to marshal and deploy multiple voices in appropriate declamation. Bellini's personal approach to both conventions of *ritmo* and *accento* had the potential to make this multivoiced inspiration audible, while his "melodie lunghe lunghe lunghe" created the impression that the singer is filled with a divine breath from elsewhere, exhaling it in song.

The fashioning of an authentic poetic voice, then—whether in melodic composition, vocal performance, or poetic recitation—depended upon the artist-author's skill in embodying the voices of others. *Improvvisatrice* Fortunata Sulgher Fantastici had this performative potential in mind when she transformed Ossianic source material in her improvised poems, at least four of which appeared in print between 1791 and 1794. Mattioda, no champion of improvised poetry (he notes that "due to its ephemeral nature, much of it—at times to our benefit—was never printed"), finds Fantastici's poems expansively sentimental, devoid of the universalism and the terseness of both Macpherson's original and Cesarotti's translation. While in the work of those authors, "pathetic and sentimental elements are circumscribed by the epic nature of the plot and are always linked to a broader sense of loss and solitude," in Fantastici's poems, "the heroines become the bearers of external sentimentalism."[65] One episode, the murder of Agandecca by her father in the third book of *Fingal*, is, according to Mattioda, "amplified in a pathetic way devoid of that sublime brevity" that characterized the originals. Macpherson's original—"She came with her loose raven locks. Her white breasts heaved with sighs, like the foam of the streamy Lubar. Starno pierced her side with steel"—is rendered by Cesarotti in a way that preserves the delectable picture of Agandecca's physical beauty, and its short and broken lines reflect the suddenness and brutality of the murder:

The beauty came,
her locks loose, her lashes wet; her white breast
heaved with sighs,
like the foam of the Lubar. Her cruel father
seized her, stabbed her.[66]

[Venne la bella, / sciolta il crin, molle il ciglio: il bianco petto / le si gonfiava all'aura de' sospiri, / come spuma del Luba. Il fero padre / l'afferrò, la trafisse.]

Fantastici's version, in contrast, depicts the scene from the perspective of the fearful Agandecca:

Disheveled, wretched,
with her lowered forehead between closed hands,
she fell desperately at his feet,
this forlorn girl; the cruel man grabbed
with one hand her delicate arm,
and with the other mercilessly pierced her heart.[67]

[Scarmigliata, squallida, / con bassa fronte fra le mani chiusa, / gli cadde al piede disperatamente / la fanciulla smarrita; il crudo afferra / con una mano il delicato braccio, / e con l'altra spietato il cor le fiede.]

Fantastici, to be sure, makes a spectacle out of this scene, but it is a spectacle designed to elicit sympathy through vividly embodying the attack in dynamic gestures. Indeed, her version is essentially a set of precise stage directions—first, Agandecca lowers her head between her fists, then she falls to her father's feet, and finally, Fantastici specifies that her father catches her by the arm with one hand and with the other stabs her in the heart.[68] Enlivened with movement, Fantastici's more personalized amplification of the original gives time for the scene to unfold in the listener's imagination, perhaps helped along in live performance with some appropriate gestures on the part of the improviser herself. Fantastici's poem is certainly in line with the broader trend to make feminine characters in Ossianic theatrical productions into "virtuous suffering personae" in order to elicit compassion.[69] But I would argue that, in addition to her emphasis on feminine distress, it is Fantastici's crucial shift from a pictorial aesthetic to a gestural one that enacts the performative values of theatrical melodrama. Fantastici's poetic voice inserts the poet powerfully in Agandecca's fictional body—while her own performing self acts as a medium for the heroine's imagined physicality. Her poetry thus seeks to capture a wholly realized and embodied theatrical scene. The improviser's voice and gesture vividly transport the listener: the chiming of *piede* (feet) and *fiede* (smites) sonically linking the father's deathly blow to the daughter's posture of supplication.

The Mystery of the Missing Harp

I end with a mystery. The distinction Angela Esterhammer draws between improvisation and inspiration is based on nineteenth-century sources that seek to quarantine these two concepts, to cordon off the unruly spectacle of public improvisation from "true" creative labor—we recall Giordani's insistence that only sustained hard work produces masterpieces discussed in this book's introduction. But of course, the two are not so easily separated; Esterhammer's account of the popularity of the poetic improviser in Italy and beyond concedes that the improviser's ability to *perform* inspiration—through physical signs such as fevered gestures, sweating brows, and the wild intensity of their declamation—was a prime attraction. But Bellini's melodic aesthetic, I would argue, often effaces this kind of effort, conveying instead the illusion of a less ornamented, more "natural" melody. In the same way, *Norma*'s indebtedness to the craze for Northern subjects is sometimes masked. If Ossian's "translators" were at pains to authenticate their work by proudly touting its Northern origins, Bellini seems, at times, to have actively suppressed sonic connections to the world of Ossian.

The mystery of the missing harp is a case in point. *Norma*'s overture originally featured a part for harp throughout. But Bellini deleted the bulk of it, saving the harp for just a brief passage at the very end. It is unclear why he made such a decision, but his choice undeniably changed the overture's sound. Instead of having the harp contribute to the somber, militaristic music of the opening, or using it to accompany the cheerful melody that follows, Bellini does something different. He reserves the harp for a kind of special effect, having it serve as a sonic marker of an otherworldly realm; strings flit about freely in figuration and melody is absent.

To be sure, Bellini was not the first to associate the sound of the harp with the beyond. But in choosing this conventional association and muting others—such as the bellicose bard singing battle songs or the improviser accompanying herself—I hear an echo of other choices by which Bellini dramatized inspiration while also obscuring it. Operatic authorship, then, could be understood as a flickering dance of veiling and unveiling, of shifting moonlight and shadow across a nocturnal landscape. Bellini's autograph reveals his own shape-shifting work as he translated both the poetic voice of the libretto and the timbre of Pasta's voice into his melodies. Attention to operatic composition as a polyvocal affair offers a new way to read Kimbell's observation that "given the state of the autographs of both the score and the libretto, there can be no doubt that 'Casta Diva' was assiduously and long toiled over."[70] Bellini labored mightily to produce an aria that enacts the effortless power of inspiration, in the process drawing a veil over the messy practicalities of his own form of creative mediumship. Although the tales we have told in the past about Bellini's creative process may portray him in a mythic light, a closer look at his creative process adds texture and depth to the myths. We have tended to uphold a hierarchy of mediumship, whereby the performer acts as a vessel for the genius of the composer while the composer is a vessel for divine inspiration. The picture looks quite different once we realize just how earthly, how material this inspiration could be—the lilting, conventional rhythms of rhymed poetry or the sound of a beautiful voice. If the work of the Romantic author has been to transmute these mundane materials into masterworks, the work of scholarship has been, up to now, to further the process of transubstantiation. But we don't have to continue this effort. We can choose, like Stendhal's Neapolitan friend, to respond to opera with our own poetic performances, to remember the once-living singer whose voice became melody—a voice that became, in John Rosselli's words, "a bright bird swooping down a moonlit sky."[71]

4

Saffo's Lyre: Improvising Operatic Authorship

The year was 1840, and Giovanni Pacini, prolific opera composer, was making a return to the stage after a hiatus of nearly five years. A series of disastrous failures in the previous decade spurred him to withdraw into a period of semiretirement, during which he set about altering his style to appeal to audiences eager for a new kind of theater. In his memoirs, Pacini described studying "new developments" in opera in an effort to infuse his music with greater "truth" and dramatic impact.[1] This attempt to develop what seems like a self-consciously innovative, Romantic aesthetic had a somewhat surprising result: Pacini made his comeback with an opera about an ancient Greek. His *Saffo* brought to the stage the story of an improvising singer-poet who wins the Olympic laurel and, as a result, loses her husband to another woman. Salvadore Cammarano's libretto, based on plays by Franz Grillparzer and Pietro Beltrame, follows Ovid's narrative of heterosexual love, desertion, and suicide: driven to despair, Saffo defiles her rival's wedding altar and then throws herself from a cliff. Before her fatal leap, she performs a single improvisation as part of a lengthy *scena finale*—a mad scene that has aspects of both open and closed forms, and combines syllabic declamation with a more florid vocal idiom. At first glance, the choice of Sappho as heroine may appear to graft neoclassical exoticism onto a typical Romantic melodrama, much as the production's costumes eschewed tunics and instead layered Greek decoration over a full-skirted 1840s silhouette (fig. 4.1). After all, while twenty-first-century audiences may view Sappho as a lesbian icon, in the early nineteenth century, she was primarily understood as a tragic figure whose unrequited love and subsequent suicide made her the ideal heroine.

To Pacini and his contemporaries, however, Sappho was also something more. She was the first *improvvisatrice*, that female improviser who, as we

FIGURE 4.1 Figurino for Pacini, *Saffo*. Title role: Francilla Pixis. Watercolor and tempera on cardstock, 194x117 mm of Biblioteca del Conservatorio di musica S. Pietro a Majella, Naples, IT-NA0059, shelf mark C23-19.

have seen, inspired enthusiasm for her ability to chant poetic verses extempore to musical accompaniment. Pacini's opera was likewise received enthusiastically, and what reviewers praised above all was its wealth of beautiful melody.[2] *Saffo* was full of "smooth and simple melodies" (canti semplice e spianati) that spoke to the heart.[3] Some imagined this melodiousness as nostalgic: "In an age in which they applaud music because the philosophers of music, those walking contrapuntists, tell them that these things are beautiful, and of the most refined school," it is rare to find a composer still able to write such beautiful tunes.[4] The fact that Pacini managed such a coup after nearly five years of silence was cause for praise, one critic reported, but he deserved even more for achieving such a feat while "European music attempts to overcome melody with the peak of complicated harmony."[5]

Such enthusiasm for Pacini's melodic genius—he had been known as the "maestro delle cabalette," and commentators more often praised the beauty of his tunes than the operas' libretti—seems to situate his opera very far from the world of poetry. But listening to Pacini's opera with the practice of improvised poetry in mind places into relief a number of issues central to the history of nineteenth-century opera, chief among them the intertwining of neoclassic and Romantic aesthetics, and the sticky distinctions between text and performance. In this chapter, I will focus on how the Sapphic improviser figure served as a nexus for both the Romantic recuperation of classical ideals as well as concerns about authorship in an age when the creation of poetry and music was increasingly separated from poetic and musical performance. Given the fact that the emergence of a more modern aesthetic in opera has been ascribed to composers' increasing control over singers, a theme elaborated most memorably, as we have seen in chapter 2, by Stendhal, it is significant that Pacini would choose to make a comeback with an opera that places a performer—one who sings her own extemporaneous compositions, no less—at the center of its plot.[6] Saffo, as envoiced by singers such as Marianna Barbieri-Nini or Francilla Pixis, the creator of the role, accordingly raises questions about the relative status of singerly versus composerly invention.[7]

What is at stake when modern authors use Sappho's tale for their own purposes and when composers base their written works on the lives of improvisers? It is more than appropriation. Considering Pacini's opera as one of a constellation of what Joan DeJean calls "Sapphic fictions" allows a more complex understanding of operatic authorship to emerge and highlights the many changes that were taking place mid-century as Pacini was attempting to reestablish his reputation as a composer to watch. By focusing on the connections between the practice and reception of poetic improvisation and how

Pacini's opera represents Saffo as *improvvisatrice*, I aim to assemble a view of operatic authorship as contingent, collaborative, and, ultimately, framed by contemporary discourses of spontaneity.

Saffo's Past

Sappho, serving as a model for the *improvvisatrice*, was an icon of spontaneous poetic performance in the moment. At the same time, however, her life story was the focus of a vast array of texts, from novels to plays and other theatrical works. This outpouring perhaps reached its apex in the Napoleonic era. Considering only Italian musical works, the period saw Simon Mayr's opera *Saffo* (1794), Nicolo Zingarelli's *monologo Saffo* (before 1800), and cantatas by Francesco Morlacchi (*Saffo in Leucade*, 1809), Ferdinando Paer (*Saffo*, 1815), and Gaetano Donizetti (*Saffo*, before 1828), all of which testify to the allure of the subject. No wonder, then, that Pacini's choice of Sappho as heroine was viewed as somewhat old-fashioned by his contemporaries.[8] The prevalence of works for solo voice in this earlier repertoire suggests that Sappho was often viewed as a solitary figure, the quintessential abandoned woman. Indeed, in a Donizetti manuscript associated with his cantata held at the Museo Donizettiano in Bergamo, Saffo expresses her manic distress over Faone's betrayal and abandonment in a cabaletta ("Son tradira, abbandonata").[9] Donizetti's almost Rossinian approach to form—every two lines of text are treated as additive units that move freely between F minor and A-flat major—portrays Saffo as alternately outraged (in forceful leaps) and breathlessly lamenting her helplessness (in rapid sighing gestures) as she describes being unable to run from Faone's image (ex. 4.1).[10]

While the author of this poetry is uncertain (perhaps it was penned by Donizetti himself), the libretto for Pacini's *Saffo* by Salvadore Cammarano drew on a play by Pietro Beltrame (performed in Naples in 1838) which itself took Franz Grillparzer's 1817 *Sapho* as a model.[11] It followed the established literary trend of focusing on the main character's tragic fate more than her poetic abilities. The Sapphic fictions of this era thus shaped the image of the poet inherited by Pacini, Cammarano, and their audience: Sappho as a symbol of doomed love, known for her suicide rather than her accomplishments.[12] In uncovering the many layers of this portrait, two intertwined themes emerge: the poet's problematic sexuality and the way her work provided a foundation upon which other authors could build their careers. As DeJean has argued, "the telltale mark of Napoleonic or proto-Napoleonic fictions of Sappho is the heroine's uncontrollable attraction to male physical beauty."[13] This

EXAMPLE 4.1 Vocal line from Saffo's "Son tradita, abbandonata," composed by Donizetti (manuscript held in the Archivio del Museo Donizettiano, Bergamo).

attraction is Sappho's downfall: her creativity is both spurred and destroyed by male beauty. And the silencing of her poetic ability is the occasion for living voices to speak.

Perhaps the most popular Italian retelling of Sappho's life was Alessandro Verri's 1782 novel *Le avventure di Saffo, poetessa di Mitilene*, which was published in fifteen Italian editions and appeared in many other languages.[14] Verri dealt with the "rumors" of Sappho's transgressive love for women by replacing one sort of sexual transgression (same-sex love) with another (uncontrollable lust for the opposite sex). He prefaced his tale, therefore, with two seemingly contradictory caveats. First, he maintains that the tales of Sappho's love for women were merely rumors put about by her rivals. But this apparently sober effort to rehabilitate Sappho's reputation is undercut by his opening gesture, when he reveals that the tale he relates is of the "most unhappy events of a profane love." Therefore, he worries about calling on the Muses to inspire him for fear of offending these chaste and celestial beings.[15] In Verri's tale, it is the sight of Phaon's nakedness after a wrestling bout that spurs the poet to improvise her first poem. Verri dwells on the moment when Phaon strips down and "appeared perfectly naked, having only the usual wrestler's girdle."[16] As DeJean puts it, "Verri exaggerates Phaon's masculinity in order to put a revitalized Phaon at the center of the Sapphic plot."[17] Later fictions would attempt yet another recuperation—not simply a "straightening" of Sappho, but a sort of purification. Grillparzer's 1817 play, which DeJean argues both "culminat[es]" past traditions and "sets the norm" for nineteenth-century Sapphic fiction, emphasized Sappho's sacrificial suicide rather than her unfulfilled lust and made the deadly leap iconic: "Grillparzer . . . makes a bold new move and scripts his Sappho's suicide as her renunciation of sexuality and a gesture of penance necessary to gain poetic immortality."[18] This notion of the leap as penance is retained in Cammerano's libretto, though it is construed as penance for Saffo's emotional outburst that defiled the altar of the gods. This purification of Sappho's reputation is, DeJean argues, "the major way in which the nineteenth century justified its reexaltation of her poetry: by denying her sexuality."[19]

This recasting of Sappho as admirably self-abnegating serves not just to recuperate her transgressive image, but also opens the door for living authors to use Sappho's life and fragmentary writings as a springboard to launch their own reputations. They do so by putting their own stamp on the long history of Sapphic fictions. DeJean argues, for example, that "Grillparzer . . . makes a name for himself and wins an authorial signature by killing Sappho, or at least the Sappho that, for two hundred years, authors following the Ovidian plots had been constructing bit by bit."[20] Perhaps no scene in Verri's novel captures the sidelining of Sappho more clearly than the one where the poet takes on the role of listener to Phaon's tale of transformation at the hands of Aphrodite. When Phaon relates the story, his is the "tongue inspired by the gods," while Sappho, placed at the fringes of the action, is made into a passive, frozen receptacle for it, one in whom "all motion was suspended."[21] This move was perhaps not uncharacteristic: recall that it was Verri who urged Italian salonnières to follow the example of their French counterparts by facilitating the creative efforts of men rather than put themselves forward.

The Improviser Absorbed

A hermeneutic reading of the texts of Pacini's opera—its libretto and score—seems to suggest that the opera continues the trend of associating Saffo not with poetic genius but with passive loyalty and suicide. Rossini's Corinna, we recall, was marked by a potential slippage between operatic diva and improvising poetess. Corinna's improvisations, precisely because they were set apart from their surroundings, opened out into the event—indeed, some reviewers complained about the fact that they stopped the action and created intolerable *longueurs*.[22] In contrast, Pacini subsumes Saffo's sole improvisation into an innovative compositional structure that seems to forestall any potential connections between the creative work of the character and that of the singer. The very first scene of Pacini's opera establishes a division between her public and private selves; indeed, Saffo does not receive an entrance aria, the standard occasion to highlight a singer's vocal prowess. Instead, the opera opens with the priest Alcandro plotting the heroine's downfall. He is joined by Saffo's husband Faone, who cannot decide whether his wife is unfaithful to him or simply obsessed with her own fame. When Saffo enters, Faone confronts her with his suspicions. In the middle of their confrontation, news arrives that Saffo has won the Olympic laurel. Her triumph, however, is bittersweet: Faone rejects her at the same moment. All the activities associated with Saffo's public acclaim (her first performance and her crowning) take place offstage. Just as Staël's novel framed Corinne with speculation and fantasy, Pacini's Saffo is circumscribed by Alcandro's plot for revenge and Faone's suspicions.

Such a plot structure means that Pacini has no opportunity to paint Saffo as a sympathetic character until the first-act finale, the first time she appears on stage. This finale is actually an extended confrontational duet between Saffo and Faone, with the couple singing mostly in dialogue rather than *a due* (ex. 4.2). In the *Allegro giusto*, Saffo's wide-ranging melody, with its forceful rhythms (m. 44), is not repeated by Faone (m. 86), who has more fragmented and plaintive utterances. But Faone does mimic one of her melodies. As Saffo insists that even when her genius takes flight she longs to be on earth with Faone (pickup to m. 64), she unleashes a big tune that begins with a leap of a sixth to a held note, then descends through triplet figuration. The driving rhythm of the accompaniment also loosens into triplets, a shift to a more obviously lyrical mode that one might hear as sincere and heartfelt. But at measure 103 Faone explicitly associates this mode with Saffo's performing persona: in echoing back the melody Saffo used to defend herself, he claims she is seduced by applause and values fame more than love. Faone's accusations are echoed in the orchestral accompaniment: in both cases, the shift in emotional register is framed by a turn figure that evokes a kind of folk dance in triple meter (see m. 63 and m. 102)—perhaps an effort on Pacini's part to create a Greek *tinta*.[23] This gesture toward what the French called *couleur locale* places Saffo's melody in a communal Greek context of public performance, making it difficult to hear her passionate outpouring as unmarked, private utterance, especially once it is undermined by Faone.

Saffo's private utterances are thus potentially public, highlighting the blurring of the two realms that characterized contemporary representations of artistic women in general and singers and improvisers in particular.[24] Dissolving the boundaries between private distress and public performance is crucial

Saffo: When my burning genius loosens its wings toward the sky, and heaven opens to receive me like a deathless spirit... as the numberless stars rush with rapid steps, and the rays of the burning sun shine all about me, although I am among the delights with which Heaven adorns itself, my spirit is not content. I long to return to earth, ah, because on earth I can live with you in love.
Faone: You have never been short of clever words to calm the frenzy of my just suspicions! But this is not enough to wipe away the stains upon your fidelity; for all the youths of Greece lie at your feet. You listen readily to seductive applause and are more inflamed by the glory of ambitions than by love... the love that burns fervently only in me!

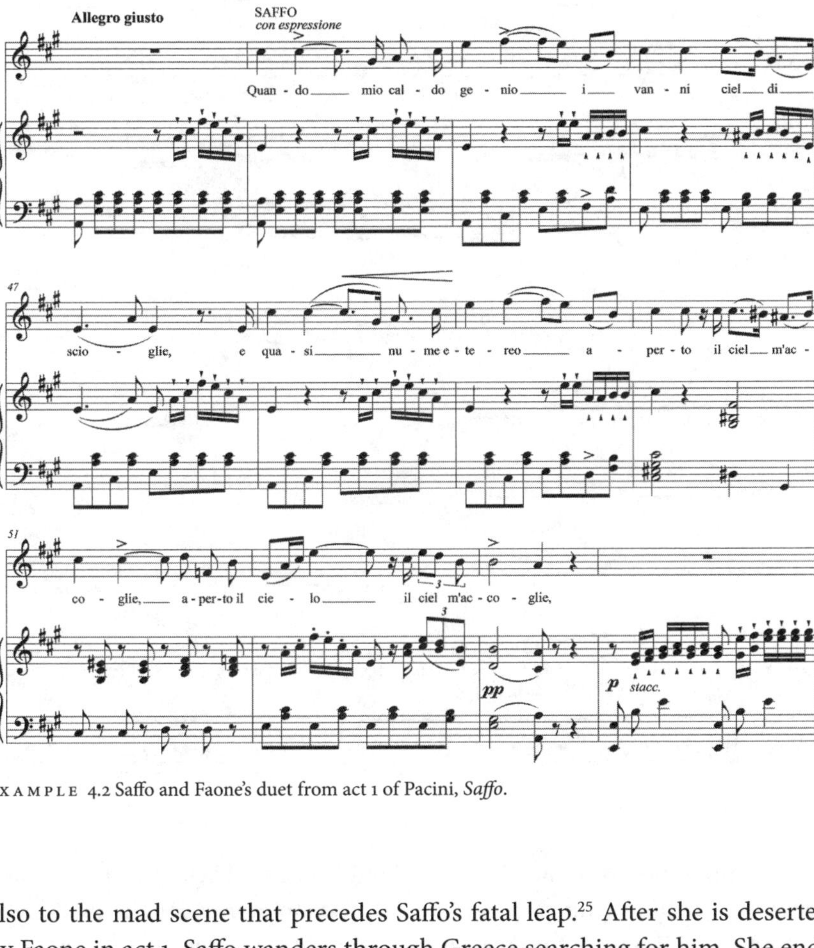

EXAMPLE 4.2 Saffo and Faone's duet from act 1 of Pacini, *Saffo*.

also to the mad scene that precedes Saffo's fatal leap.[25] After she is deserted by Faone in act 1, Saffo wanders through Greece searching for him. She ends up in Leucas, where she befriends Climene, Alcandro's daughter, who asks her to sing the nuptial hymn at her wedding. Saffo agrees, only to discover that Climene is marrying Faone. Enraged, she defiles the altar. To appease the populace's demand for restitution, Alcandro sentences Saffo to the Leucadian leap, only to discover that his revenge has backfired: Saffo is his long-lost daughter. Accepting her fate, Saffo grows distracted and loses her reason. She sings the nuptial hymn at the top of the cliff before leaping to her death.

EXAMPLE 4.2 (*continued*)

Given the success of mad heroines like Donizetti's Lucia five years earlier, perhaps it should be no surprise that Saffo—who arrives for the final scene dressed in white, with disheveled hair—should be reinvented as an operatic madwoman. But it is telling that Saffo's only onstage performance in the entire opera takes place during this scene, as if spontaneous improvisation can take place only at moments of mental extremity. In this respect, Saffo's madness seems yet another instance of the Romantic imbrication of mental illness and artistic authenticity.[26] Saffo's instability is also an opportunity to push the boundaries of the double-aria form—the standard pattern of a lyric slow movement followed by brilliant cabaletta. While the Ricordi vocal score describes the third act as consisting of a chorus followed by a *scena ed aria*, Pacini's manuscript labeled the whole act "Gran Scena Finale," which more accurately captures the way the action unfolds. The form of the scene mirrors Saffo's volatility by taking a wrong turn in the middle. After a solemn introduction and chorus, Saffo's brief, stark recitative is followed by what seems to be the slow movement (in D major and marked *Andante affettuoso*), but this melody trails off as she is interrupted by Alcandro and Climene, whom she recognizes as her onetime patron. She calls for her lyre and improvises

EXAMPLE 4.2 (*continued*)

the promised nuptial hymn, "Teco dall'are pronube," which begins in G major (ex. 4.3). Saffo's improvisation serves as the scene's true slow movement, followed as it is by a clear *tempo di mezzo* and cabaletta ("L'ama ognor qual io" in D-flat major). But its *Allegro moderato* tempo (which is not strongly contrasting with the cabaletta's *Affetuoso*) and marked rhythmic articulation might also recall one of Donizetti's moderate-tempo cabalettas and thus confuse the listener.[27]

As is the case with many operatic mad scenes, Saffo's improvisation gets its initial emotional force not from lyricism or elaborate ornament, but from the contrast between joyful, celebratory music and the tragic situation. This

4

EXAMPLE 4.2 (*continued*)

EXAMPLE 4.2 (*continued*)

moment is clearly framed as an onstage song—she tells the breeze and waves to be silent because she is about to sing—but, as with so many mad songs, it wanders. The first stanza of text is set to a modified lyric prototype (AA'BB'A"). Despite the melody's regularity, already in the second (A') phrase her music becomes more wayward (mm. 200–203) as it first heads for a cadence on the relative minor (e) but then proceeds to modulate to the dominant. By the second stanza, where one might expect a varied repetition of the melody, the orchestra abandons its role as simulacrum of Saffo's lyre in order to portray the celebrations she has just described (ex. 4.4). The marked rhythm, like that of a processional dance, the pseudo-antiphonal flutes, and the prevalence of the minor mode (m. 234) seem like further attempts to conjure up a Greek sound. Saffo sings more fragmentary statements above this processional music until the moment she steps out of her performed hymn to address her audience in the first person. She bids them farewell and speaks of leaving earth for heaven to another big tune (m. 244) nearly identical to the one she sang in her earlier duet with Faone. This time her outpouring is stripped of its prefatory pseudo-Greek turn figure; perhaps in the unraveling of her public improvisation Saffo has finally achieved an authentic personal utterance. But each time Saffo has one of these triplet-filled tunes, she is singing of a place

Saffo: Sea that roars in this broken crag, chattering breezes of heaven, be silent: I sing! With you from the wedding altar I come to my father's house. Decked with flowers, behold the bed covered in purple!

EXAMPLE 4.3 Saffo's improvisation from act 3, Pacini, *Saffo*.

EXAMPLE 4.3 (*continued*)

beyond this world—this is the song of a heroine about to die. The appearance of a heavenly topos in the aria finale allows us to understand the similar moment in the first act as a kind of musical foreshadowing: what Faone mocked as an unconvincing performance here makes an entirely convincing death.

This is, by now, a familiar story: Saffo's skill as a poet is represented on stage as anti-rational excess, and her improvisational prowess is explicitly framed by and tied to the display of her suffering body—she even throws herself in tears

Saffo: Let us go, let us go, for love does not tolerate delay. In a cloud of pink the wedding bed is ready and decked for her. Farewell; I leave you on earth and soon you shall be in Heaven!

EXAMPLE 4.4 Second stanza of Saffo's improvisation from act 3, Pacini, *Saffo*.

at Alcandro's feet before her cabaletta. Faced with an ancient poet transformed into a Romantic madwoman, we may be tempted to search for alternative, more redemptive, readings. Many earlier studies of the "problem" of women in opera wrestled with the question of whether such characters could be rescued from their oppressive plots.[28] Often salvation is thought to emerge through singing. Susan McClary's discussion of Lucia's mad coloratura as an exercise in transgression and Roger Parker's account of a Verdian heroine who sings up to her death instead of succumbing quietly each suggest that characters might escape their degraded positions via the performers who envoice them.[29] Certainly such arguments do well to draw attention away from plot and score and toward opera as an embodied, live phenomenon. Nevertheless, I would argue that distinctions between rebellious singer and controlling text imply too clear a division between work and performance, a division that perhaps speaks more to twentieth- and twenty-first-century concerns than to nineteenth-century ones. Indeed, it is worth reiterating that despite the supposed ascendency of the work concept, operatic composition in the 1840s was still essentially collaborative in nature, and the scores that resulted were often treated as anything but authoritative.[30] With this in mind, I would like to broaden the scope of my

EXAMPLE 4.4 (*continued*)

EXAMPLE 4.4 (*continued*)

discussion, resisting the false choice between performer and composer, which seems to offer a grim, one-dimensional picture of Pacini's opera as constraining and delimiting a female authorial voice. To do so, I turn back to the figure of the *improvvisatrice*, offering three vignettes—three Sapphic fragments, if you will. By examining how the rhetoric of spontaneity frames the production of both poetic and musical texts, the collaborative nature of operatic production, and the tensions inherent in Sappho as a model author, I seek to sketch out a notion of operatic authorship that is itself based on performative values—an authorship that is decentered, shared between different agents, and only incompletely legible in material traces.

I. *SOMEONE, I TELL YOU, IN ANOTHER TIME, WILL REMEMBER US.* (189)[31]

By 1840, the *improvvisatrice* herself—whether seen as a sibyl, Sappho, or a sacrifice to art—was in danger of becoming a palimpsest. The very popularity of poetic improvisation made it subject to critical scrutiny; many of Taddei's contemporaries were, like Waiblinger, preoccupied with specifying the differences between premeditated and spontaneously composed poetry. As Waiblinger makes clear, the intrusion of remembered texts into improvised performance was thought by many to invalidate the improviser's accomplishment—a theme that recurs repeatedly in nineteenth-century discussions. But the printed poems that form the foundation of Waiblinger's defense were themselves produced in a context in which, as Michael Caesar has argued, the difference between premeditated poetry and improvised poetry was becoming increasingly blurred.[32]

Caesar has suggested that by 1840 improvisers had begun to fade from view and those who remained occupied something of an embattled position. Often accused of fakery, they were subject to the unmasking efforts of scribes who used new forms of shorthand to prove that supposedly spontaneous poems were the result of tricks of memorization rather than divine inspiration or genius.[33] As published poetry grew in importance, the *improvvisatori* appear to have devised conflicting strategies for survival: the improviser Francesco Gianni, for example, published nearly simultaneous editions of premeditated and improvised poetry (1794–1795), suggesting that the latter should be judged by the same standards as the former. But he also was careful to bolster the special status of improvised poetry as an event, prefacing his improvisations with detailed information about when and where they were performed as well as which audience members participated by setting themes or meters.[34] Faced with such an example, *improvvisatrice* Teresa Bandettini was forced to negotiate a new path between the older "practice of a closed-circuit manuscript circulation" and the push to gain a larger audience through publication.[35] Bandettini yielded to this pressure despite the fact that she may have had very little control over the text published by a transcriber and that her reputation as an author of premeditated poetry might suffer if those works were compared to her improvisations. But from the 1830s on, it was more typical for poets who engaged both in improvising and in writing poetry to "merge the two activities in the act of publication, presenting the public with texts which have little or nothing to distinguish the improvised from the non-improvised."[36] For Caesar, the replication of transcriptions represents a spur to coherence and fixity that ultimately diminishes the practice of improvisation:

> Transcription is improvisation's oxygen. But there is something insidious about it too: the more that it submits to the conventions of written verse, from rules of punctuation and capitalization to the pauses and rhythms fixed by metre on the page, and the further it moves from the infinite variety of emphasis allowed by oral performance, so much the more the poem comes to

seem as though it were always already written, the improvisation no longer the focal point but rather the pre-text for what has become something else.[37]

But if improvisation was aspiring to the condition of written poetry, submitted to the standards of the "eye" as well as the "ear," the reverse was arguably also true.[38] An examination of Italian periodicals from the years around 1840, when printed poetry was supposedly crowding out improvisatory performances, reveals that improvisatory values—spontaneity, social exchange, the desire to make visible the intangible spark of inspiration—are hardly absent from poetic discourse. Alongside accounts of performances of *improvvisatori*, one finds frequent references to spontaneity as a virtue not just in performance but in the creation of texts. Indeed, even in a negative review of the improviser Cataldi, the critic seems to concede the contest to him, admitting that writing is a poor medium by which to convince someone to change his tastes or preferences—it can never compete with (or can only aspire to) the sheer persuasive force of the improvising poet.[39] In an article describing a local festival, the author expresses his gratitude that the stenographers do not yet hound writers, since he wrote down his impressions the moment they occurred.[40]

Angela Esterhammer has observed that foreign commentators on Italian improvisers tended to emphasize the differences between Italian extemporized poetry and their own native traditions of written and published poems. Many Italian writers of the day, in contrast, stressed the synergy between writing and improvising. In *Il pirata* of 28 February 1840, for example, a poem by Luigi Gaiter is introduced in a way that suggests that the published version actually offers proof of the spontaneity of the poet. Gaiter, the writer assures us, is "a rare example of modesty; he unites great understanding of genius, bursts of imagination, and a stream of fluent, spontaneous verses, which the Romanza that you have before your eyes proves beyond a doubt."[41] Although it is unclear whether Gaiter's Romanza was the product of premeditation or improvisation, the preface directs the reader to judge it by improvisation's standards—as evidence of the poet's improvisatory gifts. In such accounts, the improvised, the spontaneously created, supplies the model by which other poetic efforts are judged, complicating the narrative of decline that characterizes Caesar's history of transcription.

The fact that improvisers of this era found themselves negotiating the production of poems for publication and for a live audience does not mean that performance-oriented values were subsumed in the drive to create good texts. Giuseppe Regaldi's decision, on the Paris republication of an edition of his improvised poetry, to revise the transcriptions in much the same way he revised his premeditated poetry is understood by Caesar as "a small symptom of the gradual merging of the transcribed improvisation and the premeditated, written, poem."[42] But Regaldi apparently worked at other times to imbue his poetry with both a sense of contemporaneity and the atmosphere of a special event. Soon after *Saffo*'s premiere, Regaldi performed verses on the subject of Pacini's opera, and accounts of his triumph were reported in at least two periodicals.[43] Regaldi's move suggests that, as they were threatened by the new trend for published poetry, poetic improvisers may have looked to opera not only as a source of live *frisson* and improvisatory spark, but also as a way of lending an "up to the minute" quality to a performance, which normally was marked by a veritable excess of familiar classical and historical themes.[44] Such a survival strategy traces a circle from ancient *improvvisatrice* to her operatic representation and back to the world of the modern improviser.

Pacini also participated in this rhetoric of spontaneity, openly touting his ability to produce rapidly. In his memoirs, he recounts *Saffo*'s triumph in Naples and expresses his joy that the city celebrated his accomplishment with such fervor. He then boasts that he composed the opera in "only twenty-eight days," claiming that "the final scene of *Saffo*, consisting of the funeral chorus, recitative, improvisation, tempo di mezzo, and cabaletta was created in two hours!!! Pardon me if I am guilty of excessive vanity."[45] In Ferdinando Magnani's foreword to the memoirs, this tidbit is repeated, but this time Magnani writes that the opera was *improvvisata*—improvised—in a mere twenty-eight days. It is no coincidence, I would argue, that the nexus for these extravagant claims is Saffo's own scene of improvisation. Pacini and Magnani bolster the composer's reputation by stressing the speedy and spontaneous nature of his production; they enhance the value of the opera by pointing out how like an improvisation—perhaps one of Saffo's own—it is. Such values, of course, had a long history and a long future: in the Ricordi puff piece "How Giuseppe Verdi Composes and Rehearses," the composer is portrayed as gifted with the ability to realize his vision in a single gesture—from mind to page—that bears more than a passing resemblance to the descriptions of the improviser's gift. It paints an idealized image of a composer who never needs to create sketches: everything simply flows from him spontaneously.[46]

What is odd about Pacini's claim is that in the very next paragraph, he asserts that, thanks to the success of *Saffo*, he was no longer considered merely the master of the cabaletta, but a composer of "elaborate works" and "well-thought-out productions."[47] Just a few years after *Saffo*'s premiere, Donizetti was making similar claims about his speedy pace of production to friends. These boasts, however, were followed by requests not to reveal his secrets, as it might damage his reputation.[48] Operatic authorship was clearly in the midst of an identity crisis. As we have seen, the paradox of an operatic composer who was both spontaneous *and* studied was on full display in the forged letter attributed to Bellini (which probably first appeared in 1843) describing his compositional process as a reverse engineering of poetic improvisation. These portraits of compositional practice show that Italian opera's rapid pace of production could be seen in two ways: as evidence of genius as defined by the improvisatory values of spontaneity and speed, or as the triumph of the industry's relentless demand for novelty over artistic integrity.

II. *I COULD NOT HOPE TO TOUCH THE SKY WITH MY TWO ARMS.* (35)

Although these accounts paint operatic composition as the work of a solitary, inspired genius, it is worth reiterating here that operatic composition in the 1840s was essentially collaborative, and collaborative in ways that may seem foreign to us. Singers played a role in the creation of operas during nearly every stage of the production, from the choice of subject to the shaping of melodies, and, as we have seen, they were the celebrated creators of the ornamentation that enlivened these melodies.[49] Even a cursory glance at the manuscript of *Saffo* held at the Biblioteca del Conservatorio di San Pietro a Majella in Naples suggests that Francilla Pixis, the first Saffo, was the final arbiter of the ornamentation she performed. Perusing the manuscript of *Saffo* thus opens up a space between the text and its performance, reminding us that Pixis improvised as expected her own ornaments at cadenzas, especially in the final cabaletta, and certainly did not renounce her creative input. The manuscript contains a number of additions in Pacini's hand that evidently seek to streamline dramatic action (splitting up stage directions differently over a span of music) or to emphasize moments of intensity (by adding accent and staccato marks to the singer's line). In some places, Pacini has written in specific ornaments in a different ink, especially at cadenzas. These additions, however, are sporadic and inconsistent, which implies that Pacini's attitude to ornamentation in *Saffo* was practical and contingent rather than a sustained effort to dictate what the soprano should sing. There seems to be no rhyme or reason to which cadenzas are written in, and Pacini even neglects to copy out the melody for the repeated verse of Saffo's final cabaletta, obviously expecting the singer to supply the varied melody (fig. 4.2).

The picture that emerges from these additions to the manuscript is of the composer sitting at the keyboard with Pixis, writing in changes where the two felt more specific guidance was needed. Perhaps in the course of rehearsals with the composer, she would improvise a cadenza, the two would agree that

FIGURE 4.2 Cadenza added to manuscript of Pacini, *Saffo*, act 3, 1840. Biblioteca del Conservatorio di musica S. Pietro a Majella, Naples, IT-NA0059.

it was effective, and he would quickly write it down—the hand that wrote the cadenzas not only used a different ink, but is notably less careful. In other instances (such as the cabaletta's missing second verse), one can imagine the composer and singer agreeing that she would no doubt come up with something effective on her own. It seems too simple to conclude, then, that Pacini's opera forecloses either Pixis's creative input or the character Saffo's authorial power in order to harness the *improvvisatrice*'s spark for the composer's own gain.

It is undeniable that Sappho's life and work was a locus of appropriation.[50] Fascination with Sappho spurred an interest in relics, manuscripts, and scraps, along with the notion that her work needed to be completed by another hand. Indeed, there is a long history of writers and scholars presenting their own work as "discoveries" and "translations" of lost Sappho manuscripts. The Neapolitan general Vincenzo Imperiale, for example, was not the first to perpetuate literary fraud when he claimed to have discovered Sapphic hymns to Phaon's perfect physique.[51] The Sapphic fragment thus spurs a literary effort to "make whole" the remains of a lost past. This archaeological attitude toward the fragment places the focus on the objects of creative endeavor and thus may seem to privilege the single, unitary author—the way a shard of pottery suggests a lost whole made by, we imagine, a single pair of hands. These imagined wholes, whether reconstructed pots or completed Sapphic poems, are not just aesthetic objects, but fantasies of the past, stories that often tell us more about the concerns of those engaging in the work of reconstruction than the lost creators they describe.

It is not only fictions about Sappho's life and poetry that collect around Sapphic fragments, but fictions of authorship more broadly. As translators and authors used Sapphic fragments to tell new stories about Sappho, they also used these fragments to construct new stories of authorship. The nineteenth-century obsession with elaborating upon traces of a lost past gives rise to a fantasy of authorship that seems to privilege both a longed-for wholeness and a single creator endowed with divine genius. But, in fact, such authorship is founded upon a multiplicity of voices and a playing out of authorship as a series of performative decisions. The fact that Sapphic fragments were an excuse for new authorial performances might lead us to think differently about the material traces (or lack thereof) of operatic labor. The case of one Sapphic fiction that never saw the light of day is a case in point. Seven years before Pacini's *Saffo*, in 1833, librettist Felice Romani and Saverio Mercadante attempted to launch a Sapphic opera at La Fenice. Mercadante engaged Romani to compose a libretto on the subject, but Henriette Méric-Lalande, the soprano contracted for the season, refused to play the role. Romani, understandably, was furious: he had produced a libretto for which he was now not being paid, and his next assignment (to produce a libretto for Donizetti's *Lucrezia Borgia*) he undertook with little enthusiasm.[52]

The combined effort of numerous agents did not bring Sappho to life; everything hinged on the diva, Méric-Lalande, who decided not to be the embodiment of Sappho. This failed enterprise reveals the weaknesses and potentially abortive nature of collaborative authorship. One potential preventative measure to guard against such outcomes would be to fold the power of the performer into the person of the composer, to shift the emphasis to the composer's singular artistic vision and not the singer's capabilities. The dematerialization of the Sapphic improviser is, in some ways, a pragmatic and protective move. The nineteenth-century obsession with the Sapphic fragment is thus marked by a tension between an archaeological notion of the fragment (the shard of pottery as remnant of a lost whole) and a performative one (broken speech that demands an interlocutor). But an attention to both of these modes of fragmentation can allow us to imagine the lost social relations that escape the material stuff of artistic creation. Operatic scores are themselves built on loss. Even though we like to think of them as wholes, they are indeed fragments—incomplete traces of the collaborative network that brought these works into being and that was necessary to give them life in performance.

III. . . . *MY VOICE IS EMPTY AND CAN SAY NOTHING. . . .* (73)

Such accounts of operatic composition draw attention to the precarious position operatic "authors" occupied in mid-nineteenth-century Italy, reminding us that poetic and musical authorship was a matter not only of creating texts—it was also enacted in performance. The ubiquity of Sappho-like improvisers in the nineteenth century could therefore be ascribed partly to the ancient poet's peculiar status as an author: an icon of inspired poetic performance, her texts survived in fragments, and Sappho herself was subject to endless speculative recasting and to much rumination on the intersections of gender and creativity. Indeed, several scholars have argued that it was Sappho's nineteenth-century image as both the absent origin of feminine creativity and an impossible author, whose utterances emerge only after her death, that made her such an attractive model for women poets in particular.[53] Patrick Vincent maintains that poets adopted the identity of the abandoned Sappho or the tragic Corinne strategically. Investigating the tendency of women writers to "cast themselves in the role of the abandoned woman so as to enable their public voice," he argues that "love elegies modeled on the Sappho-Corinne myth were one of the principal ways in which women could authorize themselves as poets."[54] In his reading of poets who trope on the Sapphic myth of abandonment, it was the act of "citing" Sappho's state—forlorn, abandoned, pining for love—that allowed women writers to craft a public persona. But this persona paradoxically shunned publicity in favor of privacy, denying the efficacy of the very authorial power it seemed to carve out. Thus, the last lines of Felicia Hemans's 1830 poem "Corinne at the Capitol" undercut the previous stanzas' celebration of feminine creativity, proposing that the creation of domestic bliss for an audience of one—an admiring husband—is preferable to improvising poetry to the acclaim of an adoring public:

> Happier, happier far than thou,
> With the laurel on thy brow,
> She that makes the humblest hearth
> Lovely but to one on earth![55]

The "poetess," from this perspective, is a role to be performed: a role that allowed women to publish and gain recognition as authors while simultaneously interrogating the very possibility of feminine authority.

Yopie Prins has similarly read the prevalence of themes of extremity and loss in women's writing about Sappho as indicative of a fundamental uncertainty about the possibility of feminine authorship, an uncertainty which, as we have seen, informed Staël's representation of the *improvvisatrice*. Many poems in Sappho's voice seem to emerge from an impossible place: the recovered words uttered by a long-dead woman at the moment before her suicide. Depersonalization is the inevitable result, Prins claims, of an authorial stance characterized by the "postscript"—a poem written from the perspective of a Sappho perpetually suspended at the moment of her leap. If Ovid and later authors most often imagined Sappho's voice as irrevocably severed from her performing presence, audible only after her death, the poet's reputation is inevitably subsumed into a narrative of loss and suicide. This is especially the case in Sappho poems written by nineteenth-century women. The "success" of these verses, writes Prins, "depends on the repetition of a loss or failure that is the very means of its literary transmission."[56] And because Sappho's voice—in the nineteenth-century imagination, at least—emerges from this impossible place, it is all the more subject to ventriloquy. Sappho's texts survive in fragments, requiring extensive editorial intervention, and if her most famous song was thought to emerge spontaneously before her suicidal leap, then it must be imagined by other authors who step in to speak for her.[57]

Sappho was thus easily amenable to appropriation; she is a figure who seems to exist to be overwritten. The improviser Regaldi, in his verses of praise for Pacini's opera, for example, imagined the glory of the dead Saffo passed on to the composer. In his sonnet of admiration for the composer after *Saffo*'s success, he described the ancient poet's discarded laurel, left behind after her suicidal leap. In Regaldi's poem, a muse descends from the sky to collect the abandoned wreath, promising humankind that whoever tells Sappho's story well will be crowned with her laurel. In the final three lines—the *volta*, or turn, that rhetorical device characteristic of the sonnet—Regaldi neatly ties up the cross-millennial connection between composer and ancient poet:

> Dopo un volger di secoli, a divini
> Mesti concenti, fur spiegate l'ali . . .
> Di Saffo il lauro incoronò Pacini.

> [After the passage of centuries, to divine, sad harmonies, the wings were unfolded . . . Sappho's laurel crowned Pacini.][58]

The image of Sappho's laurel left behind on the cliff could be read as a metaphor for the authorial traces the poet has left behind. Sappho herself thus becomes an inspiring muse—a distant and unattainable ideal not unlike Dante's

Beatrice or Petrarch's Laura—to those who were moved by her story to poetic creation.

As we peruse Italian periodicals from the early 1840s, it becomes clear why some authors thought muses were desperately needed: poetry itself was understood to be in decline. Librettist and poet Felice Romani, in a lengthy 1840 review of a collection of poems by Count Linati, observes that the crisis of poetry was so common a trope that it was beginning to wear thin. "Every day . . . this poor age of ours is denounced as the enemy of poetry," he begins, and this collection of poems by Count Linati is no exception: the first poem speaks of the degradation of contemporary poetry. Nonetheless, Romani argues that "the Italian press cries out every day for poetry [whether] good or mediocre, cold or insipid; the papers and gift-books overflow with it; and women's albums are full of it. . . ."[59] Romani concludes that the era's much-discussed "antipathy to poetry" (poesefobia) is an "invention" (menzogna): as long as Italy's natural beauty and sonorous language continue to inspire its poets, "no one will ever hold poetry in contempt in Italy."[60] But what Romani does not comment on is what motivates Linati to compose poetry despite its degraded status. It is the twin influences of an "excellent woman" (the dedicatee of his poem, Maddalena Giovannini Grisati) and an imagined lyre:

> Sebben la dolce arte de' carmi a vile
> Torni a questa età nostra, e d'ogni vanto
> Oggi la spogli il rio tenor de' fati. . . .
> Sull'auree fila dell'eburnea cetra
> Per te mi giova, eccelsa donna, all'etra
> Scioglier inni soavi. . . .

> [Even though the sweet art of poetry becomes worthless in this age of ours, and the harsh deeds of the fates have stripped it of every honor. . . . Upon the golden strings of the ivory lyre, most excellent woman, it pleases me to let loose into the air sweet hymns to you. . . .][61]

Linati's conventional invocation of the exalted feminine figure who calls forth sweet hymns from the poet conjures up the figure of the muse, while the presence of the (explicitly classicized) lyre calls to mind both Sappho and Orpheus. The idealized source of inspiration for Linati's poem could not be further from the women who, Romani suggests, are significant producers and consumers of printed poetry. The modern poet, then, is able to write even in the face of the so-called crisis of poetry by calling up the memory of communal performance—of poetry enacted in the moment and composed in the presence of an appreciative listener.

Given the historic links between Sappho and improvisers, it comes as no surprise that on occasion *improvvisatrici* became muses to those who saw them perform. A poem written by a follower of Rosa Taddei is explicit in linking Sappho to the modern improviser; here, however, it is not Sappho but the *improvvisatrice* herself—or more specifically her performance—that inspires the poet to write. The anonymous writer's account begins in a manner not unlike other reviews of extemporaneous poetry—he tells us what subjects Taddei improvised and the audience's reactions. One crucial detail stands out, however: the audience members, he reports, were so enchanted by Taddei's performance that, had it not been for the presence of a master stenographer, they would have all rushed to set down her words themselves in order to "treasure" her skill—evidence, perhaps, to support Caesar's assertions concerning the drive to channel improvised poetry into written texts.[62] But, rather than merely replicate the work of the stenographer, this adoring fan is moved to compose his own poetry:

> Such beautiful poems aroused in me such enthusiasm, that in my imagination, they did not fade with [Taddei's] voice, but with the approval of the *signori Romantici* they flew to resound among the Elysian immortals, where Saffo and Corinna enraptured wished to honor Licoride Partenopea [Taddei's Arcadian name], making her one of their beautiful number. This same concept burst forth in my mind dressed in the following Latin verses. . . .[63]

Just as Sappho herself swings between exemplar of the brilliant poet and the unattainable, tragic figure who moves others to create, the real improvisers of the Italian stage were also inspiring muses, memorialized in homages such as this. Above all, this account indicates that the poetic improviser was the focal point of a strange circulation of authorial energy—her live performance of self-authored, spontaneous poetry rouses the writer to produce a text, but the text itself aspires to some of the values of spontaneous poetry, by imagining the echoes of the performer's voice. Poems of praise such as this monumentalized the work of the improviser, and textualized it, perhaps in a very conventional way, but these poems were also efforts to capture and channel aspects of extemporaneous poetry.

The notion of authorship I am sketching here suggests that in these nineteenth-century contexts the material fact of the production of texts is not as important as the aspects of authorship enacted in performance. That is, authorship is an amalgam of creative power and the performance or execution of that power, and texts themselves could only incompletely embody this amalgam. This perhaps explains why so many poets prefaced their work with explanations that situated it in real time, or borrowed markers of immediacy from extemporaneous practices. Given this context, perhaps Pacini's decision to compose an opera centered on Sappho makes more sense. To be sure, he could ventriloquize the ancient poet and win the laurel for himself, as Regaldi suggests. But he could also carve out a position as an author who paradoxically seems to place the performer at the forefront. In this way, he could elevate the values of spontaneity and inspiration associated with improvisatory practices while avoiding much of the messiness such practices entailed. I would suggest that it is precisely because Sappho embodied an ideal in which creation and execution were fused that she was invoked so often by *improvvisatori* as well as by librettists and composers. One notable review of Pacini's opera imagined Saffo both as the muse who bestows her gifts on the composer and as a fantastical performer of the work, which is here elided with her lyre: "Anyone who loves Italy and is jealous of her glory" should rejoice that Pacini's "muse has returned to strike the strings of that lyre, from which the liveliest sounds make echo every musical corner of Europe."[64] Pacini's *Saffo* throws into relief the difficulties of carving out an authorial position in an opera industry that until fairly recently valued the work of singers over that of composers. Placing this little-known opera in the context of contemporary practices of poetic improvisation also highlights values that have become lost to us as the notion of the operatic work began to crowd out the ideal of spontaneous creation in the moment. Anyone interested in inscribing his name on the ephemeral art of music in 1840 might successfully employ the figure of Sappho—a lacuna where an author should be—in a genre where the very notion of authorship was fast becoming more contested and complex.

5

A Sapphic Orpheus: Pauline Viardot and the Sexual Politics of Operatic Collaboration

> I love Fidelio, I adore Orpheus, on my knees, with tears of ecstasy, my heart is forever chained to the feet of the Queen of the Arts, Pauline Viardot!!. My tenderness for you is "without equal," O my dear beloved! You are [. . .] my most caressing, my sweetest thought! . . . Your charming graciousness toward me, touches me so profoundly that I cry . . . instead of thanking you! . . . It is near me, that crown that circled the head of a divine creature! How happy I am and how poorly I express my happiness![1]
>
> PAULINE D´ARANGE TO PAULINE VIARDOT, *letter dated 20 May 1860*

These words of thanks and devotion were addressed to Pauline Viardot by an admirer the year after the singer appeared in Hector Berlioz's revival of Christoph Willibald Gluck's *Orphée*. Pauline D'Arange wrote Viardot at least nine letters, which the singer kept in a scrapbook album bound in red leather and embossed with the opera's title. The album holds an extensive collection of fan material, including poems, paeans, and long missives, all in response to Viardot's performance as Orpheus, a role that was widely understood as the crowning achievement of her career. The correspondence from D'Arange, however, is unusual for both its fervor—her handwriting is expansive and suggests the letters were written in haste—and its intimate tone, characterized by both enthusiastic admiration and abject worship. But the missives also convey a sense of an intense, romantic familiarity even as they enact the drama of the supplicant pining for a distant beloved. Earlier, on April 7 of the same year, D'Arange had written, "Why, my dear darling, do you let me love you . . . without letting fall upon me one of your sweet rays from your splendid aureole? One line, one word, one card from you, Madame, would be for me a supreme happiness!"[2] Perhaps Viardot responded to this plea with a token or gift—possibly even sending the crown that D'Arange mentions in her letter a month later, the crown that once "circled the head of a divine creature" and is now at her side as she writes.

D'Arange's impassioned responses offer us a strikingly different way of understanding the appeal of the singer's career-capping role. Flora Willson has explored how the critical reception of Viardot as Orpheus consistently portrayed the singer as a living sculpture embodying neoclassical ideals and testified to the French reverence for the past and commitment to establishing a canonic musical "museum" at mid-century. Indeed, many of the other letters pressed between the pages of the album compliment Viardot's hard-won artistic maturity, lauding her as a cultural monument. The spacious scrawl and heated rhetoric of D'Arange's letters, however, speak not to the singer's status as immortal artistic edifice, but instead to her ability to forge passionate connections beyond the stage. D'Arange's apparent haste and enthusiasm, and especially her praise of Viardot's performance in trouser roles, thus raise the possibility of a Sapphic strand of reception. The temptation to follow this thread is only strengthened by the knowledge that eight years before *Orphée*, she had appeared on stage as another famous lyre-toting poet, creating the title role in Gounod's *Sapho.*

What would it mean to hear Viardot's Orpheus Sapphically? One approach would be to focus on the particularly electric reactions of fans such as D'Arange, seeking to untangle the ways that operatic stardom created the possibility of novel romantic and sexual identities. As Daniel Cavicchi has recently argued, the nineteenth century was an era of

> new and heightened awareness of the personal qualities of performers. In a time when romantic ideas of a core individual self were taking hold and, in romantic relationships, people were striving to achieve an intense "sharing of selfhood" (McMahon 1998: 66), the act of loving music often idealized identification with performers . . . Especially after repeated encounters with the same performers, music lovers often began to feel a strong and uniquely charged connection to that performer's unchanging, "inner" self.[3]

Female singers performing *en travesti*—dressed as men—offer an especially rich ground for the blossoming of same-sex affinities. Scholars such as Wayne Koestenbaum, Terry Castle, Elizabeth Wood, Heather Hadlock, and Wendy Bashant have all explored the imbrication of theatrical cross-dressing and queer desire.[4] That this body of work, most of which dates from the 1990s, was often explicitly autobiographical in nature speaks to, Monica Pearl claims, the existence of an "operatic closet," a "private (though shared) coded escape from an oppressive mainstream heterosexual world."[5] These accounts, however, focused as they are on fandom as an expression of hidden identities, at times emphasize the particular erotic charge of secrecy and intimacy (or even isolation) over the broader real-world connections that diva worship forged. Wood, for instance, has theorized a "Sapphonic" voice that has "overtones and resonances in and beyond voice production and hidden vestibules of the body."[6] This voice, in its ability to cross registers and the boundaries of self, continues to sound even through the spaces of historical distance and thus sings to the finely tuned listener of unheard and unacknowledged desires. Viardot plays a crucial role in defining this voice for Wood. Anecdotes relayed by her daughter of two women caught up in Viardot's spell—one a young girl who "grew thin and pale" with love for the diva, the other a widow who religiously attended Viardot's performances as Orpheus and left her flowers after each one—provide evidence of the transgressive power of a "voice that refuses standard categories."[7] It is tempting to place the letters of D'Arange next to these accounts, to try to match her declarations with the behavior of either the lovesick girl or the devoted widow. But the Viardot of D'Arange's effusions is more than a Sapphic object of desire. D'Arange's letters encourage us to understand Viardot's enduring contribution to opera as, above all, a matter of relationships—between fan and singer, between singer and the broader public, and between singer and composer.

A Sapphic hearing, then, would move beyond the notion of the diva's voice as object of secret desire to investigate other kinds of transgressive relationships. For Sappho was also an unsettling icon of the power of feminine talent, deployed variously as model and cautionary tale. The mythic account of Sappho's poetic genius first set down by Ovid claimed that her talent originated from Orpheus's lyre, which, legend had it, washed ashore on Lesbos after he was dismembered by the Furies. Here feminine creativity is predicated on masculine dismemberment—even castration—that has connotations of both sexual abandon and murderous violence.[8] In the operatic world, we can perceive echoes of this myth in the ways singerly intervention into the operatic score comes to be figured as the violation of a different kind of body: the composer's body of work. Reading against the grain, investigating not the Orphic Sappho but the Sapphic Orpheus, turns this familiar story on its head. I will focus on the Sapphic resonances in Viardot's embodiment of both Gluck's hero and Gounod's heroine not only as occasions for same-sex desire, but also as sites of real-world struggle around troubling, non-procreative feminine creativity and the problems it posed to traditional models of operatic production.

In this, the book's final chapter, I thus zoom out to a more panoramic view, traveling from Italy to France in order to consider how the figure of Sappho played a role in the nation's neoclassical turn.[9] Although Viardot was a product of the Italian *bel canto* tradition, she was a central figure in France's mid-century neoclassical craze, during which both scholarly and popular portrayals of the ancient poetess were undergoing profound transformations. As Margaret Reynolds has observed, it was in post-1850s France that we find an increasing concern with Sappho as a sexual rebel living and working outside bourgeois moral codes.[10] Women's artistic creativity, as a result, was inextricably tangled up with ideas of sexual transgression. Sappho was depicted as an "unnatural" woman as several different iconic images merged and melded: fallen woman, courtesan and muse, mentor and lover of young women, poet in a man's world.

Indeed, Viardot's biography overlaps suggestively with the Sappho myth, particularly in the way her life was understood to swing between the twin poles of creative work and romantic love. Rather than focus on Viardot as muse to male composers, I trace her own creative impact on the texts she helped create: Berlioz's renovation of *Orphée* and Gounod's *Sapho*. In so doing, I seek to illuminate the limits and possibilities for women composer-performers in the mid-nineteenth century by exploring the shifting meanings of operatic collaboration. It is in the complex work of collaboration that the collision of cultural ideas about muses and creators, singers and courtesans, is made apparent. Throughout, I will weave together biography, reception history, and study of Viardot's own compositional and creative endeavors to investigate how she negotiated the era's expectations and ideas surrounding women singer-composers in light of changing ideas about Sappho in France. Viardot's complicated friendships with male composers and her creative and interpersonal conflicts illuminate the unique way that this singer negotiated a difficult role for herself: that of singer and creator, facilitator and muse.

Attention to the mundane, everyday working life of the singer and in particular the complexity of her artistic collaborations reveals some interesting patterns. First, her relationships with both Gounod and Berlioz eventually foundered in disagreement and cool separation. The problems revolved around Viardot's supposed sexual impropriety and the issue of creative ownership, and these two strands, I argue, are not unrelated. Gounod's *Sapho* was composed largely at Viardot's country house, and she was instrumental in securing a contract for the composer. But her generosity backfired when the parents of Gounod's fiancée demanded that he cut all ties to the singer to avoid any signs of impropriety. In the series of complicated social maneuvers that ensued, Viardot's husband and close family friend were moved to come to her aid in defending her reputation from the suggestion of an affair with the composer. In the case of her work with Berlioz on *Orphée*, another intense and intimate period of collaboration gave way to coolness when the composer came to resent both the acclaim showered on Viardot's performance and her Italianate approach to ornamenting Gluck's music. In exploring these consequences, I suggest that close working relationships, and with them the notion of the composer's muse, were beginning to be viewed in a more ambivalent light. The drama of Viardot's precarious reputation and tussles over her "ownership" of the ornaments she performed thus attests to new, messier instances of the Sapphic trope. No longer the distant, unattainable Beatrice or Laura of the Renaissance, the muse was sliding into the role of courtesan, at the beck and call of the artist who sought to capture her in his chosen medium. Such a shift, I argue, contributed greatly to the ever-widening—and increasingly gendered—gulf between creators and interpreters. By confronting the relational nature of Viardot's genius, however, I show how the singer worked to offer alternative models of operatic creativity.

The Anti-Diva

Though Viardot came from a family of singers, she never comfortably inhabited the role of diva the way her sister Maria Malibran did.[11] Indeed, Beatrice Borchard has called Viardot an "anti-diva" for the ways both accidents of birth (her homely appearance, her status as a younger child) and personal preference (her desire to be a concert pianist, her intellectual and studious bent) led the singer to critique the institution of diva-hood from within.[12] Viardot's fame rested in both her distance from singerly stereotypes and her vocal "otherness." She possessed a voice that Camille Saint-Saëns described as "not velvet or crystal, but harsh . . . [like] the pungent taste of a bitter orange. It was made for tragedy, epic verse, and was more superhuman than human."[13] As Mary Ann Smart has noted, the "double" character of Viardot's voice, "combining a rich contralto register with a soprano extension . . . brought together in a single body the characteristics of grand opera's traditional contrasting sopranos—high and low, lyric and dramatic, Italianate and declamatory." This mixture of qualities and facility in both florid and speech-like styles meant that "she was somehow resistant to the 'typing' that constrained most singers, her talents spilling far beyond any single dramatic or vocal category."[14] At the time she began to work with Gounod on *Sapho*, Viardot, fresh from her triumph as Fidès in Meyerbeer's *La prophète*, had already been astonishing audiences for a dozen years with her two-and-a-half-octave range and her consummate talent as an actress.

But Viardot's creative activities also extended beyond singing. She had enjoyed a rigorous education, both humanistic and musical. From an early age she composed her own songs—her first tour featured several of her own compositions, with Robert Schumann publishing one of them in the *Neue Zeitschrift für Musik*. A fixture in the salon of George Sand, Viardot inspired Sand's 1842 novel *Consuelo*. She spoke six languages fluently and read several more, was an accomplished pianist (Franz Liszt was one of her teachers), and was also a devoted admirer of earlier—and at that time rather unfashionable—composers like Gluck and Mozart. In truth, she was something of a musical chameleon, with an insatiable taste for music of all styles and periods.[15] Most significantly, Viardot's musical and literary activities were inevitably conducted in a rich network of social relationships. As Smart puts it, "Viardot was also that rare creature, a *female* singer who enjoyed full and friendly collaboration with composers, her input welcomed by Meyerbeer, Gounod, Berlioz, Saint-Saëns, all of whom designed roles with her in mind."[16] Her contemporaries found this quality unusual enough to merit comment. Gabriel Fauré, a close friend and another sometime collaborator, wrote in *Le Figaro* on the occasion of Viardot's death: "Indeed, due to her vast intelligence, to an artistic sense, which had been marvelously developed from a serious musical education, to her sensitivity, her rare delicacy of penetration, was she not . . . better than an interpreter—more than a counselor, almost a collaborator?"[17] Fauré's cautious "almost" alerts us to the singularity of a singer so comfortable in this role. Seen from a modern perspective, Viardot's career presents no need for such equivocations. Certainly her education, her musical training, and her interpretive sensitivity prepared her well for such collective work—but so did her experience as a composer.

From the beginning of her compositional career, Viardot seemed to relish the collaborative nature of artistic production.[18] She was well known in her own circles as a composer in her own right—and her creative process was characterized by its cooperative qualities. Viardot's compositions often emerged from fruitful relationships with other artists and gave occasion for shared pleasure in performance. Her vocal arrangements of Frédéric Chopin's mazurkas, for example, grew from their friendship, and were greatly admired by Chopin himself, who accompanied her at the piano when Viardot performed the works in concert. Later in life, she composed operettas, one of which, *Le dernier sorcier*, was performed in an orchestral version in Weimar in 1869 (and in Riga and Karlsruhe a year later) to some critical acclaim. Henry Chorley wrote, "It is not possible to conceive anything of its kind more perfect in quaint fantasy, real charm and complete execution."[19] These operatic works depended upon and employed a different set of cooperative values: her intimate friend Ivan Turgenev wrote the texts, and Viardot made sure there were roles for her students. The fact that they were on a modest scale and performed in domestic settings has led them to be labeled "salon operas." But this generic marker speaks to a set of values that marked Viardot's entire creative life: they recall an earlier era of the integration of creative work and sociality in that eighteenth-century "temple of female glory," the artist's salon.

Viardot and Berlioz

Viardot's preference for collaborative work was certainly apparent in her work with Berlioz on the revival of Gluck's *Orphée et Eurydice.* That the role of Orphée needed to be rewritten and adapted for Viardot's unique voice necessarily made the undertaking a shared one. (At several points, Saint-Saëns also stepped in to reorchestrate portions of the work.) Gluck himself had reshaped the role of Orpheus for individual singers—first alto castrato, then soprano castrato, and finally *haute-contre*—in multiple versions of the opera (the first two in Italian in 1762 and 1769, respectively, the third in French in 1774). But *Orphée* in any form had nearly fallen out of the repertoire, thanks to the decline of the castrato and the growing difficulty of finding a male countertenor who could manage the role as concert pitch rose. Viardot, however, had been performing the *scène aux enfers* for many years—Berlioz admired her performance at the Bonn music festival in 1845—so she was a logical choice for the title role when the impresario Léon Carvalho had the idea to resurrect Gluck's opera.[20] Berlioz and Viardot worked together for several months in 1859—often at Courtavenel, the Viardots' country estate—to revise Gluck's score for modern performance and to recast Orpheus as a trouser role for contralto. Berlioz strove to combine the Paris and Vienna versions of Gluck's opera while accommodating the singer's capabilities.

Patrick Waddington has detailed the wide variety of roles Viardot played in this working relationship: she was a sympathetic ear, a bastion of support both emotional and practical, and she cared for Berlioz's health while he was in a fragile state.[21] Viardot was forthcoming about the explicitly sexualized dynamic in their collaboration, describing herself as the object of the composer's passionate attachment. Her correspondence portrayed Berlioz as supplicant and object of pity and made clear her emotional involvement in the project and the composer's fate. "Poor man!" she wrote to her friend Rietz, "I am extremely concerned about him—he is so very ill, embittered, and unhappy! I am very fond of him; and I know he loves me dearly, only too dearly in fact . . . Just think of it: after a long, good friendship with me, he has the ill luck suddenly to fall in love!"[22] Viardot wrote that she was in an "awkward situation" because Berlioz was in "such a sickly state that any emotion will kill him." He felt, she reported, "that he has scarcely any more time to live, and the thought of dying both revolts and horrifies him . . . I am very much aware that I, and I alone, can comfort this poor bleeding heart."[23] The opportunity to minister to the ailing Berlioz was clearly welcomed by Viardot. The composer's extreme mental, physical, and emotional distress—and his resultant dependency on Viardot—may have made him all the more receptive to the kind of collaborative working relationship she preferred.

Berlioz's gravitation toward a beloved "angel of mercy" facilitated the kind of dialogic dynamic fundamental to her creative process.

But it was the sticky question of how to appropriately ornament *Orphée* that exposed the unsteady foundation of his collaboration with Viardot. In the jockeying that resulted, we encounter the larger question of where authority resides when multiple authors revive the work of a dead composer. Audiences were more than willing to grant Viardot special status as the embodiment of Orpheus, while Berlioz occupied an unstable place—as arranger and accommodator rather than composer in his own right. There was, it seems, no space for Berlioz to insert himself as a new author of *Orphée*—when the position was already occupied by Gluck, and when Viardot was the recognizable face, voice, and body of a new Orpheus.[24] Berlioz's ensuing disgruntlement was expressed in an attempt to police the boundaries of what constituted acceptable intervention into existing masterworks, and he faulted Viardot for her singerly disregard for the score, discursively placing her back into the position of stereotypical diva. The problem was not simply status anxiety, but also the fact that Berlioz and Viardot had conflicting ideas of the opera's mythical namesake. In short: was Orpheus, the archetypal musician, more properly understood as an improviser, or was he an exemplar of noble simplicity, a monument to a golden age?

Joel-Marie Fauquet, the editor of the critical edition of Berlioz's *Orphée*, has found traces of this negotiation in the extant sources. A bundle of sixteen manuscript pages held in the Fonds du Conservatoire at the Biblioteque Nationale, for example, shows the evidence of three different hands. Positing that they are "the fragments of preparatory sketches exchanged by Berlioz and Viardot," Fauquet sees Viardot's influence in the movement of the final showstopper, "J'ai perdu mon Euridice," to the end of act 1, and in the preponderance of cadenzas, often trials of different variants for the same phrase ending (ex. 5.1).[25] Shifting the opera's most famous number to the end of the first act makes sound theatrical sense for a singer—especially one who made it famous as a recital piece—accustomed to creating a strong impression at that dramatic juncture. This alteration is later crossed out, and the aria is restored to its original position at the end of the opera, a sign, Fauquet argues, of Berlioz's "purism." Indeed, Fauquet's examination of the sources reveals, he maintains, "two opposing notions of correct interpretation: one, Berlioz's, based . . . on a kind of literal fidelity to the text; the other, Viardot's, marked by an interest in the problems of ornamentation."[26] "For Berlioz," writes Fauquet, "the sobriety of Gluck's vocal lines, inflected with the dramatic accents of the literary text, was diametrically opposed to . . . the ornate style of singing so adored by the dilettante public . . . but for Pauline Viardot it was not: she was

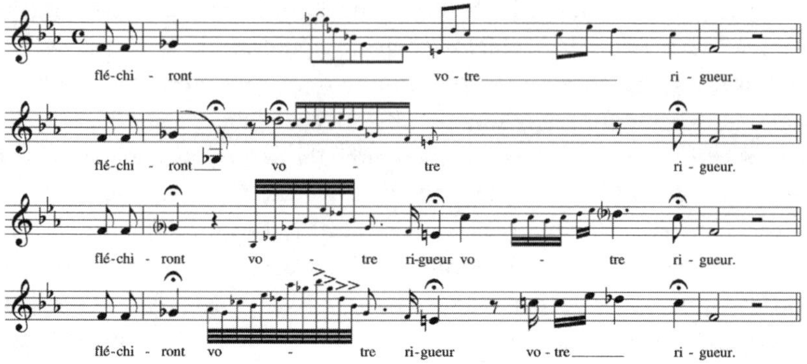

EXAMPLE 5.1 Viardot's multiple cadenza possibilities for "Ah la flamme qui me dévore," act 2 of Berlioz/Gluck, *Orphée* (Biblitèque Nationale, Musique, ms. 1522).

attached to the tradition of 'bel canto' and attempted to reconcile the two styles by adding ornaments and embellishing fermatas with cadenzas."

The conflict of values is not between fidelity and ornamentation, then, but rather involves different notions of what constitutes authentic expression. For Viardot, "classic" expression meant resurrecting earlier traditions of ornamentation; her antiquarian interests informed her belief that earlier eras understood ornament as a necessary and vital part of expressive performance.[27] But it is clear that she sought to meld this more florid idiom with the opera's gestural, declamatory style; in her own copy of the 1872 score published by Heugel, Viardot's interventions show just as much interest in shaping each parlante phrase with articulate detail as she does in crafting cadenzas. A comparison between her later annotations to the recitative "Qu'entends je? Qu'a-t-il dit?" and Berlioz's revised vocal part in the 1859 piano-vocal score (although this score was published by Escudier, its plates were also the basis for the Heugel edition) shows Viardot's exquisite attention to each expressive detail: the page is filled with accents, articulation marks, crescendi and decrescendi, dynamic markings, fermatas, and breath indications (ex. 5.2).[28] Berlioz's attraction to the "timeless" classicism of Gluck was also an interest in a vocal style—speechlike, plain, and tied to the rhythms of the text—that was quintessentially modern. And Berlioz himself was not above concerning himself with the important matter of showstopping cadenzas. In the case of the aria that concluded the first act (originally "L'espoir renait dan mon âme" and now titled "Amour, viens, rendre a mon âme"), he weighed in with his own advice on the concluding cadenza.[29] On 13 September 1859, he wrote, "I forgot to tell you that in your 'air à roulades' that concludes the first act, it is absolutely essential to sing an astounding cadenza at the last fermata. Gluck calls for it. So compose a lively mixture of vocalises for this moment and you will bring the house down as you leave the stage."[30] However, the composition was not left to Viardot alone. The next day Berlioz wrote to encourage her to reuse the melody of the earlier number "Objet de mons amours," which he notated in his letter, arguing that this strategy was something that "instrumental virtuosos do in their concertos." If they need to justify such a decision to critics, he suggests that they cite earlier performance practice: "We will say, if we have to, that *this is the cadenza sung by Legros* [. . .] The Parisians will surely swallow it whole. I think that you could leave the stage with a triple salvo of applause and thus enable us to avoid finishing on that stupid word 'appas.' "[31] The cadenza itself framed the reminiscence of "Objet de mon amour" with athletic arpeggiated gestures, startling leaps of a tenth and an eleventh, and an uncanny, two-octave chromatic ascent and descent (ex. 5.3).

EXAMPLE 5.2 Viardot's annotations to a copy of the 1872 Heugel edition of *Orphée*.

EXAMPLE 5.3 Concluding cadenza for "Amour, viens, rendre a mon âme" (act 1 of Berlioz/Gluck, *Orphée*) published as an appendix in the piano-vocal score.

Viardot's later annotated score shows that she added other, shorter cadenzas throughout the number to prepare for the final display.[32]

Then two things happened: Viardot received incandescent praise for her performance as Orpheus, and she had the temerity to allow publication of her ornaments.[33] George Sand's assessment, as biased as it no doubt was, well represents the tenor of the praise Viardot received: "This is, no doubt, the purest and most perfect artistic expression that we have seen for half a century, this Orpheus of hers—*understood, clothed, played, mimed, sung, spoken,* and *wept through* in the way that she interprets it."[34] Viardot was perceived as the total embodiment of Orpheus, credited, as Willson has argued, with single-handedly bringing back the extinct work from the dead and in the process becoming herself a kind of living monument.[35] But the overwhelming success of *Orphée*—and the fact that the acclaim most often focused on Viardot's powers of interpretation rather than Berlioz's role in the revival—caused some friction in their relationship. Waddington argues that Berlioz was jealous of the acclaim granted to Viardot, arguing that it was based on spurious grounds: "as it was, the audiences admired her most for the liberties she took with the score, and the sensation of the opera was her own 'stupendous cadenza.'"[36] The conflict between the two came to a head in 1861 when they began work on Gluck's *Alceste* in an effort to re-create *Orphée*'s stunning success. Berlioz refused to make changes to the score requested by Viardot (Waddington writes: "In view of her professional discernment, we may assume that these were not trivial in character") and unleashed a torrent of criticism of the diva in a letter to Royer:

> Absolute fidelity of interpretation is as necessary for the operas of Gluck as it is for the works of great dramatic poets, and it is just as senseless and revolting to pervert his melodies and recitatives by adding notes and changing final cadences as it would be to add words and change rhymes in the verse of Corneille. The only artists to whom one can usefully give advice are those who have a truly moral attitude towards their art, and a sincere respect for the great masters . . . As for the others, in spite of any desire they might have to take note of certain opinions, their vulgar vocalist's instincts will always carry the day.[37]

And yet, as we have seen, Berlioz's picture of the preserving composer and the revisionist diva is not entirely accurate. Viardot later defended herself to Reynaldo Hahn, telling him that the cadenza, "for which I have had the honor of being criticized . . . was manufactured by *all three of us!* . . . The first part (by Berlioz) is good; the second (by Saint-Saëns) is a bit odd; the several lines written by the singer are too 'singerish'; and the last part, by Berlioz, might also have been written by the concierge."[38] Waddington ascribes Berlioz's behavior to simple professional jealousy. "The reason Berlioz gave to Pauline for refusing to collaborate," he writes, "was that she should not have published *variants* for *Orphée*. When we remember that he had actively connived with her in these, we cannot take his new-found righteousness too seriously."[39]

I would argue that the break between composer and singer stemmed from an anxiety about the nature of collaborative creativity more generally. At Courtavenel, where opera was a family affair, and even Viardot's daughter corrected Berlioz's counterpoint, it was difficult to maintain the role of misunderstood genius laboring over his works in exile. Berlioz himself eventually chafed at all this togetherness, returning to Paris. Instead, we see a model of collective composition, which makes it difficult to know how to apportion credit or blame. Perhaps it is no wonder, then, that despite the fact that Berlioz encouraged Viardot to compose a showstopping cadenza, he conveniently forgot his own part in its creation when he used it as an excuse to break with the singer. Viardot's collaboration with Berlioz reveals conflicting values—not simply the different concerns of singer versus composer, as Berlioz suggested in his complaint. Certainly audiences were more than ready to see Viardot as the quintessential embodiment of Orpheus, the creative musician whose living performance of classic work renovated and revived it. Berlioz's competing perspective, however—that masterpieces demand "absolute fidelity"—would eventually sweep this image away.

Gounod and Viardot

A similar chain of events—close collaboration followed by friction and then a break—had played out eight years earlier in Viardot's relationship with Charles Gounod. It is no exaggeration to say that Viardot's role in the composition of Gounod's 1851 *Sapho* was fundamental to the work's very existence. She not only urged the young composer to write an opera, she advocated for his contract, which, given the composer's untested reputation, was issued only because she agreed to perform the title role.[40] Gounod and Viardot met sometime in 1849 or early 1850, introduced by a mutual friend: Charles was thirty-one, Pauline twenty-eight. Although he was her elder, Pauline was by far the more famous and influential figure. Gounod was not yet widely known; he had won the Prix de Rome in 1839, but after returning to Paris he worked as a church musician (even briefly pursuing ordination as a priest), and his oeuvre consisted mostly of liturgical music and some secular songs. During the conversation, the two seem to have connected over their shared interest in the ancient world, Gounod coming at it from the biblical angle, Viardot from her studies of Latin and Greek. After he played and sang some of his music for her (accompanying himself on the piano), Viardot asked him why he had not yet composed an opera, and a collaboration was born. The libretto, by Emile Augier, was ready in April of 1850, and Gounod signed a contract with the Opera on April 3. Later that month, Pauline and her husband opened Courtavenel, their country home, to the composer and his mother upon the death of Gounod's older brother; he stayed there throughout the summer and into the fall while Viardot was on tour. During that time, the two corresponded frequently—Gounod wrote her nearly every day, often multiple times per day. His letters to the singer have been collected in a recent volume edited by Melanie von Goldbeck, but Viardot's side of the exchange has been lost, perhaps, as Gérard Condé has argued, destroyed by a composer "jealous" of his own reputation and eager to erase the "traces of a collaboration."[41] Viardot's absence from Courtavenel during the summer months, as well as the loss of her letters, has led to a somewhat misty picture of her influence on *Sapho*: Barbara Kendall-Davies argues, for example, that "Although Pauline was far away . . . the memory of her voice haunted [Gounod] as he composed the music she would sing."[42] Yet Gounod's correspondence, the evidence of an unpublished letter from Pauline's husband Louis Viardot, and a closer examination of the score paint a more nuanced picture of *Sapho*'s creation, suggesting that Viardot was not content to be merely a distant muse.

Several things complicate the familiar picture of the solitary composer inspired by a remote, ethereal figure. First, Gounod's letters to Viardot were emotionally intense, detailed, and confessional—Goldbeck calls them an intimate diary of his creative process and state of mind—and in them he repeatedly engaged in what I would call a discursive merging with Viardot, as if the two were fused into a single creative force. This fusion seems to exist in both an ideal realm and a practical one. In letters written over the course of a single week in May of 1850, for example, he asks for help with the finale of the first act ("Aidez-moi donc, que je le sente d'ici cette collaboration de coeur qui en vaut bien en autre"), and anticipates writing Sapho's ode, addressing Viardot as a kind of patroness divinity ("C'est ici que je vais vous invoquer avec toute la devotion et toute la ferveur imaginable. O ma patronne, exaucez-moi!").[43] Throughout the correspondence, the word "our" occurs with some frequency, as when he refers pointedly to *Sapho* as "*our* oeuvre."[44]

Second, the setting at Courtavenel was fairly crowded—in addition to Gounod's own mother and Viardot's family, the Russian author Ivan Turgenev was already in residence, and Louis Viardot, Pauline's husband, was also present at various points. Turgenev was a bemused witness to the young composer's struggles:

> "It is very beautiful today. Gounod has walked all day in the woods . . . searching for an idea. But inspiration, capricious as a woman, did not come, and he found nothing . . . At this moment he is lying on the bearskin in labor-pains. He has an obstinacy and a tenacity in his travail that arouse my admiration. His unproductiveness of today makes him very unhappy; he heaves sigh after sigh, as big as an arm, and is unable to distract himself from his preoccupation . . ."[45]

The "labor" of composition, then, was far from solitary, but performed both for the absent Viardot (via letters) and for the household, Gounod's audience acting variously as sympathetic observers, troubleshooters, or midwives. Gounod and Turgenev were engaged in a friendly—or not-so-friendly—rivalry, going so far as to compare their letters from Viardot to see who had received the most pages (Turgenev complaining that Gounod's were always longer than his). But Gounod's creative imagination was fired when the two men gathered in the evenings to imagine the singer's successes on her tour. Waddington has described how Turgenev wrote to Viardot, revealing to her that "Gounod and he had stayed up late to follow her imagined progress in *Le Prophète* in Berlin, telling each other when she would have reached

'Ah, mon fils,' applauding at the end of acts, and throwing down sprays of white lilac (a piece of which he included with his letter)."[46] The atmosphere was thus one of intense triangulation as Viardot's devotees gathered to burnish her aura, and to channel their own creative efforts through their affective relationships to both the absent ideal and her present admirers.[47]

A thorny problem facing Gounod was the question of Sapho's final scene. Augier's libretto presents a version of Sapho's life that was fairly conventional for the time: her performance of sung, improvised poetry wins her the Olympic laurel and Phaon's love, stealing him away from the courtesan Glycère. But his former lover has her revenge when she reveals Phaon's involvement in a political plot and demands that Sapho repudiate him in order to save his life. When he sails away with Glycère for voluntary exile, Sapho flings herself from a cliff into the deep. On June 28, Gounod wrote of his struggles with this last number, describing Sapho's final moments and copying in several lines of text he had decided would serve him well. He continued, "From the last four lines—'Maintenant reçois-moi . . .' to the end, the music becomes turbulent; the roaring of the sea combines with these last expressions of sorrow until the final big orchestral entry, which occurs at the moment when Sapho throws herself into the sea."[48] In short, Gounod envisioned Sapho's suicidal leap as a big theatrical climax. A few days later, Gounod wrote to Pauline that he had completed the scene and performed it for his mother and Louis Viardot's sister Berthe. The event, he boasted, was a "Huuuuuuuge success. They found the last number grippingly dramatic and were greatly moved by it. As was I. I can hardly wait to *give* you all of this: *you for whom* and a bit *by whom* I have made it."[49]

But Louis Viardot wasn't so sure. Just a few days later, in a letter written with the meticulous expertise of a former impresario, he sent Pauline a detailed précis of the opera, described what was left to be composed, and shared his impressions of the work's potential for success.[50] This unpublished letter, held in Harvard's Houghton Library, reads something like a foreman's report to the boss, with Gounod cast as laborer. Louis is clearly confident in his own opinions, but many of them rest on his intimate knowledge not just of public taste but also of Viardot's capabilities and preferences. At times he clearly acknowledges that final judgment is not possible until he hears her perform the work, as when he admits that a number in the second act "did not touch and move" him as much as expected; he determines that he must "blame" himself until Viardot arrives—one assumes to give it the performance it deserves. That tricky finale was a cause for much concern. Louis reported that he had urged Gounod to streamline the finale by cutting eight lines of text before Sappho's prayer and the shepherd's song to avoid unnecessarily "lengthen[ing] the scene, and cool[ing] it down." And, despite the enthusiastic reception of "Maman et Berthe," Louis found that Sapho's final song "had a major defect." The problem was pacing and sentiment: "The song of despair for Sapho must be magnificent and awesome—at least I believe that you will *make* it have that effect," he wrote, but Gounod, by setting the words "horrid torments, have an end with me" to music that expressed "mad and enraged" despair, had evoked not the death of a noble figure but instead "a gambler who is about to commit suicide."[51] The solution Louis proposed was to make the final scene sound more like Gluck:

> At my suggestion, Gounod [now] has Sapho sing this whole phrase at the bottom of the cliff, while the sea roars. Then she climbs the rock of Leucas, the sea becomes calm, and—from on high—she now says: "Oh, you who leave, cursing the woman who loves you, be blessed by a woman who is dying" and then she leaps into the sea. These added words, very different in expression from the preceding ones—tender and noble—need to be like the last words of Armide [in act 2 of Gluck's *Armide*] in the "hatred" duet, added by Gluck. This will be more appropriate, and more beautiful. Gounod did not hesitate to accept my suggestion, and he is pleased with himself [for having done so].[52]

But Louis's solution, however confidently offered and enthusiastically accepted by Gounod, did not make the final cut. Though in the score Sapho does utter similar words to the ones in this letter, they do not occur right before her suicidal leap but instead provide a calm interlude before her final aria.

So neither Louis's suggestion—end with a nod to Gluckian restraint—nor Gounod's original idea—a climax marked by high melodrama—were ultimately deemed suitable for the ancient poet's final song. The solution our team of collaborators arrived at was an unusual one, and it was most likely sparked by Viardot's return to Courtavenel. When Pauline arrived in September, she was in a position to assess the opera for herself. After Gounod played through the work, singing at the keyboard, she impressed the composer by learning the entire score herself in just a few days—well enough, as James Harding says, to "accompany nearly all of it by heart at the piano."[53] After this period of study she proposed "even bigger changes," as she wrote to Turgenev, who had in the meantime returned to Russia. The two areas of most concern for her were Sapho's first act ode and, no surprise, the end of the opera—of the latter she wrote, "the whole last scene will be reworked." Viardot seems to have proposed that Gounod scrap the music he had written for these two numbers and instead use previously composed songs—his "Le soir" (text by Alphonse de Lamartine) from 1840 for Sapho's first-act ode and the 1841 "Lamento—La chanson du pêcheur" (text by Théophile Gautier) for the final number.

The choice had much to do with wanting to end the opera with a strong, pathetic effect, as she explained to Turgenev: ". . . the *Lamento* will be inserted—this has been decided—but only as a purely lyrical number: as the last song of Sapho. Her lyre in her hand, she will bid farewell to Phaon, to the sun, to her lyre, and finally to her life, and she will dive headfirst and go drown herself in the tears that she has made the spectator[s] shed."[54] In this final sentence, Viardot wittily slips between the "elle" who is Sapho and the "elle" who is Viardot, as she suggests that the audience's tears will be copious enough for the suicidal poet to drown herself. The reuse of "Lamento" is thus important to her primarily because of the effect that it will allow her to create on stage as a performer—she displays a sort of knowingness about her own power to arouse the audience's feelings. It also explicitly presents Sapho as a performer, although a very un-diva-like one.

A Drawing-Room Sappho?

Nevertheless, all this attention to the final scene—and to the third act more broadly—went largely unappreciated. One contemporary critic complained that the opera was a puzzling hybrid, noting that "one of the most annoying aspects of the libretto is that the accumulation of choral sound and massed effects happens in the first act, whereas the third [. . .] consists entirely of a succession of solos."[55] Stephen Huebner has argued that this uncoupling of dramatic tension from spectacle robbed *Sapho* of the end-weightedness—the buildup to a dramatic finish—that spectators had come to expect from grand opera.[56] The work's portrayal of its title character may have also undermined audience expectations. This Sapho is an unusual operatic heroine: most of her musical utterances have a plainness and simplicity about them that speaks of a vocal idiom foreign to the stage. Indeed, the effect of reusing previously composed songs for Sapho's two big numbers—songs written not for an opera, but for domestic consumption and to be performed by solo vocalist with piano—cannot be underestimated. Instead of a fiery, creative poet or even a flamboyantly tragic figure, she seems to have emerged from a more intimate domestic space.

Let us examine more closely the almost-decade-old song entitled "Lamento—La chanson du pêcheur" that Gounod reused for Sapho's big finale (ex. 5.4). "Lamento" acquired new words to serve as Sapho's last song, but the melody changed very little in the journey from parlor to stage, with only minor emendations to accommodate Augier's new text. The most obvious change the song underwent is the shift in narrator—from anonymous male fisherman to historic female poet. Gautier's narrator grieves the death of a beloved in a simple and naïve tone.

> Ma belle amie est morte:
> Je pleurerai toujours;
> Sous la tombe elle emporte
> Mon âme et mes amours.
> Dans le ciel, sans m'attendre,
> Elle s'en retourna;
> L'ange qui l'emmena
> Ne voulut pas me prendre.
> Que mon sort est amer!
> Ah ! sans amour, s'en aller sur la mer!
> [. . .]
> Sur moi la nuit immense
> S'étend comme un linceul;
> Je chante ma romance
> Que le ciel entend seul.

> [My beautiful love is dead, / I shall weep always; / Into the tomb, she has taken / My soul and my love. / Without waiting for me, / She has returned to heaven. / The angel which took her there / Did not want to take me. / How bitter is my fate! / Ah! without love, to go to sea! [. . .] Above me the immense night / Spreads itself like a shroud; / I sing my romanza / That heaven alone hears.]

That brief moment of Romantic self-consciousness at the lines "I sing my romanza / That heaven alone hears" heightens the sincerity effect, as the narrator is explicitly singing a song to nature instead of an audience. As for Gounod's music, a rolling, arpeggiated accompaniment figure and the triple meter clearly mark this piece as oceanic in nature, making it well suited to do double duty for both a lamenting fisherman and the soon-to-drown Sapho. The piece is in two stanzas, each of which begins in B-flat minor and modulates to D major, and the melody is almost austere. A focus on repeated notes and a strict absence of melisma characterize the vocal line, whose expressive touches consist of downward leaps and long, sustained notes. The plainness of the melody perhaps shows how rustic, folklike simplicity and noble classicism are two sides of the same coin.

Sapho's poem is, in contrast, more elevated, but it too speaks of its own status as song. However, this is a failed performance: Sapho addresses her lyre (embodied by the orchestra's harp), whose murmuring cannot console her in her extremity and cannot prevent her death.

EXAMPLE 5.4 Gounod, "Lamento" (text Gautier).

O ma lyre immortelle,
Qui dans les tristes jours
A tous mes maux fidèle
Les consolait toujours!
En vain ton doux murmure
Veut m'aider à souffrir,
Non, tu ne peux guérir
Ma dernière blessure;
Ma blessure est au coeur
Seul le trépas peut finir ma douleur.

[O my immortal lyre, / Who, in sad times, / Faithful through all my woes, / Always consoled me! / In vain your gentle murmuring / Tries to aid me in my suffering; / No, you cannot heal / My latest wound; / My wound is in my heart! / Only death can end my anguish!]

Remaking the earlier song, placing the melody of the mourning fisherman in the mouth of the suicidal poetess, could be thought of as a form of ventriloquy or perhaps an uncanny doubling, as if Sapho were both the (already) dead beloved and her own mourner.[57] Sapho's lyre is even made to imitate the sound of the ocean, as the harp voices the moody, roiling arpeggios originally given to the piano. Here the lyre is no longer the vehicle of the poet's genius but instead the instrument of her destruction. Sapho's death song is at once folksy and cerebral—it seems to anticipate its future life as a successful recital piece, where, coming full circle, the iconic lyre would be replaced with the domestic piano (ex. 5.5).

The Break

The intense collaboration and friendship between Gounod and Viardot was short-lived. In the spring of 1852, the year after *Sapho*'s premiere, Gounod announced his engagement to Anna Zimmermann, the daughter of Pierre-Joseph-Guillaume Zimmermann, one of his teachers at the Conservatoire. The connection may have been instrumental in securing him positions as director of the Orphéon (an organization of choral societies) and as chief of vocal instruction in Paris city schools. The news of his impending marriage spurred a series of social missteps and breaches of protocol that eventually ended friendly relations between Gounod and the Viardot family. This almost novelistic tragedy of manners turned on a repeatedly canceled dinner engagement, a hasty wedding, and a returned bride gift. It ended with Louis Viardot writing Gounod, "Since you have had the weakness, I should say the cowardice, to make yourself the intermediary and accomplice of an insult addressed to a lady

EXAMPLE 5.5 Gounod, "Ô ma lyre immortelle," from *Sapho*.

whom you should at least respect, you will not be surprised that I am closing to you henceforth the door of our home. You will be without doubt a great musician, sir, and you will have admirers, but I doubt if you will keep any friends."

Pauline detailed what happened in a long letter to George Sand (she even copied out entire letters sent by the principal actors, as if presenting evidence in a court of law).[58] After Gounod's sudden announcement of his engagement, Viardot tried twice to plan a dinner in honor of his fiancée, only to have the Zimmermanns cancel. On the third attempt, Gounod arrived at the door "shamefaced" the evening of the party and said that it must again be canceled because his fiancée was ill (Pauline wrote to Sand that "my chickens were roasted and the table almost set").[59] Viardot herself was pregnant with her second child—she would give birth to her daughter Claudie on May 21—and Gounod, along with his mother and the Zimmermanns, had insisted to Viardot that the couple would wait to marry until after the soprano delivered, so that she could attend. Two days after the birth, however, Viardot heard secondhand from Gounod's mother that the couple was to be married that very day in a small ceremony with only a few witnesses—not even Louis was invited. Her later gift to the bride of a bracelet was returned by Gounod with a brusque and ambiguously worded excuse. Unfortunately, he had planned to buy his wife a bracelet as well (it would be the "only one she plans to wear"), and in returning her gift he wanted to spare Viardot the refusal that would surely come from Anna.[60] The damage was done: Louis sent Gounod the angry letter barring him entrance to the house.

EXAMPLE 5.5 (*continued*)

When Gounod arrived to plead his case to Louis, he revealed that the source of the unpleasantness was "malicious gossip" that the Zimmermann family had heard. There had long been speculation about the relationship between Pauline and Turgenev, who were believed to be lovers; Harding writes that when Gounod "became an intimate of the Viardot household . . . malicious tongues suggested that the triangle had become a square."[61] Gounod explicitly acknowledged this gossip in a later letter to Louis attempting to defend his behavior:

> The extreme intimacy with which you favored me, the continuous and very cordial welcome which I have received, your unique patronage to which I owe the first steps of my career, finally, all that constituted the complete familiarity of our relations has been, as you know, the subject of slanderous interpretations, which your character and the knowledge of your wife's character have made you despise; that was all they deserved. These evil sentiments have been whispered recently to my new family and troubled their minds to such a degree that I was obliged, when they finally confided in me, to declare on my honor that although very close to the time of my marriage, I would renounce it rather than fail to obtain the trust I deserved in this respect; that faced by such uneasiness on one side and devoted friends on the other, I felt compelled in all conscience to a double line of conduct: a line of reserve, it is true, sufficient to insure peace of mind of those who are confiding to me their dearest treasure, their child; but also a line of fidelity to the memory of those from whom I had received much and to whom I was still indebted.[62]

At issue for Gounod's bourgeois parents-in-law, then, was the composer's close connection to the seemingly scandalous singer; they pressured him to break ties with Viardot, doubtful that their collaboration was merely professional. The Zimmermanns' outrage certainly concerned sexual propriety, and perhaps more specifically the paternity of Viardot's child. Pauline's bridal gift of a bracelet for Anna arrived in the midst of this domestic storm. She wrote to Sand, explaining the reasons for the bracelet's return: "He [Gounod] confessed [to Scheffer, a friend of the Viardots] that his new family had had their minds troubled for some time by an anonymous letter and some gossip, both malicious and injurious, about him and myself, but that he had indignantly denied it; that nevertheless he thought he was doing well to forestall a refusal which would perhaps have been sent to me . . ."[63] Gounod's attempt to appease both parties, however, was unsuccessful. After his pleading visit to speak to Louis, he was given the chance to make amends by paying a wedding visit to Pauline within ten days—but the deadline passed, not without much waffling after the fact from Gounod. As he had promised, Louis revealed Gounod's behavior to the wider circle of their friends, and Pauline's male defenders publicly stepped in to ward off the suggestion of impropriety and maintain her reputation. That was the end of the collaboration between Gounod and Viardot.

Whatever the facts of the matter were, Viardot's letter to Sand "vibrates with betrayed affection and with anger," in the words of Thérèse Marix-Spire. As Louis put it, she wrote, either Gounod had not really defended Pauline's honor or he had, the Zimmermans had not believed him, and he married into the family anyway; in either case, he had acted abominably. Viardot wrote: "After that, you may understand, my Ninounne, that there is nothing further to reply to so much vileness and stupidity. We have resolved to write [to Gounod] no more . . . And nevertheless, I tell you in all sincerity, in spite of the sorrow, in spite of the wrong all this has done to me, I do not regret the help I have been able to give this ingrate. Here he is launched on his career, and if his *entourage* and his own character do not destroy his genius, which is much to be feared, he will compose some masterpieces which will do honor to art and delight those who hear them."[64] In one respect, her disappointment hinged on Gounod's inability to manage public perception of their collaborative relationship even after she had taken "him in like a child of the house" and worked in so many ways to advance his career. But Viardot also seems to have been truly shocked that someone in possession of such musical gifts should be willing to bow to the strictures of bourgeois society (never mind that the Viardots' sense of outrage was itself predicated on bourgeois manners and morals), and that he could act so blatantly out of self-interest: "With all his appearance of feeling, that *heart* of which he talks so much in such eloquent language is nothing more than a sac of egoism, vanity, and calculation—in a word, he is a *Tartuffe*. Good God, what a disillusionment! . . . How is it that such genius can exist where there is no *genuine heart!*"[65] Sand replied, sagely: "It is very rare when there is not side by side with genius a dose of vanity which turns greatness into meanness."[66]

Owning Sappho

That gossip circulated about Viardot's propriety is not surprising. Because they put themselves on display before audiences of men, traveled freely, and generally operated outside the bounds of domestic respectability, performing women had long been subject to speculation about their sexual availability. But that such scandal erupted in the wake of Viardot's performance as Sapho is suggestive, especially considering the new taste for sexualized representations of the ancient poet at this time. As Margaret Reynolds has argued, French authors, artists, and consumers in the middle decades of the century increasingly saw the ancient poet not as a creator, but as a courtesan. According to Reynolds, the transformation of Sappho from poet to prostitute had its roots in the era's hunger for prurient images of the wages of sexual transgression, especially representations of suicides who drowned themselves: "As [one] who was well known for having thrown herself into the water, Sappho came to be metaphorically associated with the idea of the fallen woman. In France this trend was confirmed by various pseudo-scholarly publications that proposed or disputed her role as courtesan."[67] But there was more: Reynolds has argued that "in the popular mind the life of the independent and artistic woman was inextricably mixed with the slur of sexual availability. In Sappho's case this became literally true as she was bought and sold throughout Europe."[68]

The vogue for cheaply reproduced statuettes of Sappho in the few years immediately preceding the appearance of Gounod's opera exemplifies the poet's transformation into a kind of degraded muse.[69] In 1848, just three years before Gounod's opera appeared on stage at the Opera, James Pradier sculpted an image of this new type of Sappho in silvered bronze and gilt. She was in clinging drapery, posed seductively against a column, lyre in hand, her thrusting hip and downcast eyes suggesting sensuality. The work was the subject of rapid commodification; as Reynolds notes, Pradier produced "a number of luxurious copies of his statuette in silver" and "licensed the Maison Suisse with the right to sell small-scale reproductions."[70] The same pattern was followed in 1852 with his larger seated Sappho carved in marble, whose pensive pose allows her robe to slip, revealing her shoulders.[71] A miniature bronze copy of Pradier's statue transformed Sappho into an ornament to adorn a domestic space. These copies of Pradier's work and of many similar works produced by other sculptors had multiple afterlives in bourgeois drawing rooms, libraries, and studies. Such figurines skirted the boundary between salacious and classicist; in one notable case, a reproduction of William Theed's statue of Sappho (which initially represented Sappho's nude torso) was covered with a modest scrap of fabric and necklace for domestic consumption (figs. 5.1 and 5.2). By 1884, the ubiquity of commodified Sappho figurines was a central theme of the novel *Sapho* by Alphonse Daudet that thirteen years later served as the source for yet another opera, this one by Jules Massenet. Here the heroine is not a poet from ancient Greece, but a prostitute who is nicknamed Sapho because she posed for just such a statue; the hero is "disgusted at the thought of how her body in miniature can be pawed by many a lecher admiring the adornments of his own mantelpiece."[72] It is hard to say whether or not Viardot's performance as Sapho brought to mind these new Sapphic courtesans, who allied artistic independence with sexual voracity. But in one respect, the rather odd domestication of Gounod and Viardot's operatic Sappho makes perfect sense—the deliberately untheatrical, simple style both recalls her classical roots and hints at her place in the bourgeois drawing room. Perhaps such simplicity is an effort to cover Sappho with the mantle of respectability and chaste modesty, just as Theed's reproductions for domestic use draped a scrap of fabric over the poet's naked bosom.

FIGURE 5.1 William Theed, *Sappho*, 1851. Marble, 99.7 cm. Royal Collection Trust / © Her Majesty Queen Elizabeth II 2019.

FIGURE 5.2 Desktop copy in Parian ware of Theed's *Sappho* with added drapery and necklace. Image courtesy of Chris Copeland, from *Parian: Copeland's Statuary Porcelain* by Robert Copeland (Antique Collectors' Club, 2007).

A Final Lament

These desktop Sapphos could not be further from the heated praise of Viardot as cultural monument and ancient statue come to life after her performance as Orpheus eight years later. This begs the question of why Viardot herself would advocate for the domestication of her own role as Sapho. Why assist in creating a character who not only recalled an intimate space incongruous with the operatic stage but perhaps brought to mind these other Sapphos—*objets d'art*, decorative possessions, seductive seminudes? Perhaps she didn't—the evidence for Viardot's intervention here, while strong (it was in part through his songs that she came to know and admire Gounod's talent, and the decision to reuse the earlier songs was not made until she had returned to Courtavenel), is not watertight.[73] But I would like to resist the idea that, in collaborative relationships between singer and composer, the only influence that matters is that which is exerted upon the musical text. Viardot's collaborations were in fact characterized by the sheer variety and volume of affective and practical labor she performed—labor that often left no obvious traces on the work.

Such labor is often feminized, and although it can be invisible to historians, it was a source of both satisfaction and conflict for creative women at the time. The matter of *Sapho*'s "remade songs" raises more important questions than who exactly deserves the credit for compositional decisions. Instead, the songs open out onto the larger issue of what ideals of creative effort were embraced by the mid-nineteenth-century operatic world. In this respect, it is significant that Viardot, throughout her life, both practiced and advocated for a model of creative endeavor that was decidedly utopian and in some sense nostalgic—one that was domestically focused and involved a multitude of creative actors. We see this at play not just in the case of *Sapho* and *Orphée*, but also in Viardot's later salon operas, whose texts and melodies were crafted by and for her friends and students. We can understand the domestication of Sapho not simply as a capitulation to restrictive ideals concerning feminine creativity, but more importantly as a means for Viardot to both enact and advocate for an openly collaborative ethos of artistic production, one that persisted even in an era beginning to be dominated by the myth of the solitary genius.

And, of course, Viardot was well able to speak with her own authoritative compositional voice. Her own version of "Lamento—Le chanson du pêcheur" was published in 1886 by Enoch Frères and Costallat, and dedicated to contralto Madame Evelyn Enoch, a cousin of Gabriel Astruc (ex. 5.6).[74] Viardot's *mélodie* was written earlier than its publication, however; a manuscript held at Houghton Library is inscribed "Bougival 26 October 1884."[75] That Viardot should revisit the text of the song that had been transformed into Sapho's final aria at her behest could be a simple coincidence—Gautier's poem was set by many composers. But it is significant that her manuscript dates from the very same year that Gounod revived *Sapho*, this time crafting a four-act version (never published) with Gabrielle Kraus singing the title role.[76] Viardot's "Lamento" has several qualities that might make a listener ask whether, returning to this text over three decades after her collaboration with Gounod, she was hearing a Sapphic echo in Gautier's verses.

The first indication of these faint echoes is a small word change—almost a Freudian slip. Where Gautier's poem reads "Sur moi la nuit immense / S'étend comme un linceul [Over me the immense night spreads itself like a shroud]," Viardot changed "nuit" to "mer" (fig. 5.3). The sinister result—"Over me the immense sea spreads itself like a shroud"—significantly changes the mood and meaning of the stanza. No longer a lonely, grief-stricken fisherman sailing out under gloomy skies, Viardot's narrator now sounds like the desperate Sappho, contemplating suicide by drowning—the sea-shroud that will cover her more starkly literal than Gautier's original metaphor.[77] The familiar image of Sappho singing her final song ("Je chante ma romance") and then leaping into the sea intrudes on the fisherman's lament and is hard to banish.

EXAMPLE 5.6 Viardot, "Lamento" (text Gautier).

EXAMPLE 5.6 (*continued*)

Other (sometimes puzzling) aspects of the song encourage a Sapphic hearing as well. Zoltan Roman has noticed that Viardot creates a "timeless . . . archaic" mood through "'open' intervals (mostly 4ths and 5ths, but also some octaves) and parallel chords, an induced rhythmic monotony, and—perhaps most importantly—the unmistakably modal inflection of the melody and harmony."[78] While noting that she may have been influenced by her roles as Sapho and Orphée, he does not draw a direct link between her compositional choices and her participation in reworking Gounod's earlier setting of Gautier's poem for use in *Sapho*. But, studying the song more closely, it is hard not to hear it as a kind of rewriting of Gounod's song-turned-aria. In this case, instead of domesticating Sapho by giving her an art song as operatic finale, Viardot subtly theatricalizes the art song, importing several small-scale operatic gestures to dramatic effect.

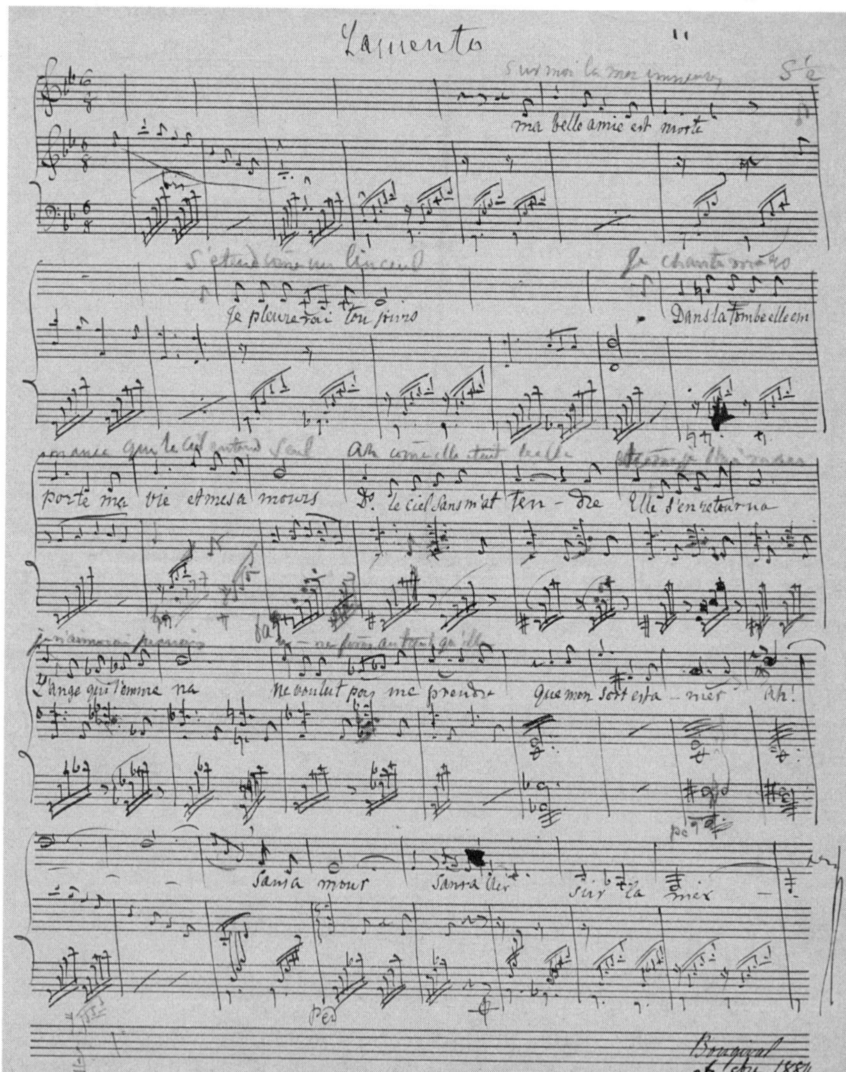

FIGURE 5.3 Viardot-García, Pauline. "Lamento," words by Theophile Gautier. Autograph manuscript score, 1884. Pauline Viardot-García additional papers, 1838–1912. MS Mus 264 (150). Houghton Library, Harvard University, Cambridge, MA.

Each stanza of Viardot's song builds via a stepwise ascent to a dramatic climax, including what Roman has called "an exquisitely calculated interpolation of four measures of *tremolandi*" that underpin the singer's declamatory double-forte outburst on the words "Que mon sort est amer [How bitter is my fate]!" "In general," Roman argues, "this device has been regarded as too dramatic for an art song." Indeed, this quasi-operatic moment disrupts the song's tranquil oceanic flow with declamatory force. As the singer resumes, softly exhaling the most basic of lyric expressions (the wordless "Ah!" on a long-held F), the watery accompaniment is subtly transformed. The harmony shifts to flat-VI7 on the word "amour," and the addition of rolled broken chords evokes the strummed gestures of a stringed instrument—perhaps even a lyre. Sapho's final aria in Gounod's opera began with a similarly evocative gesture—a timpani roll (that became left-hand tremolos in the piano-vocal score) and an expansive ascending arpeggio for the harp. But where Gounod attached an operatic opening to his interpolated art song, Viardot interpolates operatic gestures into her domestic *mélodie*, allowing an otherworldly Sapphic song to whisper through the folksy fisherman's lament.

It is a queer moment. Viardot "travesties" the song of the simple fisherman, which is here sung by a female voice to a female beloved, with the expressive echoes of the operatic stage, ever so slightly rending the sonic fabric of this timeless archaic lament. We recall Metastasio's dismissal of the art of the improviser: the sonic seduction of the improviser's voice, shaping ideas to fit the already-tailored costume of rhyme and meter, can lead to dangerous confusions—Angelicas dressed in Orlando's breastplate, Rinaldos wearing Armida's coif. We have come full circle—close your eyes and you hear not Gautier's fisherman, but Sappho on the cliff, lamenting her lost beloved, and contemplating the distance to the sea. That Viardot allows her singer to interject with an expressive, operatic voice brings the ancient figure to life rather than solidifying her into a monument—or decorative figurine.

Acknowledgments

This book has been many long years in the making and owes its existence to a multitude of helpers, both human and animal.

First, many thanks to Marta Tonegutti for her enthusiasm, patience, and vision—and to the entire staff at the University of Chicago Press. My gratitude also goes to Mary Ann Smart for being such a brilliant mentor who always gives the best advice. Roger Parker and Hilary Poriss were careful readers of the entire manuscript and offered invaluable assistance and suggestions. Hilary also deserves special commendation—along with the indefatigable Suzanne Cusick and Emanuele Senici—for cheering words at crucial moments and for giving me hope when things looked dark.

My appreciation goes to my colleagues and deans at the Eastman School of Music for facilitating the research leaves that allowed me the time and space to complete this project. I am grateful to the National Endowment for the Humanities for the Summer Stipend that allowed me to travel to Italian archives and encounter the sources that first sparked my interest in poetic improvisation. The staffs of the Istituto Nazionale di Studi Verdiani and the Centro Internazionale di Ricerca sui Periodici Musicali (CIRPeM) in Parma and the archives of Conservatorio di Musica San Pietro a Majella in Naples were warmly welcoming, extremely patient, and accommodating. Andrea Cawelti was an invaluable resource as I explored the Viardot-Garcia collection at Harvard's Houghton Library. Closer to home, David Peter Coppen and Gail Lowther at Sibley Music Library's Special Collections rendered speedy assistance at the eleventh hour.

The seeds of this book were presented in 2011 at the American Musicological Society meeting in San Francisco and two years later appeared in an expanded form in the *Journal of the American Musicological Society*; thanks to Annegret Fauser and the anonymous readers for their many helpful and detailed comments. Thanks are also due to the AMS for awarding the piece the 2014 Einstein Award, which gave me the courage to explore the *improvvisatrice* in a book-length project. Many of my chapters were presented in various venues, and I am grateful to both the hosts and respondents at these events. Chapter 1 benefited from discussion at Cornell University, where Roger Moseley organized a Central New York Humanities Corridor event on improvisation, and at SUNY-Fredonia, where a lively discussion was facilitated by Michael Markham. Chapter 3 was presented at the colloquium series at the Music Department of the University of California, Berkeley at the invitation of Mary Ann Smart. Thanks also to Sherry Lee and Ellen Lockhart for the invitation to the Jackman Humanities Institute at the University of Toronto and for the opportunity to workshop this chapter with the Center's fellows and with Angela Esterhammer. Warm appreciation goes to Angela for her generosity, as well as her groundbreaking work on poetic improvisation. Chapter 5 was presented at the first Transnational Opera Studies Conference in Bologna in 2015, as well as at the Phelps Colloquium series at the University of Rochester, and a brief portion of it was published in the *Cambridge Opera Journal* in a 2016 special issue ("Remaking the Aria") in honor of Roger Parker.

The Eastman students who have taken my seminars on improvisation have shown a willingness to explore new ideas that is truly inspiring. Jane Sylvester and Gail Lowther both deserve special recognition for their research help at crucial moments of the project, while Sarah Fuchs read portions of the draft and was always a good sounding board. Stephen Armstrong, Gabby Cornish, Mary McArthur, Alex Stefaniak, and Jane Sylvester also stepped in as dog sitters when needed.

I have been blessed with friends and colleagues who have smoothed my path. Thanks to ethnomusicologist Cristina Ghirardini for speaking to me of her work on *ottava rima* when we met in Bologna. Nicholas Baragwanath read several chapters of the manuscript, and I appreciate both his time and his recommendations. Ben Walton was always willing to talk about Stendhal, while Roger Moseley offered a listening ear. Lisa Jakelski gave timely encouragement and cheerleading. I owe much to Tim Scheie for his help with the French. I would especially like to thank the tireless and sharp-eyed Ralph Locke for his extremely generous assistance in translating Stendhal as well as his translation of the letter from Louis Viardot that appears in chapter 5. I have often been cheered to know that Wendy Pascoe is only a Skype call away. Katie Fittipaldi's infectious enthusiasm for fruitful exchange has made many days brighter. Joel Burges makes a perfect counselor-by-text and gave me the motto that spurred me through the last stages of writing. Moira Killoran delivered expert help in overcoming roadblocks. My gratitude also goes to the healers who kept me in good working order—Carrie, Jane, Mark, and the excellent staff at Strong Hospital's Heart and Vascular Department.

The ties of family have held me together in difficult times. My father, who is now gone, and my mother, whose body is still present but whose mind is not, will never read this book, but their deep influence on me and on my writing can be seen in every line. Holly Watkins has read drafts, commented, discussed, and taken on more than her share of domestic responsibilities when I've been in tight spots—I owe her more than I can say. The late Lukaçs served as my much-beloved meditation partner and master of the well-timed sigh, while Lodi and Aengus have brought joy and spontaneity to each day and encouraged me to step away from the computer and reconnect with the natural world. My brothers-in-law (Kyle and Brian) and my nieces and nephews (Gemma, Fiona, Luke, and baby Owen) have continually reminded me of what is truly important. Finally, this book is dedicated to my sisters, Juliana Wallace and Katie Esse, whose unfailing humor, support, and unconditional love—as well as the inspiring example of their own grit and resilience—have given me the strength to keep going when it seemed impossible.

Notes

Introduction

1. Daitz's recording can be heard on SoundCloud (https://soundcloud.com/rhapsodoi/sappho-1-perf-by-stephen-g-daitz). This rendition seems to differ slightly from his earlier recording of the poem, made in 1981 and published as part of a series of recorded recitations, entitled *The Living Voice of Greek and Latin Literature* and published by Bolchazy-Carducci. Another recent effort to reconstruct the music of Sappho is Ioannis Stratakis's composition using the Mixolydian mode, featuring a singer and guitarist, and performed in 2015 at the Aition cultural café (https://www.youtube.com/watch?v=XTHE-P4oZ9w).

2. Mendelsohn, "Hearing Sappho," accessed online at https://www.newyorker.com/books/page-turner/hearing-sappho.

3. Mendelsohn, "Hearing Sappho."

4. The overlap between the figure of the poetic improviser and Sappho was a common theme in eighteenth- and nineteenth-century literature. For example, in Madame de Staël's 1811 play *Sapho*, the ancient poet is presented as the "archetypal woman writer," who composed "orally, effortlessly, instantly" (DeJean, "Staël's *Corinne*: The Novel's Other Dilemma,"119). Staël's 1807 *Corinne* presented her improvising heroine "not only as a Sappho figure, but as the direct successor to Sappho" (*Fictions of Sappho*, 177). Understanding Sappho as an improviser has a long history; Dimitrios Yatromanolakis has discussed how certain textual clues in Sappho's poetry suggest they were perceived by ancient audiences as generically participating in the improvisatory context of symposiastic drinking songs (*skolia*) "performed, improvised, and reperformed on related occasions." See chapter 4, "Traditions in Flux," from his *Sappho in the Making: The Early Reception*. Accessed online at https://chs.harvard.edu/CHS/article/display/6019.4-traditions-in-flux.

5. Antonella Giordano, "Italian Women Improvisers," 141.

6. An eighteenth-century audience, she writes, whether in "salons, academies [or] theatres . . . was more accustomed to listening than reading and was therefore better disposed towards oral expression as compared with nineteenth century private reading practices."

7. Stendhal, *Life of Rossini*, trans. Richard Coe, 341–42. Throughout this book, I will cite Coe's translation only when it closely corresponds to the original French. Elsewhere, I have heavily emended and altered his translations to more accurately reflect Stendhal's text; in these cases, I will cite both the French edition and the relevant pages from Coe.

8. See, for example, Will Crutchfield, "Vocal Performance in the Nineteenth Century," 611 and 618. The classic explication of the emergence of the work concept in nineteenth-century music remains Lydia Goehr's *The Imaginary Museum of Musical Works.*

9. Hilary Poriss, *Changing the Score*, 5.

10. Susan Rutherford, *The Prima Donna and Opera*, 177–78.

11. A comprehensive survey is beyond the scope of this introduction, but notable works include Bruno Nettl and Melinda Russell, eds., *In the Course of Performance*; Gabriel Solis and Bruno Nettl, eds., *Musical Improvisation*; Bruce Ellis Benson, *Improvisation of Musical Dialogue*; Paul Berliner, *Thinking in Jazz*; Angela Esterhammer, *Romanticism and Improvisation*; a special issue of *Music Theory Online* in 2013 entitled "Theorizing Improvisation (Musically)," edited by August Sheehy and Paul Steinbeck; Georgina Born, Eric Lewis, and Will Straw, eds., *Improvisation and Social Aesthetics*; George Lewis and Ben Piekut, eds., *The Oxford Handbook of Critical Improvisation Studies*; Ajay Fischlin and George Lipsitz, *The Fierce Urgency of Now*; Dana Gooley, *Fantasies of Improvisation*; and the open-access journal *Critical Studies in Improvisation*, founded in 2004.

12. Edited by George E. Lewis and Benjamin Piekut, the volumes appeared online in 2013 and in print in 2016.

13. Gooley, *Fantasies of Improvisation*, 3–5.

14. Moseley, "Entextualization and the Improvised Past," para. 9, accessed online at http://mtosmt.org/issues/mto.13.19.2/mto.13.19.2.moseley.php.

15. Gooley, *Fantasies of Improvisation*, 9.

16. Matthew Head, "Rethinking Authorship through Women Composers," 39.

17. Head, "Rethinking Authorship through Women Composers," Jacqueline Letzer and Robert Adelson, *Women Writing Opera*, and Sin Yan Hedy Law, "Composing *Citoyennes* through *Sapho*," all show the necessity of considering gender in accounts of the history of operatic authorship. Also see Head, "Cultural Meanings for Women Composers," which explores the intersection of posthumous authorship with femininity; the notion that the ideal female author was a dead one (and an occasion for male authorial intervention) resonates strongly with eighteenth- and nineteenth-century tales of Sappho. Accounts of singers' creative input on operatic texts include Mary Ann Smart, "The Lost Voice of Rosine Stoltz" and "Verdi Sings Erminia Frezzolini"; Poriss, *Changing the Score*; and Rutherford, "Giuditta Pasta" and *The Prima Donna and Opera.*

18. Some representative studies include Yopie Prins, *Victorian Sappho*; Joan DeJean, *Fictions of Sappho*; Margaret Reynolds, *The Sappho History*; and Ellen Greene, ed., *Re-Reading Sappho.*

19. Cited in Giordano, "Eighteenth-Century Women Improvisers," 139.

20. Giordano, "Eighteenth-Century Women Improvisers," 149.

21. Giordano, "Eighteenth-Century Women Improvisers," 154.

22. Letter written to Algarotti dated 1 August 1751. Metastasio, *Lettere*, 327–28.

23. Giordani, "Intorno allo Sgricci."

24. Giordani, "Intorno allo Sgricci," section 9.

25. Giordani, "Intorno allo Sgricci," section 10.

26. Giordani, "Intorno allo Sgricci," section 4.

27. Giordani, "Intorno allo Sgricci," section 11.

28. Smart, "In Praise of Convention," 30.

29. Reynolds, *The Sappho History*, 196–97.

30. See Lewis and Piekut, eds., *Oxford Handbook of Critical Improvisation Studies*, for a capacious approach to improvisation, represented here as a group of strategies that "inform . . . a vast array of human activities."

Chapter 1

1. "Ist das erste Erscheinen der Improvvisatrice beängstigend, sieht man sie gleichsam wie ein Opfer an, und deutet ihre Todesblässe auf die gewaltige Wirkung, die ein solcher höherer Geisteszustand auf den physischen Teil der Begeisterten ausübt, schweigt das gesamte Publikum, und lauscht und schaut die Sinnende, Schwankende an, während sie die präludierende Harfe in den Zauber des Rhythmus einwiegt, so pocht wohl jedes Herz, wenn sie plötzlich vortritt, und anhebt zu singen. Nun verschwindet nach und nach auch die Blässe ihres Angesichts, Feuer und Begeisterung atmet aus ihm, unaufhaltsam folgen sich Verse auf Verse, einer lockt den andern hervor, keinem Reime fehlt der andere, das Auge des sibyllenartigen Wesens blickt irrend ins Unendliche, das heftigste Mimenspiel begleitet den Gesang und seinen oft dramatischen Inhalt, und wenn sie zuweilen—doch ist's höchst selten—fehlt und den Vers wiederholen muss, so erinnert uns das nur daran, dass sie tätig, dass sie Dichterin, Schöpferin ist, und nicht bloss vorträgt, was nicht mehr lebendig ist." Waiblinger, "Rosa Taddei, unter den Arkadiern Licori Partenopea," in *Werke und Briefe*, 3:458.

2. Ellen Lockhart has recently explored how Staël's fictional *improvvisatrice* posits a unified national voice in her *Animation, Plasticity, and Music in Italy*, 94–96.

3. The phrase is Charles des Brosses's, describing the improviser Bernardino Perfetti. See Esterhammer, *Romanticism and Improvisation*, 19.

4. di Ricco, *L'inutile e maraviglioso mestiere: Poeti improvvisatori di fine settecento*, 9. Robert Casillo has argued that Germaine de Staël's accounts of Italian life in her *Corinne* and *On Literature* both synthesized and perpetuated long-standing assumptions about Italy. See Casillo, *The Empire of Stereotypes: Germaine de Staël and the Idea of Italy*.

5. See her *Romanticism and Improvisation*.

6. In-depth study of the musical aspects of poetic improvisation is rare: some exceptions include Roberto Leydi, "Erminia monta in gondola"; Saverio Franchi, "Prassi esecutiva musicale e poesia estemporanea italiana"; and two articles by Cristina Ghirardini, "*L'improvvisatore* in Genre Scenes" and " 'L'improvvisazione poetica in ottava rima.' "

7. See Esterhammer's discussion of Tommaso Sgricci's influence on the Shelley-Byron circle (*Romanticism and Improvisation*, 110–28). Anna Celenza has written about the figure of the *improvvisatore* in the work of Hans Christian Andersen (*Hans Christian Andersen and Music*, 39–66). Although she notes that Andersen's first novel describes the improviser as putting on an "operatic, one-man performance" at the Teatro San Carlo, she mistakenly asserts that actual performances of improvised poetry "were strictly literary in nature; they were never sung" (49). Sgricci, the model for Andersen's improviser, was known for his ability to improvise tragedies without the aid of music, but other improvisers sang or chanted their verses.

8. ". . . la dolcezza delle voci femminili, la mobilità della loro fantasia e la scioltezza delle loro lingue le rendano più adatte degli uomini alla poesia estemporanea." Foscolo, "The Women of Italy," 12:435–36. English translation appears in Paola Giuli, " 'Monsters of Talent,' " 305.

9. Giuli, "Monsters of Talent," 323.

10. Waiblinger, *Werke und Briefe*, 3:458.

11. Vincent, *Romantic Poetess*, 97. The scholarship on Staël has inspired a renewed scholarly interest in Corilla Olimpica; see for example Moreno Fabbri, ed., *Corilla Olimpica e la poesia del Settecento europeo* (Pistoia: Maschietto, 2002); and Morelli, ed., *Il carteggio tra Amaduzzi e Corilla Olimpica, 1775–1792* (Florence: Olschki, 2000).

12. Staël, *Corinne*, 28. When *Corinne* was published in Italian, Staël hired an *improvvisatrice* to translate the French prose into Italian verse. Margaret Reynolds writes of a similar decision

for the English translation of 1833; Letitia Elizabeth Landon (L.E.L.), the poet known for reworking Staël's novel in her verse narrative *The Improvisatrice* (1824), was commissioned to produce "metrical versions" of Corinne's improvisations. See Reynolds, *The Sappho History*, 110–11.

13. Gutwirth, *Madame de Staël, Novelist*, 193.

14. Gutwirth, *Madame de Staël, Novelist*, 194–95.

15. See Giuli, "'Monsters of Talent'"; and Maria Pia Donato, "The Temple of Female Glory."

16. Donato, "The Temple of Female Glory," 76.

17. Donato, "The Temple of Female Glory," 64.

18. Donato, "The Temple of Female Glory," 66.

19. Donato, "The Temple of Female Glory," 69.

20. Donato, "The Temple of Female Glory," 71.

21. Donato, "The Temple of Female Glory," 72.

22. Donato, "The Temple of Female Glory," 72.

23. Donato, "The Temple of Female Glory," 73.

24. Donato, "The Temple of Female Glory," 75.

25. Donato, "The Temple of Female Glory," 75, from De Rossi, *Vita di Angelica Kauffmann*.

26. For example, Donato describes the activities of three women (Enrica Dionigi, Adelai de Lucangeli, and Maria Fulvia Bertocchi) who declared themselves Pizzelli's "pupils and emulators," in a manner that suggests she considers their accomplishments of greater value: "Unlike Boccapaduli and Pizzelli, they presented their own writing to society rather than simply facilitating the talents of others." Donato, "The Temple of Female Glory," 73.

27. ". . . man hat Gelegenheit, zu bemerken, dass mancher im Theater ist, der eben nicht den feinsten Sinn für Poesie hat; gewöhnlich sind es Themen aus der Mythologie, aus der Geschichte, die sich unzähligemal wiederholen . . ." Waiblinger, *Werke und Briefe*, 3:457.

28. "Je nach Ton und Inhalt werden sie für dies oder jenes Versmass bestimmt, und in eine Kapsel geworfen, sie wird dem Publikum zur Ziehung präsentiert, und gleich nachdem die Themen gezogen worden, beginnet die Improvvisatrice die Ausführung." Waiblinger, *Werke und Briefe*, 3:457.

29. ". . . sie die Reime mit ihr zu finden suchen, und wenn ihr eine schwere Stelle, ein schöner Gedanke, ein glücklicher Schluss gelungen, wird allgemeines Entzücken laut." Waiblinger, *Werke und Briefe*, 3:457.

30. Esterhammer, *Romanticism and Improvisation*, 109.

31. Corinna is believed to have lived during the sixth century BCE. During the nineteenth century, she was thought to be a contemporary (and rival) of Pindar. See Michel Orcel, "Le sacre de l'antiphrase," 13n6.

32. Staël, *Corinne*, 233. Emphasis in original.

33. Staël, *Corinne*, 235.

34. Staël, *Corinne*, 236.

35. Staël, *Corinne*, 236.

36. Staël, *Corinne*, 238.

37. Staël, *Corinne*, 237.

38. Chard, *Pleasure and Guilt*, 133.

39. Chard, *Pleasure and Guilt*, 127.

40. ". . . trois beaux songes de vie égarés dan les régions de la mort." From Lamartine's "fourth note" (titled "Pompei: Fragment of a voyage to Naples") following his poem "The last canto of Childe Harolde's pilgrimage." Original French cited in Chard, *Pleasure and Guilt*, 146.

41. Chard, *Pleasure and Guilt*, 146.

42. Chard, *Pleasure and Guilt*, 146, 133–35.

43. Cowgill, "Performance, Femininity, and Spectatorship," 244. Catalani interpolated her "attitudes with a shawl" into at least two operatic performances (in London and Dublin) in 1808. The libretto for her King's Theatre performance shows that the attitudes appeared during scene 5 of Sarti's opera *Gli amanti consolati,* framed and justified dramatically as a "lesson in grace." Reviews of the Dublin performance suggest that it was accompanied by the tenor's performance of a song. See Cowgill, "Performance, Femininity, and Spectatorship," 220–22.

44. Cited in Kate Williams, *England's Mistress*, 145.

45. On Hamilton's props, see Williams, *England's Mistress*, 142.

46. Astarita, *Between Salt Water and Holy Water*, 240.

47. Letter of 16 March 1787, in Goethe, *Italienische Reise*, 209. English translation in Goethe, *Italian Journey*, 170–71.

48. The duration of Hamilton's performance and quantity of poses are described by eyewitness Louis-Jérôme De Goujon Thuisy. See Cowgill, "Performance, Femininity, and Spectatorship," 225.

49. Fraser, *Emma, Lady Hamilton*, 155–56.

50. Cowgill, "Performance, Femininity, and Spectatorship," 226.

51. Giovanni Andrea Gallini apparently offered Emma two thousand pounds to perform in an opera followed by a London concert series. Cowgill, "Performance, Femininity, and Spectatorship," 226.

52. Fraser, *Emma, Lady Hamilton*, 114.

53. She had struck up a friendship with Paisiello, who gave her a duet ("Per pietà da questo istante non parlarmi, O Dio d'Amor") to perform at Carnival time with the tenor Casacelli. Fraser, *Emma, Lady Hamilton*, 119–20.

54. Fraser notes that the painter George Romney had earlier noticed the likeness between Emma and Raphael's "early series of Madonnas and lady saints," images that she claims would have been familiar to Neapolitans from copies in local churches. Fraser, *Emma, Lady Hamilton*, 117–18.

55. Fraser, *Emma, Lady Hamilton*, 143. Some found her acting too outré; Mrs. Trench complained that "she acts her songs, which I think the last degree of bad taste" (237).

56. Cowgill, "Performance, Femininity, and Spectatorship," 223.

57. Fraser, *Emma, Lady Hamilton*, 237.

58. Cowgill, "Performance, Femininity, and Spectatorship," 234.

59. Fraser, *Emma, Lady Hamilton*, 142.

60. Cowgill, "Performance, Femininity, and Spectatorship," 224. For a contrary perspective, one that understands Hart's attitudes as a species of *tableau vivant* and thus primarily frozen and statue-like, see Lockhart, *Animation, Plasticity, and Music in Italy*, 139–40.

61. Pop, "Sympathetic Spectators," 941–42.

62. Kate Davies has seen the interplay between "atomised" stillness and the rapid shifting between poses as appealing to audiences not because of their recollection of antiquity but because of their modernity. See her "Pantomime, Connoisseurship, and Consumption: Emma Hamilton and the Politics of Embodiment," 28–29.

63. She was also rumored to have had an affair with Pacini; he dedicated the score of *L'ultimo giorno di Pompei* to her when Ricordi published the full opera in piano-vocal score in the early 1830s.

64. For a useful survey of literature on historical reenactment, see Magelssen, *Living History Museums*, 3–9.

65. Giovanna Ceserani, *Italy's Lost Greece*, 89.

66. Gapps, "On Being a Mobile Monument," 50–62.

67. Waiblinger, *Werke und Briefe*, 3:456.

68. Waiblinger, *Werke und Briefe*, 3:456.

69. Staël, *Corinne*, 33.

70. "Es möchte mancher Versklauber über den Alpen glauben, dass ein solches Improvisieren durchaus Scharlatanerie sei, auf nichts al Betrug und Täuschung beruhe, und dass eine Dichterin der Art nicht ohne äusserste Anmassung auftreten könne. Ein solcher aber würde weder das italienische Volk, noch seine Sprache, noch überhaupt irgend Poesie kennen. Bekant ist, welche glückliche Gabe, welchen Hang zur Dichtkunst selbst der römische Pöbel hat. Er hat eine Art von volkstümlichem Rezitativ, das äusserst biegsam ist, immer variieren, sich ausdehnen un zusammenziehen kann, je nachdem sich dem Sänger Reime und Gedanken mehr oder minder schnell auf die Zunge drängen. Dies Rezitativ kennt jeder Vassallo, jeder Strassenjunge, und nun unterhält man sich auf der Strasse, auf dem Spaziergang, im Cancelletto, in der Osterie Stundenlang mit einem Wechelgesang, der allerdings eine fröhlichere geistreichere Unterhaltung ist, als die Klagen über Steuern und Schultheissen, womit unser Volk seine traurigen Abende hinzieht. 'Er ist ein Dichter', heisst es, und darunter versteht man immer einen Improvvisatore, den das ist im Begriffe unzertrennlich, das Dichten oder Improvisieren selbst aber nennt man geradezu cantare." Waiblinger, *Werke und Briefe*, 3:454–55.

71. See for example Fernow's description of improvised poetry as half-sung, half-recited (*Über die Improvisatoren*, 2:315). Lockhart explores the antique implications of this mode of delivery in her *Animation, Plasticity, and Music in Italy*, 107.

72. Staël, *Corinne*, 33.

73. Treccani gives an alternate definition of *cantilena:* "intonazione monotona della voce di chi parla o recita o legge [monotonous intonation of the voice of a speaker or reciter or reader]" (http://www.treccani.it/vocabolario/cantilena, accessed 6 June 2018). For more on Staël's association of *cantilena* with reading (rather than composing poetry in the moment), see Lockhart, *Animation, Plasticity, and Music in Italy*, 95.

74. See Ghirardini, "L'improvvisazione poetica in ottava rima," 64–86, for a rich discussion of the eighteenth- and nineteenth-century sources that demonstrate the place of music in poetic improvisation.

75. The essay appeared in three installments in the *Merkur* (Esterhammer, *Romanticism and Improvisation*, 46) and was later reprinted in Fernow, *Über die Improvisatoren*, in *Römische Studien* (Zurich, 1806), 2:298–416. On Fernow's ethnomusicological project, see Lockhart, *Animation, Plasticity, and Music*, 104.

76. Fernow, *Über die Improvisatoren*, 315–16. "Für jede Art des Silbenmasses hat der Sänger eine eigene Melodie, in der er seine Verse halb singt, halb rezitirt; die immer einfach und gefällig ist, und sich um so leichter jedem Stoffe anschmeigt, da die Musik hier, wie in den ältesten Zeiten, ganz der Poesie untergeordnet ist, und blos zu Verzierung des Gesanges und Ausfüllung der Lücken dient, welche zwischen den Stanzen und einzelnen Versen entstehen. Die meisten vorhandenen Melodien dieser Art, von denen wir am Schlusse des Aufsazes einige mittheilen werden, sind von berühmten Improvisatoren selbst erfunden."

77. Lockhart, *Animation, Plasticity, and Music*, 107.

78. Fernow, *Über die Improvisatoren*, 312–13.

79. "Wir glauben damit dem Freunde der Musik ein um so willkommeneres Geschenk zu machen, als er damit ausser den versi accentati alle gewöhnlichen lyrischen Versmasse der Italiener begleiten kann." Waiblinger, *Werke und Briefe*, 3:475.

80. Such accents were known as *accenti grammatici* (grammatic accents); for a fuller discussion of the distinction between grammatic, musical, and expressive accent in Italian theories of text setting, see Baragwanath, "Giovanni Battista De Vecchis and the Theory of Melodic Accent," 163. Also note that Italian verse forms are identified by the number of syllables per line rather than the pattern of stressed syllables because the latter can vary considerably from line to line within a single stanza. *Settenari* verses could thus prompt a wide variety of accompaniments in either duple or triple/compound meters. See Kimbell, *Italian Opera*, 260–62.

81. ". . . non contenta sull'aria di questa, o di quella canzonetta, che udiva cantar per la strada, vi adattava all'improvviso versi di mia invenzione con gran sorpresa di mia madre la quale era sempre il subbietto delle mie rime. Ella per mia fortuna sapeva pur anco improvvisare in ottava rima, nè sempre si recusava a rispondermi quand'io la invitava a cantare." Cited in Di Ricco, *L'inutile e meraviglioso mestiere*, 92–93.

82. See Kittler's discussion of the place of the mother's voice in phonetic approaches to literacy in the early nineteenth century: "the Mother's Mouth thus freed children from books. Her voice substituted sounds for letters . . ." Kittler, *Discourse Networks*, 25–69.

83. Gjerdingen, "The Perfection of Craft Training in the Neapolitan Conservatoires," 49. See also his *Music in the Galant Style* for a detailed examination of how these models and exemplars were used in galant music.

84. Gjerdingen, "The Perfection of Craft Training in the Neapolitan Conservatoires," 50.

85. Certain questions remain: Waiblinger doesn't say whether or not Taddei used these same accompaniments every time she recited a poem in the specified meter, but the implication seems to be that the German readers of his essay would use these same melodies over and over as they became more adept at fitting poetry to music. It also is not clear whether or not she used the same melodies from one performance to another.

86. "Es ist nicht zu leugnen, dass gewisse Kunstgriffe damit verbunden sind, dass ein gebildeter Improvvisatore ein völliges Studium verfolgen, sich mit Mythologie und Geschichte, wie mit den italienischen Klassikern vollkommen bekannt machen, dass er sogar ganze Reden, Darstellungen von allen möglichen Affekten, Sinnsprüche und Sentenzen im Vorrat haben muss; aber was ist mit all' dem zu beginnen, wenn die schnellverbindende Phantasie, das feine Gefühl, die vollkommene Gewalt der Sprache, die besonnenste Denkübung nicht vorhanden ist, um auch nur das Gelernte richtig vorzutragen und zusammenreihen!" Waiblinger, *Werke und Briefe*, 3:455.

Chapter 2

1. One famous precedent: in the opening duettino in Mozart's *Le nozze di Figaro*, Susanna tries on a new hat and asks Figaro's opinion of it.

2. See James Trilling, *Ornament: A Modern Perspective*, esp. 137–200. Gurminder Kaur Bhogal has explored how the denigration of ornament has affected scholarly approaches to vocal embellishment in "Lakmé's Echoing Jewels," 188–90.

3. C. P. E. Bach, "From *Essay on the Proper Manner of Playing a Keyboard Instrument*," 851.

4. Quoted in Nicholas Cook, *The Schenker Project*, 92. See John Koslovsky, "Tracing the Improvisatory Impulse in Early Schenkerian Theory," and John Rink, "Schenker and Improvisation," for more on the role of improvisation in Schenker's music-theoretical project.

5. Stendhal, *Life of Rossini*, trans. Coe, 263. See Cindy Kim, "Changing Meanings of Ornamentation," 66–69, for further discussion of this passage.

6. Bhogal, "Lakme's Echoing Jewels," 187.

7. Bhogal, "Lakme's Echoing Jewels," 188.

8. Bhogal, "Lakme's Echoing Jewels," 90.

9. Gossett, *Divas and Scholars*, 530.

10. Rutherford, *The Prima Donna and Opera*, 177–78. Will Crutchfield similarly argues that at the end of the nineteenth century, "contemporary opera had banished improvisation and embraced modern symphonic procedures," though he does concede that "in the Italian repertoire . . . the tradition of incidental ornamentation still had surprising vigour." Crutchfield, "Vocal Performance in the Nineteenth Century," 611 and 618. See also Poriss, *Changing the Score*, 5.

11. See Vincent, *Romantic Poetess*, 97–121, for a discussion of the many writers who "inhabited Corinne," including Letitia Landon, Jane Taylor, Felicia Hemans, Evdokia Rostopchina, and Adélaïde Dufrénoy.

12. Janet Johnson, introduction to the critical edition of *Il viaggio a Reims*, lxi. When the opera was revived in a 1984 staging by Luca Ronconi, the work's own reflexive gestures were highlighted by the presence of televisions, microphones, and reporters; by having the action take place both within and without the theater; and by adding an extra to play the role of the king sitting in the hall. See Gossett, *Divas and Scholars*, 513, for a brief account of this production.

13. Benjamin Walton, "The Operatic Coronation of Charles X," 3–4.

14. Walton, "The Operatic Coronation of Charles X," 5.

15. Walton, "The Operatic Coronation of Charles X," 7–8, 19. What Walton might call the "staged realism" of productions such as *Il viaggio* was contrasted by other, more allegorical, efforts to breach the fourth wall. In the concluding tableau of the opera *Pharamond*, for example, the skies parted, and a long line of French kings appeared. One critic wrote that "the past, in all its glory, was on the stage, and the future, with all its potential, was in the hall." Walton writes, "The blurring of boundaries between stage and life suggested by the direct link from the historical kings to Charles stands as a powerful symbol of the symbiotic relationship between the Opera and the coronation as a whole." Walton, "The Operatic Coronation of Charles X," 7.

16. See Auslander, *Liveness: Performance in a Mediatized Culture*

17. Other offstage songs on either side of *Il viaggio* include the gondolier's song in act 3 of Rossini's *Otello* (1816) and Alaïde's *romanza* in act 1 of Bellini's *La straniera* (1829).

18. Damien Colas, discussing the norms of Rossinian melodic construction, observes that the composer's vocal phrases often end with ornamental flourishes, however small. Colas partitions the typical Rossinian phrase into three parts—the anacrusis, the kernel, and the desinence—noting that "melodic desinences have a special rôle to play in that they are the melodic equivalents of the rhyme, and hence signs of closure with decisive importance in linking together the melodic phrases. Their periodic return, often emphasised by ornamentation . . . plays a crucial rôle in the coherence of the 'melodic strophe' . . ." Colas, "Melody and Ornamentation," 107–8.

19. Orcel, "Le sacre de l'antiphrase," 10.

20. Walton, "The Operatic Coronation of Charles X," 14. In subsequent performances, several verses were cut, and Rossini chose not to reuse this music when he recycled much of *Il viaggio* to craft *Le comte Ory*.

21. See Johnson, introduction to the critical edition of *Il viaggio a Reims*, and "L'histoire d'une decouverte," 20.

22. Stern, "A Documentary Study of Giuditta Pasta on the Operatic Stage," 131.

23. Some Parisians would have certainly encountered Italian improvisers, either abroad or at home: the *improvvisatore* Tommaso Sgricci, for example, had performed in Paris in March 1824.

24. See Rutherford, "Giuditta Pasta"; and Paolo Russo, "Giuditta Pasta: cantante pantomimica."

25. Cited in Johnson's introduction to the critical edition of *Il viaggio a Reims.*

26. For a discussion of various anti- and pro-ornamentation discourses, see Kim, "Changing Meanings of Ornamentation," 11–60.

27. Stendhal, *Life of Rossini*, trans. Coe, 340–42.

28. Stendhal, *Vie de Rossini*, 256–57 (*Life of Rossini*, trans. Coe, 353). In this and all other cases where I have significantly altered Coe's translation to more closely correspond to Stendhal's original French, I owe immense thanks to Ralph Locke for his assistance.

29. Gossett, *Divas and Scholars*, 297.

30. See Gossett's discussion of the material evidence of Rossini's participation in a collaborative system that treated scores as a "point of departure" rather than a "blueprint." The composer's annotations to scores, as well as the over thirty manuscripts in his hand that contain variations and cadenzas, assume that performers will consistently make their own original interventions. Gossett, *Divas and Scholars*, 194–97.

31. Gossett, *Divas and Scholars*, 293.

32. Stendhal, *Life of Rossini*, trans. Coe, 372.

33. Gossett, *Divas and Scholars*, 299.

34. Colas, "Melody and Ornamentation," 120.

35. Colas, "Melody and Ornamentation," 122.

36. Colas, "Melody and Ornamentation," 123.

37. Baragwanath, *The Italian Traditions and Puccini.* See also Gjerdingen's *Music in the Galant Style* for an exploration of similar practices in the Neapolitan partimento tradition.

38. Baragwanath, *The Italian Traditions and Puccini*, 310.

39. Baragwanath, *The Italian Traditions and Puccini*, 266. Emphasis in original.

40. Baragwanath, *The Italian Traditions and Puccini*, 257. Indeed, the practical use of the voice was so much a part of music pedagogy that even didactic texts were memorized by singing them in canon. Baragwanath, *The Italian Traditions and Puccini*, 8.

41. Baragwanath, *The Italian Traditions and Puccini*, 16–17, 256.

42. This musical example is also reproduced and discussed in greater detail in Baragwanath, *The Italian Traditions and Puccini*, 258–59.

43. Baragwanath, *The Italian Traditions and Puccini*, 261.

44. Baragwanath, *The Italian Traditions and Puccini*, 261.

45. Baragwanath, *The Italian Traditions and Puccini*, 260–61.

46. Baragwanath, *The Italian Traditions and Puccini*, 262–63.

47. Baragwanath, *The Italian Traditions and Puccini*, 265.

48. Dahlhaus, *Nineteenth-Century Music*, 59.

49. Caswell, "Mme Cinti-Damoreau," 467–68.

50. Caswell, "Mme Cinti-Damoreau," 468.

51. Caswell, "Mme Cinti-Damoreau," 468–69.

52. Laure Cinti-Damoreau, *Classic Bel Canto Technique*, x.

53. Cinti-Damoreau, *Classic Bel Canto Technique.*

54. Cinti-Damoreau, *Classic Bel Canto Technique*, xi. Elsewhere Cinti-Damoreau gestures to a more Romantic transcendence of words: "In fact," she writes, "it is never enough to cope with

the notes or to be able to perform passages of greater or less difficulty; one must color the notes, give them life, and accent them, and this is why it is essential that the artist *go beyond the words, and enter into the spirit of the piece or scene* . . ." Cinti-Damoreau, *Classic Bel Canto Technique*, ix.

55. Cinti-Damoreau, *Classic Bel Canto Technique*, x–xi. As Hilary Poriss points out, such accounts of improvisational battles between singers (including the narrative detail of "one singer surprising the other by improvising live . . . ornamentation that was far more complicated than what was planned during rehearsals") were commonplace; see Poriss, *Changing the Score*, 128–33, for a discussion of such battles featuring Maria Malibran. Both Poriss and Colas ("Melody and Ornamentation," 123) remain skeptical of the veracity of these accounts, with Poriss drawing attention to the exaggerated nature of singers' rivalries. However, improvisational battles between singers were an operatic version of the *contrasti* of improvising poets, where each poet took a stanza in turn and attempted to trip up an opponent by leaving them to grapple with a difficult rhyme.

56. Caswell, "Mme Cinti-Damoreau," 481.

57. Caswell, "Mme Cinti-Damoreau," 482.

58. See the bibliography of Robert Toft's *Bel Canto*, 253–58, for a substantial list of the vocal tutors and treatises published during this era. Of course, publishing cadenzas may have led amateur singers to borrow them; see Toft for examples of pedagogues who encouraged students unskilled at improvisation to memorize cadenzas in advance and to "achieve the appearance of spontaneity by slowing down the concluding notes" (*Bel Canto*, 153).

59. See Michael Caesar's "Poetic Improvisation and the Challenge of Transcription."

60. Matsumoto, "Manacled Freedom," 315. Matsumoto's argument is based upon the findings of Romana Margherita Pugliese's "The Origins of *Lucia di Lammermoor*'s Cadenza," which dated the cadenza to Melba's 1889 Paris performances and noted that it was not until the later nineteenth century—long after *Lucia*'s premiere—that the mad scene was "regarded as the highlight of the opera, the excesses of the cadenza resonating with the new vogue for violent and hysterical heroines on the operatic stage" (Pugliese, 23).

61. Rutherford, *The Prima Donna and Opera*, 96–97.

62. See Poriss, "Verdi Meets Bellini," 69–70, for a brief overview of the composer's correspondence with Ricordi that attempts to "protect his scores against modifications." Francesco Degrada has discussed the founding of the *Gazetta Musicale di Milano* as an attempt to bolster the reputation of Italian music as a serious art, noting that journal's manifesto made its text-centric agenda quite clear: "We shall refuse from the outset to report in detail the triumphs or failures of performances, the glories and downfalls of virtuosi." Degrada, *175 Years of Casa Ricordi*, 16.

63. Curioni, *Mercanti dell'opera*, 62.

64. Gossett, "Piracy in Venice," 125.

65. Gossett, "Piracy in Venice," 126.

66. Gossett, "Piracy in Venice," 127, 129.

67. Gossett, "Piracy in Venice," 130.

68. Moeckli focuses on MS Foà-Giordano 631. The unsigned and undated notebook contains fifty-eight different entries suggesting ornamentation for Italian opera arias; works by Rossini are heavily represented. Moeckli proposes that the author was most likely a singer or singing teacher who was active in both Italy and France, and that the majority of entries were compiled around 1835. See Moeckli, "Further Evidence of Creative Embellishment," 285.

69. Moeckli, "Further Evidence of Creative Embellishment," 289.

70. Crutchfield, "Early Vocal Ornamentation," 368–69.

71. Crutchfield, "Vocal Performance in the Nineteenth Century," 618–20.

72. Kallberg, *Chopin at the Boundaries*, 220. For more on how Chopin inscribed improvisational values into his published works, see Robert S. Hatten, "Opening the Museum Window."

73. My argument here resonates with Roger Moseley's recent discussion of Karin Barber's work on "entextualization," which argues that "entextualized elements are not to be identified with the literary and scripted and thus opposed to the oral and extemporized." Rather, both oral and written traditions can encourage reproduction of discourse in other contexts—via memorized or recalled formulas and written notation. Moseley, "Entextualization and the Improvised Past," para. 4.

74. For more on the history of the appoggiatura, see Crutchfield, "The Prosodic Appoggiatura." In the late eighteenth and early nineteenth centuries, repeated notes of the same value at feminine phrase endings were a clear signal to the performer to insert an appoggiatura. But in the music of Bellini and Verdi, the appoggiatura began to be notated with more precision.

75. For more on the proliferation of vocal treatises designed for an emerging amateur market, see Toft, *Bel Canto*, 16–18.

76. Sacks, *The Man Who Mistook His Wife for a Hat*, 8.

77. Sacks, *The Man Who Mistook His Wife for a Hat*, 13.

Chapter 3

1. "Chiuso quindi nella mia stanza, comincio a declamare la parte del personaggio del dramma con tutto il calore della passione, e osservo intanto le inflessioni della mia voce, l'affrettamento e il languore della pronunzia in questa circostanza, l'accento insomma ed il tuono dell'espressione, che dà la natura all'uomo in balía delle passioni, e vi trovo i motivi ed i tempi musicali adatti a dimostrarle e trasfonderle in altrui per mezzo dell'armonia. Li getto tosto sulla carta, li provo al clavicembalo, e quando ne sento io stesso la corrispondente emozione giudico di esserci riuscito." Bellini, *Epistolario*, 182. Translation in Smart, "In Praise of Convention," 30.

2. See Smart, *Waiting for Verdi*, 58–59.

3. Baragwanath, *The Italian Traditions and Puccini*, 75. Though Baragwanath does not maintain that this account is genuine ("it was added as an afterthought . . . years after the original recollection was published, and has all the hallmarks of a manufactured myth"), he points out that the account presents such an approach as a conventional method.

4. Smart, "In Praise of Convention," 30.

5. See my "Speaking and Sighing: Bellini's *canto declamato* and the Poetics of Restraint."

6. See Kimbell, *Norma*, 23–24.

7. Davies, "Gautier's 'Diva': The First French Uses of the Word."

8. Romani's *Dizionario d'ogni mitologia e antichità*, coauthored with Antonio Peracchi, was published in six volumes from 1809 to 1825. Kimbell, *Norma*, 20.

9. See the references to Ossian in Romani, *Critica Letteraria*, ed. Emilia Branca (Torino, 1883), 137, 142, 149, 330. https://books.google.com/books?id=Y9NAAAAYAAJ&printsec=front|cover&dq=critica+letteraria+felice+romani&hl=en&sa=X&ved=0ahUKEwiQmIfV6ZTZAhUM9IMKHbCFAcAQ6AEILzAB#v=onepage&q=ossian&f=false.

10. Cesarotti likely learned of the work while in Venice, from Charles Sackville, who may have been the one to initially translate the work from English to Italian.

11. Mattioda, "Ossian in Italy," 276.

12. Mattioda, "Ossian in Italy." *Versi sciolti* was the form taken by the chivalric epics of the fifteenth and sixteenth centuries; it had also been used to translate classical literature, in particular Annibal Caro's sixteenth-century version of the *Aeneid*.

13. Michele Leoni, who later translated the additional Ossian material in John Smith's *Gaelic Antiquities* under the title *Nuovi Canti di Ossian* (1813), decided to versify the songs. Francesca Broggi-Wüthrich, "The Making of the Italian Ossianic Tradition Revisited," 308.

14. Mattioda points out that these metrical innovations would later be adopted by Romantic poets ("Ossian in Italy," 277).

15. Moore, *Ossian and Ossianism*, 87.

16. Cesarotti, *Poesie di Ossian*, 2:5.

17. Mattioda, "Ossian in Italy," 290. Cesarotti's decision to craft a libretto is an obvious choice, given both Macpherson's note and the fact that the poem ends with a chorus of bards singing the praises of the departed heroine. Others were similarly inspired by Macpherson's translation. "Comala" was to music by Miss Harriet Wainwright in a performance at the Hanover-Square Rooms in 1792. This version featured the singer "Miss Corri" as Comala, and that libretto clearly distinguished between "Recit (Accompanied)" and "Air." See Moore, *Ossian and Ossianism*, 4:190. This 1792 libretto does not versify the text, instead maintaining the free verse of the original. But an 1819 adaptation of Comala by Charles Collins is billed as "A Dramatic Poem Versified," and features regular stanzas of ten-syllable lines with the rhyme scheme AABBCC (etc.). Moore, *Ossian and Ossianism*, 4:319.

18. This decision recalls Calzabigi's libretto for *Orfeo*, but "by introducing caesurae and dividing the hendecasyllables into different lines of verse—some of which were quite short—Cesarotti was able to bring the arias and recitative closer together in terms of metre, thereby going even further beyond the reforms introduced by Calzabigi." Mattioda, "Ossian in Italy," 291.

19. Mattei was a scholar of ancient Greek poetry fascinated by the question of whether or not Greek tragedy was sung. His *Nuovo metodo d'interpretare i tragici greci* argued that all parts of tragedy must have been sung (not simply the choruses), and that "Metastasio's melodramas represent the most perfect form of tragedy." Mattioda, "Ossian in Italy," 290.

20. Mattioda, "Ossian in Italy," 290–91. Mattei supports his critique with recourse to the ancients, arguing that "after all, neither the Greeks not the Latins, nor any other civilized nation even dreamed of jumbling together all the different metres." Mattioda, "Ossian in Italy," 291n15.

21. Mattioda, "Ossian in Italy," 292.

22. Mattioda, "Ossian in Italy," 293–300.

23. Mattioda, "Ossian in Italy," 294.

24. Mattioda concedes that "Ossianic themes and Nordic settings" justified the inclusion of tragic elements (especially tragic endings) so important to the development of operatic Romanticism. Mattioda, "Ossian in Italy," 294.

25. Published in *Biblioteco Italiana* in October 1817. Quoted in Broggi-Wüthrich, "The Making of the Italian Ossianic Tradition Revisited," 305.

26. Broggi-Wüthrich, "The Making of the Italian Ossianic Tradition Revisited," 328.

27. Broggi-Wüthrich, "The Making of the Italian Ossianic Tradition Revisited," 333–34, emphasis mine.

28. Gambarota, *Irresistible Signs*, 155.

29. Gambarota, *Irresistible Signs*, 155.

30. This appeared in Cesarotti's 1772 "Ragionamento storico-critico intorno le controversie sull'autenticità dei poemi di Ossian." See Gambarota, *Irresistible Signs*, 157.

31. Gambarota, *Irresistible Signs*, 157.

32. Cesarotti makes a similar metaphor in discussing the work of a translator, but insists that translations cannot be "servile . . . a slave wearing his master's clothes." Gambarota, *Irresistible Signs*, 161.

33. ". . . la musica di Bellini colpisce per la sua singolarità. Quasi costantemente tutta l'attenzione dell'ascoltatore viene indirizzata verso la linea melodica; Bellini si esprime principalmente attraverso il canto dei solisti, e soprattutto attraverso le melodie loro affidate." Pierluigi Petrobelli, "Antiche radici e nuove funzioni della melodia belliniana," in Della Seta and Ricciardi, eds., *Vincenzo Bellini: Verso l'edizione critica*, 15.

34. Stendhal, *Life of Rossini*, trans. Coe, 372 and 380–81.

35. Stendhal, *Life of Rossini*, trans. Coe, 375.

36. Rutherford, "Giuditta Pasta," 111.

37. Stendhal, *Life of Rossini*, trans. Coe, 376 and 383.

38. Stendhal identifies only the second and third acts of Vaccai's *Giulietta e Romeo* as suited to the "characteristics of her voice" and the "way in which she manages it." But, despite the fact that the vast majority of the music she sings was not designed for her, she "has cast a spell upon every heart" even through "music that persistently contradicts [the timbre of] her voice." *Vie de Rossini*, 280–81 (*Life of Rossini*, trans. Coe, 373).

39. Stendhal, *Vie de Rossini*, 280 (*Life of Rossini*, trans. Coe, 373).

40. Stendhal, *Vie de Rossini*, 286–87 (*Life of Rossini*, trans. Coe, 381).

41. Stendhal, *Vie de Rossini*, 279–80 (*Life of Rossini*, trans. Coe, 372).

42. Stendhal, *Vie de Rossini*, 281n1 (*Life of Rossini*, trans. Coe, 374).

43. Quoted in Kimbell, *Norma*, 11.

44. Rutherford, "Giuditta Pasta," 123–24.

45. Rutherford, "Giuditta Pasta," 136.

46. Rutherford, "Giuditta Pasta," 138.

47. Kimbell, "Vincenzo Bellini," 52.

48. Stendhal, *Vie de Rossini*, 288. Stendhal uses the phrase *l'astre des nuits*, a conventional poetic name for the moon that could be translated as "heavenly (or celestial) body." Coe fancifully renders this as "Huntress of the Night" and later "Diana." Alas, nothing in the original supports these mythological references. *Life of Rossini*, trans. Coe, 383–84.

49. Stendhal, *Life of Rossini*, trans. Coe, 375. These different timbres are not mere effects, but instead physical facts: Pasta's "several different *registers*," he insists, are "*clearly distinguishable physical aspects*, varying in accordance with the region of the scale into which the singer chances to venture."

50. Stendhal, *Vie de Rossini*, 282 (*Life of Rossini*, trans. Coe, 375).

51. Stendhal, *Vie de Rossini*, 281–82 (*Life of Rossini*, trans. Coe, 374). Rutherford points to this passage as evidence of the agency of Pasta's voice—its ability to create an effect in listeners ("Giuditta Pasta," 112).

52. This line of inquiry was first suggested to me by Christina Schiffner's work on Pasta during her time as a graduate student at UC Berkeley.

53. See Gossett, *Divas and Scholars*, 345–49, for a discussion of this transposition. Although he notes that there is no smoking gun to unequivocally support the notion that the change to F major was Bellini's decision, the autograph does show that at one point the orchestral introduction with flute was crossed out, perhaps to solve the problem of transitioning to the new key. It was later reinstated.

54. See Philip Gossett's introduction to Garland's facsimile of the autograph manuscript of *Norma* published in 1983.

55. Colas, "Le revisioni delle parte vocali negli autografi di Bellini," 316–17.

56. See Smart, "In Praise of Convention," 32–36, for a discussion of the journalistic debates about the perceived similarity between the two numbers.

57. Gossett, *Divas and Scholars*, 345.

58. Baragwanath reproduces more of Lippmann's "rhythmic musical types" and compares them to Neapolitan maestro Michele Ruta's "incises," theorized in 1884. *The Italian Traditions and Puccini*, 78–81.

59. Baragwanath, *The Italian Traditions and Puccini*, 89–90.

60. Kimbell, *Norma*, 53; and Baragwanath, *The Italian Traditions and Puccini*, 120.

61. Baragwanath, *The Italian Traditions and Puccini*, 72.

62. Baragwanath, *The Italian Traditions and Puccini*, 72.

63. Maguire, *Vincenzo Bellini*, 57–58. Maguire notes that, according to Italian treatises, "The moving of the affections in song came through the careful pronunciation and oratorical delivery of the words rather than in their interpretation in the manner of Romantic music." *Vincenzo Bellini*, 53 and 55.

64. Caesar, "Poetic Improvisation in the Nineteenth Century," 706.

65. Mattioda, "Ossian in Italy," 300.

66. Mattioda, "Ossian in Italy," 301. I have altered Mattioda's translation slightly.

67. Quoted in Mattioda, "Ossian in Italy," 301. I have altered his translation slightly.

68. The fact that Agandecca falls at her father's feet recalls a long-lived melodramatic convention of women falling to their knees to plead for mercy or offer penitence. See Roger Parker, "Lina Kneels, Gilda Sings," in *Remaking the Song*; and Mary Ann Smart's "Uneasy Bodies: Verdi and Sublimation" from her *Mimomania*.

69. Broggi-Wüthrich, "The Making of the Italian Ossianic Tradition Revisited," 322.

70. Kimbell, *Norma*, 10.

71. Rosselli, *The Life of Bellini*, 98.

Chapter 4

1. Pacini, *Le mie memorie artistiche*, 79.

2. "Pacini scrive la *Saffo,* e la *Saffo* è per lui trasmutata in effluvio di deliziosa melodi," *La Fama* 4 (14 January 1841): 16.

3. *Il pirata* 6 (25 December 1840): 208.

4. "In un'epoco in cui si applaudiscono le musiche perché i filosofi delle cose musicali, que' contrappunti ambulanti, dicono che sono belle, e della scuola più raffinata. . . ." *La Fama* 4 (14 January 1841): 16.

5. ". . . tutta la musica Europea tenta vincer la melodia coll'armonia somma e complicata." *Il pirata* 6 (25 December 1840): 208. This response to Pacinian melody—especially the suggestion that he was reviving a lost art of simpler melody—shares certain characteristics with debates concerning Bellini's melodies from a decade earlier. Indeed, *La Fama* argues in the previously cited article (14 January 1841) that Pacini took Bellini's place. Bellini's stark, syllabic melodic style in *Il pirata* and *La straniera* was labeled "filosofico" by critics: his admirers lauded the young composer for revivifying lost ideals of melody that found beauty in simplicity. See Esse, "Speaking and Sighing."

6. Stendhal, *Life of Rossini*, trans. Coe, 353. More recently, Poriss (*Changing the Score*, esp. 5 and 136) has linked the decline in the practice of aria substitution (in which singers altered the score by adding or replacing numbers) to the solidification of the notion of an operatic work.

7. Pacini himself, in a candid listing of his strengths and shortcomings, noted that he paid more attention to the vocal part than to anything else, carefully considering the abilities of his singers and adapting his music to their talents in the same way a "good tailor knows how to cut and adapt a suit for a man, concealing his natural imperfections" ("come il bravo sarto sa tagliare ed adattare l'abito all'uomo, nascondendo i difetti di natura"). *Le mie memorie artistiche*, 72.

8. See the review in *Rivista musicale di Firenze* (1 December 1840): 78.

9. The manuscript of "Son tradita, abbandonata" (BG0044 Museo Donizettiano MUSMU. MS.28) is accessible online at http://www.internetculturale.it/jmms/iccuviewer/iccu.jsp?id=oai%3Awww.internetculturale.sbn.it%2FTeca%3A20%3ANT0000%3ALO11064322&mode=all&teca=MagTeca+-+ICCU. This number, scored for solo soprano, orchestra, and chorus, is not included in the printed piano-vocal score published in Naples (around 1828?) and dedicated to Virginia Vasselli (accessible online at https://search.bibliotecadigitale.consmilano.it/explore?bitstream_id=467235&handle=20.500.12459/2827&provider=iiif-image#?c=0&m=0&s=0&cv=0&xywh=447%2C1854%2C3041%2C946).

10. I thank Adam Waller for this transcription of the vocal line of the Donizetti manuscript.

11. George Maxwell Howe, "A Probable Source of Grillparzer's Sappho," investigates an even earlier source by Amalie von Imhoff entitled *Die Schwestern von Lesbos* (1800).

12. Indeed, Verri's novel emphasizes Sappho's reaction to Phaon's beauty and physical prowess; DeJean (*Fictions of Sappho*, 173) has argued that it was one of a number of attempts to place "a revitalized, masculinized Phaon at the heroic center of Sapho's plot."

13. DeJean, *Fictions of Sappho*, 168.

14. Most, "Reflecting Sappho," 12.

15. Verri, *The Adventures of Sappho, Poetess of Mitylene*, 7.

16. In a later version of Sappho's life by Lantier, DeJean writes that "a vision of glistening male flesh awakens both Sapho's sexuality and her poetic voice. The writer who makes Phaon the origin of Sappho's poetic gift fulfills the Ovidian fiction: the beautiful young man now inspires, in addition to destroying, Sapho's poetic voice." *Fictions of Sappho*, 173.

17. DeJean, *Fictions of Sappho*, 169.

18. DeJean, *Fictions of Sappho*, 193–94.

19. DeJean, *Fictions of Sappho*, 194–95.

20. DeJean, *Fictions of Sappho*, 195.

21. DeJean, *Fictions of Sappho*, 170.

22. See the reviews cited in Johnson's introduction to the critical edition of *Il viaggio a Reims*.

23. Pacini describes his studies of Greek theater and ancient Greek modes in preparation for *Saffo*, as well as his efforts to "approximate their art of melody [approssimarmi alla loro Melopea]," in *Le mie memorie artistiche*, 80.

24. Several scholars have noticed that singers' biographies and their roles tend to overlap. See Smart, "Lost Voice of Rosine Stoltz"; and Rutherford, *Prima Donna and Opera*, 27–57.

25. This is, of course, a characteristic of many operatic mad scenes, in which the afflicted party plays out private aspirations or fantasies to a shocked onstage audience. Smart has pointed out that nineteenth-century representations of madness tended to portray personal distress as "popular entertainment," creating tension between public and private expression; "Silencing of Lucia," 121–22.

26. Esterhammer has noticed the tendency of accounts of improvisation to emphasize the strain inspiration placed on the nervous system; *Romanticism and Improvisation*, 206–9.

27. The form of this final scene is also similar to Anna's final scene in Donizetti's *Anna Bolena*, which contains three, rather than two, lyric sections before the cabaletta.

28. Much of the literature on women in opera deals, at least tangentially, with the question of how operatic plots work to suppress female power and agency. Catherine Clément's *Opera, or The Undoing of Women* is perhaps the most well-known critique of such plots; responses to her argument include Katherine Bergeron, "Clément's Opera," and Ralph Locke, "What Are These Women Doing." See also Karen Henson, "Introduction: Divo Worship," for a summary of approaches to gender in opera and an argument for looking beyond the "problem" of women in opera to an exploration of gender more broadly.

29. McClary has suggested that Donizetti's Lucia escapes her oppressive plot via transgressive ornament in *Feminine Endings*, 92–98. Parker, writing of the crucial differences between Lina in *Stiffelio* and Gilda in *Rigoletto*, argues that "one heroine is reduced to mute gestures, while the other seems to articulate a final understanding of her opera musically, lyrically, where it is most alive and humanly expressive"; *Leonora's Last Act*, 167.

30. Perhaps the most familiar account of the emergence of the work concept in the nineteenth century is Goehr, *Imaginary Museum*. For more on the collaboration between singers and composers, see Alessandro Roccatagliati, "Felice Romani"; Smart, "The Lost Voice of Rosine Stoltz"; and Henson, "Verdi, Victor Maurel." Pacini's manuscript for *Saffo* also bears traces of interventions (in a messier hand and different ink) at places where Francilla Pixis would have been expected to display her skill at ornamentation.

31. The three epigraphs are taken from *Sweetbitter Love: Poems of Sappho*. Page numbers are provided in text.

32. Caesar, "Poetic Improvisation," esp. 174 and 182.

33. Fillipo Delpino, for example, who created his own system of stenography, was known as the "scourge of all living improvisers." Caesar, "Poetic Improvisation," 178.

34. Caesar, "Poetic Improvisation and the Challenge of Transcription," 177.

35. Caesar, "Poetic Improvisation and the Challenge of Transcription," 182.

36. Caesar, "Poetic Improvisation and the Challenge of Transcription," 182.

37. Caesar, "Poetic Improvisation and the Challenge of Transcription," 182–83.

38. Gianni published several guidelines for improvisers, telling them to write down their improvisations because the judgment of the eye was more sure [*sicuro*] than the judgment of the ear; *Poesie*, 2:16.

39. *Il pirata* 5 (4 February 1840): 258–59.

40. *Figaro* 8 (21 November 1840): 337.

41. ". . . un raro esempio di modestia, congiunge molta sapienza d'ingegno, slancio di fantasia, ed una vena di versi facili, spontanei, di che vi sia non dubbia prova la Romanza, che avete sott'occhi." *Il pirata* 5 (28 February 1840): 286.

42. Caesar, "Poetic Improvisation," 181.

43. *Il pirata* 6 (26 December 1840): 208. The announcement mentions an earlier account in *L'Omnibus*.

44. One critic, for example, complained that improvisers reused too many topics; see *Il pirata* 6 (15 December 1840): 195.

45. ". . . io composi quest'opera in soli 28 giorni, e che l'ultima scena della *Saffo*, cioé *coro funebre, recitativo, improvviso, tempo di mezzo* e *cabaletta* fu creata in due ore!!! Mi si perdoni, se pecco d'eccessivo amor proprio." Pacini, *Le mie memorie artistiche*, 83.

46. The entire essay is reproduced in James Hepokoski, "Under the Eye of the Verdian Bear," 150–54. Hepokoski points out that this vision of Verdi's work habits is more marketing ploy than anything else (141).

47. Pacini, *Le mie memorie artistiche*, 83.

48. See Donizetti's letter to Antonio Vasselli dated 4 January 1843; Guido Zavadini, *Donizetti*, 647. My thanks to Roger Parker for drawing my attention to this letter.

49. See Roccatagliati, "Felice Romani, Librettist by Trade," for more on how singers shaped operatic production from the earliest stages.

50. Elizabeth D. Harvey argues that Sappho's sexuality can give male writers the opportunity to assert their superiority, showing how Donne's "Sappho to Phlaenis" "uses a lesbian erotic ethics as an implicit strategy for overcoming a male poetic rival." See "Ventriloquizing Sappho, or the Lesbian Muse," 100.

51. DeJean, *Fictions of Sappho*, 174–75.

52. The history is recounted in William Ashbrook, *Donizetti and His Operas*, 80–81.

53. Elizabeth Bronfen has discussed the prevalence of dead poetesses as muses for women poets in *Over Her Dead Body*, 395–435.

54. Vincent, *Romantic Poetess*, 52.

55. Quoted in Vincent, *Romantic Poetess*, 102–3.

56. Prins, *Victorian Sappho*, 244–45. Prins argues that the Sappho poems of several Victorian women—including Mary Robinson, L.E.L., Christina Rossetti, and Felicia Hemans—all engage, in different ways, with the "self-negating" aspects of Sapphic authorship.

57. In a similar vein, Matthew Head has explored how posthumous publication after her death both granted and withheld the status of "author" from composer Charlotte Brandes in his "Cultural Meanings for Women Composers."

58. *Il pirata* 6 (25 December 1840): 208. The context makes clear that Regaldi refers here to the ancient poet, not to Pacini's opera or the operatic character; it is Sappho the historical figure who somehow "authorizes" Pacini's creative effort.

59. ". . . tutto giorno gemono i torchi italiani per buone o mediocri, per fredde of scipite poesie: e ne riboccano i giornali e le strenne; e ne son pieni gli *Album* delle dame. . . ." Romani, "Rivista Bibliografica," *Il pirata* 5 (24 January 1840): 246.

60. ". . . la poesia non sarà mai tenuta a vile in Italia." Romani, "Rivista Bibliografica."

61. Romani, "Rivista Bibliografica." Ellipses in original.

62. Caesar, "Poetic Improvisation," 181–83.

63. "Ed in me sì belle poesie destarono tale entusiasmo, che innanzi alla mia immaginazione esse non si dileguarono colla voce, ma con buona pace de' signori Romantici volarono a risonare fra gl'immortali Elisi, ove Saffo e Corinna maravigliate vollero onorare Licoride Partenopea, facendola del loro bel numero una. Il qual concetto mi rampollò nella mente vestito de' seguenti versi latini. . . ." *Il pirata* 6 (17 November 1840): 162.

64. "A chi ama l'Italia ed è geloso della gloria di lei . . . la sua Musa tornasse a toccare le corde di quel plettro, ai cui vivacissimi suoni fe' eco ogni angolo musicale d'Europa." *Il pirata* 7 (7 January 1842): 221.

Chapter 5

1. "J'aime Fidelio, J'adore Orphée, à genoux, avec des larmes d'extase, mon coeur est pour toujours enchaîné aux pieds de la Reine des arts, Pauline Viardot!! . . . Ma tendresse pour vous est 'sans égale,' O ma chère bienaimée! Vous êtes [illeg.] ma plus caressante, ma plus douce pensée! . . . Votre ravissante gracieuseté pour moi, me touche si profondément, que je pleure . . . au lieu de vous en remercier! . . . Elle est là prés de moi, cette couronne qui a ceint la tete d'un être

Divin! . . . Que je suis heureuse et que j'exprime mal mon bonheur! . . ." Letter dated 20 May 1860. Held at Harvard's Houghton Library: MS MUS 264 box 3 (38).

2. Letter dated 7 April 1860. Held at Harvard's Houghton Library: MS MUS 264 box 3 (29).

3. Cavicchi, "Origins of Music Fandom," 238.

4. Koestenbaum, *The Queen's Throat*; Wood, "Sapphonics," in *Queering the Pitch*; Hadlock, "The Career of Cherubino, or the Trouser Role Grows Up," in *Siren Songs*; Bashant, "Singing in Greek Drag"; and Castle, "In Praise of Brigitte Fassbaender," in *En Travesti*.

5. Pearl, "The Opera Closet," 46.

6. Wood, "Sapphonics," 27.

7. Wood, "Sapphonics," 29–30.

8. Orpheus has long been opera's foundational archetype, invoked to explain the power of song to move and persuade. But Carolyn Abbate has argued that the Orpheus myth—especially the oft-overlooked, gruesome detail of the final song by his severed head—is representative of "the uncanny aspects of musical performance, operatic performance in particular, precisely because one cannot say how it sings, who is in charge, who is the source of the utterance." *In Search of Opera*, 5.

9. See Göran Blix, *From Paris to Pompeii*, for a thorough account of how an "archaelogical gaze" (often turned on Italy) was imbricated with the development of French Romanticism.

10. Reynolds, *The Sappho History*, 196–97.

11. Viardot-Garcia's father was the tenor and singing teacher Manuel Garcia, and her mother the soprano Joaquina Sitchès. Her brother, the famed researcher and pedagogue Manuel Garcia Jr., gained fame for his work with the laryngoscope and exploration into the vocal mechanism.

12. Borchard, "Eine 'Anti-Diva'?"

13. Harding, *Gounod*, 60.

14. Smart, "Singers at the Opéra, 1828–1849," 123–25.

15. This tendency drew her to perform all kinds of music as well; according to James Harding, near the end of her life Viardot reportedly advised a student not to sing such a varied repertoire because it had ruined her voice. Harding does not cite his source for this piece of advice (*Gounod*, 60).

16. Smart, "Singers at the Opéra," 124.

17. "En effet, par sa vaste intelligence, par us sens artistique, qu'avait merveilleusement developpé une sérieuse éducation musicale, par sa sensibilité sa rare finesse de pénétration, n'a-t-elle pas été [. . .] mieux qu'une interprète—plus qu'une conseillère, presque une collaboratrice?" Cited in Borchard, "Eine 'Anti-Diva'?," 115.

18. For more on Viardot's compositional strategies, including their indebtedness to improvisation and to "composing in dialogue," see Borchard, *Pauline Viardot-Garcia*, 243–73.

19. Chorley, *The Athenaeum* (12 October 1867). Cited in Borchard, "Viardot."

20. Berlioz praised Viardot's performance of the *scene aux enfers* in 1842 in Vienna, where she seems to have added ornaments found in an eighteenth-century manuscript from the Sistine Chapel. "Despite a cadenza added at the end of the third verse," he wrote, "Mme Viardot reproduced those noble and touching melodies with scrupulous fidelity." Fauquet, "Berlioz's Version of Gluck's *Orphée*," 194.

21. Waddington, "Pauline Viardot-Garcia as Berlioz's Counselor and Physician."

22. Waddington, "Berlioz's Counselor," 386–87.

23. Waddington, "Berlioz's Counselor," 387.

24. Berlioz himself participated in the mythmaking that credited Viardot with special status as the embodiment of Orpheus in his two reviews. In his review of 22 November 1859, Berlioz

credits Viardot alone for the famous cadenza that ends act 1, then deleted that passage when republishing the review in *A Travers Chant* (Fauquet, "Berlioz's Version of Gluck's *Orphée*," 213). Flora Willson has noted that Berlioz strengthened the idea of Viardot's performance as a monumental occasion when he claimed in his 9 December 1859 review that painters and sculptors were inspired to capture Viardot's "poses, [her] sculptural *attitudes*" in quick sketches during the performance (Willson, "Classic Staging," 314–15).

25. Bibliotèque Nationale, Musique, ms. 1522. See Fauquet, "Berlioz's Version of Gluck's *Orphée*," 204–10.

26. Fauquet, "Berlioz's Version of Gluck's *Orphée*," 194.

27. Reynaldo Hahn mentions that Viardot showed him an ornamented version of "Che farò" in a Sistine Chapel manuscript to support her decision to add her own embellishments. Fauquet, "Berlioz's Version of Gluck's *Orphée*," 214.

28. See Fauquet, "Berlioz's Version of Gluck's *Orphée*," 237–53, for a side-by-side comparison of several numbers in the two scores.

29. There is disagreement on what led Berlioz to this rather uncharacteristic involvement in crafting a cadenza. Fauquet argues that he believed the aria was not Gluck's at all, and rather had been borrowed from Ferdinando Bertoni. For evidence, he cites Saint-Saëns's later memoirs: "We took up the task [of writing the cadenza] with even greater enthusiasm as we were convinced we were fooling about with a piece whose composer merited no fidelity" ("Berlioz's Version of Gluck's *Orphée*," 212n73). Waddington, however, believes this to be a red herring ("Berlioz's Counselor," 391).

30. Fauquet, "Berlioz's Version of Gluck's *Orphée*," 211.

31. Fauquet, "Berlioz's Version of Gluck's *Orphée*," 212.

32. Fauquet, "Berlioz's Version of Gluck's *Orphée*," 232.

33. Waddington lists the sources where the cadenza was published ("Berlioz's Counselor," 391).

34. Waddington, "Berlioz's Counselor," 395.

35. Willson, "Classic Staging."

36. Waddingon, "Berlioz's Counselor," 395–96.

37. Waddingon, "Berlioz's Counselor," 396.

38. Cited in Fauquet, "Berlioz's Version of Gluck's *Orphée*," 212.

39. Waddington, "Berlioz's Counselor," 397.

40. See Harding, *Gounod*, 58–71.

41. Condé, preface to von Goldbeck, ed., *Lettres de Charles Gounod à Pauline Viardot*, 16.

42. Kendall-Davies, *Life and Work of Pauline Viardot-Garcia*, 1:289.

43. Gounod to Pauline Viardot, 18 May 1850 (*Lettres*, 128) and 11 May 1850 (*Lettres*, 112).

44. Gounod to Pauline Viardot, 17 May 1850 (*Lettres*, 127).

45. Thérèse Marix-Spire, "Gounod and His First Interpreter, Part I," 199.

46. Waddington, "Turgenev and Gounod: Rival Strangers," 17–18.

47. This sort of triangular dynamic—here, one of masculine jockeying over both creative output and attention from an absent and idealized woman—was most memorably theorized by Eve Kosofsky Sedgwick in her book *Between Men: English Literature and Male Homosocial Desire*.

48. "À partir des quartre derniers vers . . . la musique se désordonne jusqu'à la fin; le mugissement de la mer se joint à ces derniers accents de douleur jusqu'au dernier grand coup d'orchestre qui a lieu au moment où Sapho se jette dans la mer." Gounod to Pauline Viardot, 28–29 June 1850 (*Lettres*, 158).

49. "Grrrr'andissime succès. Elles ont trouvé le dernier morceau d'un dramatique saisissant, et en étaient tout émues. Et moi aussi. Il me tarde de vous donner tout cela à vous pour qui et un peu par qui je le fais." 30 June–2 July 1850 (*Lettres*, 161). "Par qui" could also mean "with whose assistance" or "thanks to."

50. Louis Viardot to Pauline Viardot, Courtavenel, 2 August 1850. Houghton Library, Harvard University: MS Mus 264 box 2 (64). I am indebted to Ralph Locke for his assistance with both deciphering Louis's handwriting and translating the letter. Louis had been the director of the Théâtre Italien; not only was he intimately familiar with Pauline's voice and capabilities, but he had an impresario's professional knowledge of operatic convention and theatrical pacing.

51. "Le chant de désespoir de Sapho doit être d'un grand et terrible effect—je crois du moins que tu le feras ainsi—mais il avait un grand défaut, si je ne m'abuse: c'était de [illeg.] dans ce même sentiment de désespoir insensé et furieux, sur les mots: 'tourments affreux, avec moi finissez.' C'est un joueur qui se suicide."

52. "Sur mon avis, Gounod fait dire à Sapho toute cette phrase désespérée au bas du rocher, pendant les mugissements de la mer. Puis elle monte la roche de [Leucas], la mer s'apaise, et, de là[-]haut, elle dit encore: 'Oh toi qui pars maudissant ton amante, sois béni par une mourante' et le saut de carpe. Ces mots ajoutés d'une expression toute autre que les précédents, tendres et nobles, doivent être comme les derniers mots a'Armide dans le duo de la 'Haine,' ceux ajouté par Gluck. Ce sera plus juste, et plus beau. Gounod n'a pas hésité à me croire, et s'en applaudit." Louis is referring to the duet for Armide and Hidraot in act 2 of Gluck's *Armide* ("Esprits de haine et de rage"). He had invoked the Gluck/Mozart dichotomy earlier in the letter—and it became a shorthand for the difference between lyrical melody and recitative. The connection between *Sapho* and Gluck is significant, given the fact that Viardot would cap her career as Orphée less than a decade later.

53. Harding, *Gounod*, 63–64.

54. "Le Lamento sera mis, c'est décidé, mais alors comme morceau purement lyrique, comme dernier chant de Sapho. La lyre en main, elle dira adieu à Phaon, au soleil, à sa lyre, à sa vie enfin, et s'en ira piquer sa tête et se noyer dans les larmes qu'elle aura fait verser au spectateur." Viardot, letter to Ivan Turgenev dated 10–15 September 1850, cited in Friang, *Pauline Viardot*, 108. Gounod set the text of Gautier's poem for a second time in his 1872 "Ma belle amie est morte (Lamento)."

55. Huebner, *Operas of Gounod*, 188.

56. This aspect of the work has been described as a problem of genre—as if *Sapho* was attempting but failing to be an opéra-comique. Huebner, *Operas of Gounod*, 188.

57. Contrafacta such as this are of course common in the history of vocal music; however, devising new words for existing melodies was one working method of poetic improvisers, as we recall from Teresa Bandettini's account of learning to improvise as a child in chapter 1.

58. Marix-Spire, "Gounod and His First Interpreter" (Parts I and II), reproduces the correspondence related to this event, and my discussion draws from this source.

59. Marix-Spire, "Gounod and His First Interpreter, Part II," 308.

60. A later intimate of Gounod's, the soprano (and possible unreliable narrator) Georgina Weldon, wrote in her memoirs that when Anna received Pauline's gift of a bracelet, she "furiously declared that she did not accept gifts from her husband's mistress." Cited in Harding, *Gounod*, 76.

61. Harding, *Gounod*, 61. Gossip about the paternity of Viardot's children has been a mainstay of the singer's biography; her relationship with Turgenev has received the most scrutiny. Hilary Poriss has discussed the sources contradicting such rumors, suggesting that it is unlikely that Turgenev fathered any of Viardot's children (Poriss, review of *Life and Work of Viardot*, by Kendall-Davies, 697).

62. Marix-Spire, "Gounod and His First Interpreter, Part II," 310.

63. Marix-Spire, "Gounod and His First Interpreter, Part II," 309–10.

64. Marix-Spire, "Gounod and His First Interpreter, Part II," 316.

65. Marix-Spire, "Gounod and His First Interpreter, Part II," 302.

66. Marix-Spire, "Gounod and His First Interpreter, Part II," 303.

67. Reynolds, *The Sappho History*, 77.

68. Reynolds, *The Sappho History*, 78–79.

69. This new Sappho was often defined by a transgressive sexuality. Reynolds notes that "a contemporary fashion for lesbianism, in literature and in life, meant that Arsene Houssaye could begin a gossipy account of the *amours* of Georges Sand with the much quoted statement: 'At this time Sapho was resuscitated in Paris, not knowing if she loved Phaon or Erinna.' Allier de Hauteroche wrote an 1822 article that proposed there were two Sapphos—one a famous poet, one a courtesan." *The Sappho History*, 77.

70. Reynolds, *The Sappho History*, 78.

71. The model for this sculpture may have been the tragic actress Rachel [Elisabeth Félix] or perhaps Louise Colet, author and mistress of Flaubert, both independent and artistic women. Reynolds, *The Sappho History*, 79.

72. Reynolds, *The Sappho History*, 79.

73. Gerard Condé has recently argued that the letters leave some room for the possibility that Gounod might have made the decision himself. It seems significant, however, that the decision to reuse the existing songs was made after Pauline arrived home.

74. Jean-Michel Nectoux notes that Evelyn Enoch was a member of Fauré's circle and would sing to his piano accompaniment at salon gatherings. "Fauré: Voice, Style, Vocality," 371.

75. Patrick Waddington notes that another manuscript, with corrections and alterations, was advertised in the Lisa Cox catalogue, no. 39 (2001), item 122. Patrick Waddington has named this manuscript in his unpublished catalogue of the musical works of Viardot.

76. Viardot no doubt encountered numerous settings of this text: Faure's version was written around the time he met Viardot, in 1872, and was performed by her in 1876. It was published with Viardot as the dedicatee in 1877. See Zoltan Roman, "Selected Early Songs of Faure," 27–28.

77. Perhaps Viardot's use of "mer" instead of "nuit" was a simple mistake; however, she chose to retain it throughout the revision process, and the substitution was left to stand in the published version.

78. Roman, "Selected Early Songs of Fauré," 32.

Bibliography

Abbate, Carolyn. *In Search of Opera*. Princeton, NJ, and Oxford: Princeton University Press, 2001.

Ashbrook, William. *Donizetti and His Operas*. Cambridge: Cambridge University Press, 1983.

Astarita, Tommaso. *Between Salt Water and Holy Water*. New York and London: W. W. Norton & Company, 2005.

Auslander, Philip. *Liveness: Performance in a Mediatized Culture*. London: Routledge, 1999.

Bach, C. P. E. "From *Essay on the Proper Manner of Playing a Keyboard Instrument*." In *Strunk's Source Readings in Music History*, edited by Leo Treitler, 851–55. New York: Norton, 1998.

Baragwanath, Nicholas. "Giovanni Battista De Vecchis and the Theory of Melodic Accent from Zarlino to Zingarelli." *Music and Letters* 95/2 (2014): 157–82.

———. *The Italian Traditions and Puccini*. Bloomington and Indianapolis: Indiana University Press, 2011.

Bashant, Wendy. "Singing in Greek Drag: Gluck, Berlioz, George Eliot." In *En travesti: Women, Gender Subversion, Opera*, edited by Corinne E. Blackmer and Patricia Juliana Smith, 216–41. New York: Columbia University Press, 1995.

Bellini, Vincenzo. *Epistolario*. Edited by Luisa Cambi. Verona: Mondadori, 1943.

Benson, Bruce Ellis. *The Improvisation of Musical Dialogue: A Phenomenology of Music*. Cambridge: Cambridge University Press, 2003.

Bergeron, Katherine. "Clément's Opera, or One Woman's Undoing." *Cambridge Opera Journal* 2 (1990): 93–98.

Berliner, Paul. *Thinking in Jazz: The Infinite Art of Improvisation*. Chicago Studies in Ethnomusicology. Chicago: University of Chicago Press, 1994.

Bhogal, Gurminder Kaur. "Lakme's Echoing Jewels." In *The Arts of the Prima Donna in the Long Nineteenth Century*, edited by Rachel Cowgill and Hilary Poriss, 186–205. New York: Oxford University Press, 2012.

Blix, Göran. *From Paris to Pompeii: French Romanticism and the Cultural Politics of Archaeology*. Philadelphia: University of Pennsylvania Press, 2009.

Borchard, Beatrix. "Eine 'Anti-Diva'? Zur Rezeption Pauline Viardot-Garcias im 19. Jahrhundert." In *Diva—Die Inszenierung der übermenschlichen Frau. Interdisziplinäre Untersuchungen zu einem kulturellen Phänomen des 19. Und 20. Jahrhunderts*, edited by Rebecca Grotjahn, Dörte Schimidt, and Thomas Seedorf, 114–25. Schliengen: Edition Argus, 2011.

———. *Pauline Viardot-Garcia: Fülle des Lebens.* Cologne: Böhlau Verlag, 2016.

———. "Viardot [née Garcia], (Michelle Ferdinande) Pauline." *Grove Music Online.* 2001; accessed 19 November 2019. https://www-oxfordmusiconline-com.ezp.lib.rochester.edu/grovemusic/view/10.1093/gmo/9781561592630.001.0001/omo-9781561592630-e-0000029283.

Born, Georgina, Eric Lewis, and Will Straw, eds. *Improvisation and Social Aesthetics.* Durham, NC: Duke University Press, 2017.

Broggi-Wüthrich, Francesca. "From Smith's *Antiquities* to Leoni's *Nuovi Canti*: The Making of the Italian Ossianic Tradition Revisited." In *The Reception of Ossian in Europe*, edited by Howard Gaskill, 303–34. New York: Thoemmes Continuum, 2004.

Bronfen, Elisabeth. *Over Her Dead Body: Death, Femininity, and the Aesthetic.* Manchester: Manchester University Press, 1992.

Caesar, Michael. "Poetic Improvisation and the Challenge of Transcription." In *Theatre, Opera, and Performance in Italy from the Fifteenth Century to the Present: Essays in Honour of Richard Andrews*, edited by Brian Richardson, Simon Gilson, and Catherine Keen, 173–84. Egham, UK: Society for Italian Studies, 2004.

———. "Poetic Improvisation in the Nineteenth Century: Giuseppe Regaldi and Giannina Milli." *Modern Language Review* 101 (2006): 701–14.

Casillo, Robert. *The Empire of Stereotypes: Germaine de Staël and the Idea of Italy.* New York: Palgrave Macmillan, 2006.

Castle, Terry. "In Praise of Brigitte Fassbaender: Reflections on Diva-Worship." In *En Travesti: Women, Gender Subversion, Opera*, edited by Corinne E. Blackmer and Patricia Juliana Smith, 20–58. New York: Columbia University Press, 1995.

Caswell, Austin. "Mme Cinti-Damoreau and the Embellishment of Italian Opera in Paris: 1820–1845." *Journal of the American Musicological Society* 28 (1975): 459–92.

Cavicchi, Daniel. "Loving Music: Listeners, Entertainments, and the Origins of Music Fandom in Nineteenth-Century America." In *Fandom: Identities and Communities in a Mediated World*, edited by Jonathan Gray and C. Lee Harrington, 235–49. New York and London: New York University Press, 2007.

Celenza, Anna Harwell. *Hans Christian Andersen and Music: The Nightingale Revealed.* Aldershot, UK, and Burlington, VT: Ashgate, 2005.

Cesarotti, Melchiorre. *Poesie di Ossian*, vol. 2. Florence: Molini, Landi and Co., 1807.

Ceserani, Giovanna. *Italy's Lost Greece: Magna Graecia and the Making of Modern Archaeology.* Oxford: Oxford University Press, 2012.

Chard, Chloe. *Pleasure and Guilt on the Grand Tour: Travel Writing and Imaginative Geography 1600–1830.* Manchester: Manchester University Press, 1999.

Clément, Catherine. *Opera, or The Undoing of Women*, translated by Betsy Wing. Foreword by Susan McClary. Minneapolis: University of Minnesota Press, 1988.

Colas, Damien. "Le revisioni delle parte vocali negli autografi di Bellini." In *Vincenzo Bellini: Verso l'edizione critica. Atti del convegno internazionale, Sienna, 1–3 giugno 2000*, edited by Fabrizio Della Seta and Simonetta Ricciardi, 315–46. Florence: Olschki, 2004.

———. "Melody and Ornamentation," translated by Cormac Newark. In *The Cambridge Companion to Rossini*, edited by Emanuele Senici, 104–23. Cambridge Companions to Music. Cambridge: Cambridge University Press, 2004.

Cook, Nicholas. *The Schenker Project: Culture, Race, and Music Theory in Fin-de-siècle Vienna.* Oxford: Oxford University Press, 2007.

Cowgill, Rachel. "'Attitudes with a Shawl': Femininity, Performance, and Spectatorship at the Italian Opera in Early Nineteenth-Century London." In *The Arts of the Prima Donna in the Long Nineteenth Century*, edited by Rachel Cowgill and Hilary Poriss, 217–51. New York: Oxford University Press, 2012.

Crutchfield, Will. "Appendix V: Early Vocal Ornamentation." In Gioachino Rossini, *Il barbiere di Siviglia*, edited by Patricia B. Brauner. Works of Gioachino Rossini, 2:361–420. Kassel: Bärenreiter, 2008.

———. "The Prosodic Appoggiatura in the Music of Mozart and His Contemporaries." *Journal of the American Musicological Society* 42 (1989): 229–74.

———. "Vocal Performance in the Nineteenth Century." In *The Cambridge History of Musical Performance*, edited by Colin Lawson and Robin Stowell, 611–42. Cambridge: Cambridge University Press, 2012.

Curioni, Stefano Baia. *Mercanti dell'opera: storie di casa Ricordi*. Milan: Il Saggiatore, 2011.

Dahlhaus, Carl. *Nineteenth-Century Music*. Translated by J. Bradford Robinson. Berkeley and Los Angeles: University of California Press, 1989.

Daitz, Stephen. *A Recital of Ancient Greek Poetry*. 2nd ed. Series: The Living Voice of Greek and Latin Literature. Mundelein, IL: Bolchazy-Carducci, 2010.

Damoreau, Laure-Cinthie. *Classic Bel Canto Technique*. Translated by Victor Rangel-Ribeiro. Mineolo, NY: Dover, 1997 [1849].

Davies, James Q. "Gautier's 'Diva': The First French Uses of the Word." In Cowgill and Poriss, eds., *The Arts of the Prima Donna in the Long Nineteenth Century*, 123–46. New York: Oxford University Press, 2012.

Davies, Kate. "Pantomime, Connoisseurship, Consumption: Emma Hamilton and the Politics of Embodiment." *CW3 Journal* 2 (2006), http://www2.shu.ac.uk/corvey/CW3journal/issue%20two/davies.html.

Degrada, Francesco. *Music Musicians Publishing: 175 Years of Casa Ricordi, 1808–1983*. Milan: Ricordi, 1983.

DeJean, Joan. *Fictions of Sappho, 1546–1937*. Women in Culture and Society. Chicago: University of Chicago Press, 1989.

———. "Stael's *Corinne*: The Novel's Other Dilemma." In *The Novel's Seductions: Stael's* Corinne *in Critical Inquiry*, edited by Karyna Szmurlo, 117–26. Lewisburg: Bucknell University Press, 1999.

Della Seta, Fabrizio, and Simonetta Ricciardi, eds. *Vincenzo Bellini: Verso l'edizione critica. Atti del convegno internazionale, Sienna, 1–3 giugno 2000*. Florence: Olschki, 2004.

Di Ricco, Alessandra. *L'inutile e maraviglioso mestiere: Poeti improvvisatori di fine settecento*. Milan: Angeli, 1990.

Donato, Maria Pia. "The Temple of Female Glory." In *Italy's Eighteenth Century: Gender and Culture in the Age of the Grand Tour*, edited by Paula Findlen, Wendy Wassyng Roworth, and Catherine M. Sama, 59–78. Stanford, CA: Stanford University Press, 2009.

Esse, Melina. "Speaking and Sighing: Bellini's canto declamato and the Poetics of Restraint." *Current Musicology* 87 (2009): 7–45.

Esterhammer, Angela. *Romanticism and Improvisation, 1750–1850*. Cambridge: Cambridge University Press, 2008.

Fabbri, Moreno, ed. *Corilla Olimpica e la poesia del Settecento europeo*. Pistoia: Maschietto, 2002.

Fauquet, Joel-Marie. "Berlioz's Version of Gluck's *Orphée*." In *Berlioz Studies*, edited by Peter Bloom, 189–253. Cambridge: Cambridge University Press, 1992.

Fernow, Carl Ludwig. *Über die Improvisatoren*. In *Römische Studien* 2: 298–416. Zurich: Gessner, 1806.

Fischlin, Ajay, and George Lipsitz. *The Fierce Urgency of Now: Improvisation, Rights, and the Ethics of Cocreation*. Durham, NC: Duke University Press, 2013.

Foscolo, Ugo. "The Women of Italy." In *Edizione nationale delle opere di Ugo Foscolo*, vol. 12, *Scritti vari di critica storica e letteraria 1817 al 1827*, edited by Urberto Limentani and John Lindon, 418–69. Florence: F. Le Monnier, 1978.

Franchi, Saverio. "Prassi esecutiva musicale e poesia estemporanea italiana." In *Oralita: cultura, letteratura, discorso*, edited by Bruno Gentili and Giuseppe Paioni, 409–27. Rome: Ateneo, 1985.

Fraser, Flora. *Emma, Lady Hamilton*. New York: Alfred A. Knopf, 1987.

Friang, Michèle. *Pauline Viardot au miroir de sa correspondance*. Paris: Hermann Éditeurs, 2008.

Gambarota, Paola. *Irresistible Signs: The Genius of Language and Italian National Identity*. Toronto: University of Toronto Press, 2011.

Gapps, Stephen. "On Being a Mobile Monument: Historical Reenactments and Commemorations." In *Historical Reenactment: From Realism to the Affective Turn*, edited by Iain McCalman and Paul A. Pickering, 50–62. Basingstoke, UK: Palgrave Macmillan, 2010.

Ghirardini, Cristina. "La 'naturale acuta sensibilità all'armonia, al numero ed al metro.' L'improvvisazione poetica in ottava rima in Italia centrale dal Settecento alla prima metà del Novecento." *Fonti musicali italiane: Periodico di ricerca musicologica* 22 (2017): 55–90.

———. "*L'improvvisatore* in Genre Scenes by Foreign and Italian Artists in the 19th Century." *L'Idomeneo* 21 (2016): 37–64.

Gianni, Francesco. *Poesie de Francesco Gianni*, vol. 2. Naples: Nella Tipografia San Giacomo, 1806.

Giordani, Pietro. "Intorno allo Sgricci ed agl'improvvisatori in Italia [Of Sgricci and the Improvisers in Italy]." *Biblioteca Italiana Ossia Giornale di Letteratura Scienze ed Arti* 4 (1816): 365–75. Accessed at http://romanticimprov.utoronto.ca/?p=2974, 15 December 2018.

Giordano, Antonella. "'Donna il cui carme gli animi soggioga': Eighteenth-Century Italian Women Improvisers." *Journal of Early Modern Studies* 7 (2018): 139–55.

Giuli, Paola. "Monsters of Talent: Fame and Reputation of Women Improvisers in Arcadia." In *Italy's Eighteenth Century: Gender and Culture in the Age of the Grand Tour*, edited by Paula Findlen, Wendy Wassyng Roworth, and Catherine M. Sama, 303–30. Stanford, CA: Stanford University Press, 2009.

Gjerdingen, Robert O. *Music in the Galant Style*. Oxford: Oxford University Press, 2007.

———. "The Perfection of Craft Training in the Neapolitan Conservatoires." *Rivista di analisi e teoria musicale* 15/1 (Lucca, Italy: 2009): 29–52.

Goehr, Lydia. *The Imaginary Museum of Musical Works: An Essay in the Philosophy of Music*. Oxford: Oxford University Press, 1994.

Goethe, Johann Wolfgang von. *Italian Journey*. Translated by Robert R. Heitner; edited by Thomas P. Saine and Jeffrey L. Sammons. Princeton, NJ: Princeton University Press, 1994.

———. *Italienische Reise*. Edited by Eric Trunz. Munich: Beck, 2007.

Gooley, Dana. *Fantasies of Improvisation: Free Playing in Nineteenth-Century Music*. Oxford and New York: Oxford University Press, 2018.

Gossett, Philip. *Divas and Scholars: Performing Italian Opera*. Chicago: University of Chicago Press, 2006.

———. "Piracy in Venice: The Selling of *Semiramide*." In *Words on Music: Essays in Honor of Andrew Porter on the Occasion of His 75th Birthday*, edited by David Rosen and Claire Brook, 120–37. Hillsdale, NY: Pendragon Press, 2003.

Gounod, Charles. *Lettres de Charles Gounod à Pauline Viardot*. Edited by Melanie von Goldbeck; preface by Gérard Condé. Arles: Actes Sud, 2015.

Greene, Ellen, ed. *Re-Reading Sappho: Reception and Transmission*. Berkeley: University of California Press, 1996.

Gutwirth, Madelyn. *Madame de Staël, Novelist: The Emergence of the Artist as a Woman*. Urbana: University of Illinois Press, 1978.

Hadlock, Heather. "The Career of Cherubino, or the Trouser Role Grows Up." In *Siren Songs*, edited by Mary Ann Smart. Princeton, NJ, and Oxford: Princeton University Press, 2000.

Harding, James. *Gounod*. London: George Allen and Unwin Ltd., 1973.

Harvey, Elizabeth D. "Ventriloquizing Sappho, or the Lesbian Muse." In *Re-reading Sappho: Reception and Transmission*, edited by Ellen Greene, 79–104. Classics and Contemporary Thought 3. Berkeley and Los Angeles: University of California Press, 1996.

Hatten, Robert S. "Opening the Museum Window: Improvisation and Its Inscribed Values in Canonic Works by Chopin and Schumann." In *Musical Improvisation: Art, Education, and Society*, edited by Gabriel Solis and Bruno Nettl, 281–95. Urbana and Chicago: University of Illinois Press, 2009.

Head, Matthew. "Cultural Meanings for Women Composers: Charlotte ('Minna') Brandes and the Beautiful Dead in the German Enlightenment." *Journal of the American Musicological Society* 57 (2004): 231–84.

———. "Rethinking Authorship through Women Composers." *Women and Music* 6 (2002): 36–50.

Henson, Karen. "Introduction: Divo Worship." *Cambridge Opera Journal* 19 (2007): 1–9.

———. "Verdi, Victor Maurel and Fin-de-Siècle Operatic Performance." *Cambridge Opera Journal* 19 (2007): 59–84.

Hepokoski, James A. "Under the Eye of the Verdian Bear: Notes on the Rehearsals and Première of *Falstaff*." *Musical Quarterly* 71 (1985): 135–56.

Howe, George Maxwell. "A Probably Source of Grillparzer's Sappho." *Journal of English and Germanic Philology* 22 (1923): 503–29.

Huebner, Steven. *The Operas of Charles Gounod*. Oxford and New York: Clarendon/Oxford University Press, 1990.

Johnson, Janet L. "L'histoire d'une découverte." In *Le Voyage à Reims; Le comte Ory, Rossini. L'avant scène Opéra* 140 (1991): 14–21.

Johnson, Janet L., ed. Introduction to the critical edition: *Il viaggio a Reims ossia l'albergo del giglio d'oro*, ed. Janet L. Johnson, in *Edizione critica delle opere di Gioachino Rossini*, serie 1, vol. 35, xxi–lxiv. Pesaro, 1999.

Kallberg, Jeffrey. *Chopin at the Boundaries: Sex, History, and Musical Genre*. Cambridge, MA: Harvard University Press, 1996.

Kendall-Davies, Barbara. *The Life and Work of Pauline Viardot-Garcia, Volume I: The Years of Fame, 1836–1863*. Amersham: Cambridge Scholars Press, 2003.

Kim, Cindy Lee. "Changing Meanings of Ornamentation in Nineteenth-Century Italian Opera." PhD diss., University of Rochester (Eastman School of Music), 2011.

Kimbell, David. *Cambridge Opera Handbooks. Vincenzo Bellini:* Norma. Cambridge: Cambridge University Press, 1998.

———. *Italian Opera. National Traditions of Opera*. Cambridge: Cambridge University Press, 1991.

———. "Vincenzo Bellini." In *New Penguin Opera Guide*, edited by Amanda Holden, 46–55. London: Penguin, 2001.

Kittler, Friedrich. *Discourse Networks 1800/1900*. Stanford, CA: Stanford University Press, 1990.

Koestenbaum, Wayne. *The Queen's Throat: Opera, Homosexuality, and the Mystery of Desire*. Boston: DaCapo Press, 2001 [1993].

Koslovsky, John. "Tracing the Improvisatory Impulse in Early Schenkerian Theory." *Intégral* 24 (2010): 57–79.

Law, Sin Yan Hedy. "Composing *Citoyennes* through *Sapho*." *Opera Quarterly* 32 (2017): 5–28.

Letzer, Jacqueline, and Robert Adelson. *Women Writing Opera: Creativity and Controversy in the Age of the French Revolution*. Berkeley: University of California Press, 2001.

Lewis, George, and Ben Piekut, eds. *The Oxford Handbook of Critical Improvisation Studies*, 2 vols. Oxford and New York: Oxford University Press, 2016.

Leydi, Roberto. "Erminia monta in gondola." In *Tartini: il tempo e le opera*, edited by Andrea Bomba and Maria Nevilla Massaro, 417–42. Bologna: Il Mulino, 1994.

Locke, Ralph P. "What Are These Women Doing in Opera?" In *En Travesti: Women, Gender Subversion, Opera*, edited by Corinne E. Blackmer and Patricia Juliana Smith, 59–98. New York: Columbia University Press, 1995.

Lockhart, Ellen. *Animation, Plasticity, and Music in Italy, 1770–1830*. Berkeley and Los Angeles: University of California Press, 2017.

Magelssen, Scott. *Living History Museums: Undoing History Through Performance*. Lanham, MD: Scarecrow Press, 2007.

Maguire, Simon. *Vincenzo Bellini and the Aesthetics of Nineteenth-Century Italian Opera*. New York: Garland, 1989.

Marix-Spire, Thérèse. "Gounod and His First Interpreter: Pauline Viardot, Part I." Translated by Gustave Reese. *Musical Quarterly* 31 (1945): 193–211.

———. "Gounod and His First Interpreter: Pauline Viardot, Part II." Translated by Erminie Huntress. *Musical Quarterly* 31 (1945): 299–317.

Matsumoto, Naomi. "Manacled Freedom: Nineteenth-Century Vocal Improvisation and the Flute—Accompanied Cadenza in Donizetti's Lucia di Lammermoor." In *Beyond Notes: Improvisation in Western Music of the Eighteenth and Nineteenth Centuries*, edited by Rudolf Rasch, 295–316. Speculum musicae 16. Turnhout: Brepols, 2011.

Mattioda, Enrico. "Ossian in Italy: From Cesarotti to the Theatre." In *The Reception of Ossian in Europe*, edited by Howard Gaskill, 274–303. New York: Thoemmes Continuum, 2004.

McClary, Susan. *Feminine Endings: Music, Gender, and Sexuality*. Minneapolis: University of Minnesota Press, 1991.

Mendelsohn, Daniel. "Hearing Sappho." In *The New Yorker*, 12 March 2015. Accessed at https://www.newyorker.com/books/page-turner/hearing-sappho.

Metastasio, Pietro. *Tutte le opere*: *Lettere*, vol. 3. Edited by Bruno Brunelli. Milan: Mondadori, 1954.

Moeckli, Laura. " 'Abbellimenti o fioritura': Further Evidence of Creative Embellishment in and beyond the Rossinian Repertoire." In *Beyond Notes: Improvisation in Western Music of the Eighteenth and Nineteenth Centuries*, edited by Rudolf Rasch, 277–94. Speculum musicae 16. Turnhout: Brepols, 2011.

Moore, Dafydd, ed. *Ossian and Ossianism*. Routledge: London and New York, 2004 [1762].

Morelli, Luciana, ed. *Il carteggio tra Amaduzzi e Corilla Olimpica, 1775–1792*. Florence: Olschki, 2000.

Moseley, Roger. "Entextualization and the Improvised Past." *Music Theory Online* 19 (2013). www.mtosmt.org/issues/mto.13.19.2/toc.19.2.html.

Most, Glen W. "Reflecting Sappho." In *Re-reading Sappho: Reception and Transmission*, edited by Ellen Greene, 11–35. Classics and Contemporary Thought 3. Berkeley and Los Angeles: University of California Press, 1996.

Nectoux, Jean-Michel. "Fauré: Voice, Style, Vocality." In *Regarding Fauré*, edited and translated by Tom Gordon, 369–402. Abingdon and New York: Routledge, 2013.

Nettl, Bruno, and Melinda Russell, eds. *In the Course of Performance: Studies in the World of Musical Improvisation*. Chicago: University of Chicago Press, 1998.

Orcel, Michel. "Le sacre de l'antiphrase." In *Le Voyage à Reims; Le comte Ory, Rossini. L'avant scène Opéra* 140 (1991): 9–13.

Pacini, Giovanni. *Le mie memorie artistiche*. Edited by Ferdinando Magnani. Florence: Le Monnier, 1875. Reprint, Bologna: Arnaldo Forni Editore, 1978.

Parker, Roger. *Leonora's Last Act: Essays in Verdian Discourse*. Princeton Studies in Opera. Princeton, NJ: Princeton University Press, 1997.

Pearl, Monica B. "The Opera Closet: Ardor, Shame, Queer Confessions." *Prose Studies* 37 (2015): 46–65.

Pop, Andrei. "Sympathetic Spectators: Henry Fuseli's Nightmare and Emma Hamilton's Attitudes." *Art History* 34 (2011): 934–57.

Poriss, Hilary. *Changing the Score: Arias, Prima Donnas, and the Authority of Performance*. AMS Studies in Music. Oxford: Oxford University Press, 2009.

———. Review of *Life and Work of Pauline Viardot Garcia*, vol. 1, *The Years of Fame, 1836–1863*, by Barbara Kendall-Davies, and *The Life and Work of Pauline Viardot Garcia*, vol. 2, *The Years of Grace, 1863–1910*, by Barbara Kendall-Davies. *Journal of the American Musicological Society* 68 (2015): 692–98.

———. "Verdi Meets Bellini: *I Lombardi* in *Beatrice di Tenda*'s Castle." In *Verdi 2001: Atti del Convegno internazionale / Proceedings of the International Conference, Parma—New York—New Haven, 24 January–1 February 2001*, edited by Fabrizio Della Seta, Roberta Montemorra Marvin, and Marco Marica, 69–81. Florence: Leo S. Olschki, 2002.

Prins, Yopie. *Victorian Sappho*. Princeton, NJ: Princeton University Press, 1999.

Pugliese, Romana Margherita. "The Origins of *Lucia di Lammermoor*'s Cadenza." *Cambridge Opera Journal* 16 (2004): 23–42.

Reynolds, Margaret. *The Sappho History*. Basingstoke, UK: Palgrave Macmillan, 2003.

Rink, John. "Schenker and Improvisation." *Journal of Music Theory* 37 (1993): 1–54.

Roccatagliati, Alessandro. "Felice Romani, Librettist by Trade." *Cambridge Opera Journal* 8 (1996): 113–45.

Roman, Zoltan. "*Gradus ad Parnassum*: Selected Early Songs of Gabriel Fauré in the Socio-Cultural Context of His Time." *Studia Musicologica* 48 (2007): 5–44.

Rosselli, John. *The Life of Bellini*. Cambridge: Cambridge University Press, 1996.

Russo, Paolo. "Giuditta Pasta: cantante pantomimica." *Musica e storia* 10 (2002): 497–532.

Rutherford, Susan. "'La cantante delle passioni': Giuditta Pasta and the Idea of Operatic Performance." *Cambridge Opera Journal* 19 (2007): 107–38.

———. *The Prima Donna and Opera, 1815–1930*. Cambridge Studies in Opera. Cambridge: Cambridge University Press, 2006.

Sacks, Oliver. *The Man Who Mistook His Wife for a Hat and Other Clinical Tales*. New York: Touchstone, 1998.

Sappho. *Sweetbitter Love: Poems of Sappho*. Translated by Willis Barnstone. Boston and London: Shambhala, 2006.

Sedgwick, Eve Kosofsky. *Between Men: English Literature and Male Homosocial Desire*. 30th-anniversary ed. New York: Columbia University Press, 2015 [1985].

Sheehy, August, and Paul Steinbeck. "Introduction: Theorizing Improvisation (Musically)." *Music Theory Online* 19 (2013). www.mtosmt.org/issues/mto.13.19.2/toc.19.2.html.

Smart, Mary Ann. "In Praise of Convention: Formula and Experiment in Bellini's Self- Borrowings." *Journal of the American Musicological Society* 53 (2000): 25–68.

———. "The Lost Voice of Rosine Stoltz." *Cambridge Opera Journal* 6 (1994): 31–50.

———. *Mimomania: Music and Gesture in Nineteenth-Century Opera*. Berkeley: University of California Press, 2004.

———. "Roles, Reputations, Shadows: Singers at the Opéra, 1828–1849." In *The Cambridge Companion to Grand Opera*, edited by David Charlton, 108–28. Cambridge: Cambridge University Press, 2003.

———. "The Silencing of Lucia." *Cambridge Opera Journal* 4 (1992): 119–41.

———. "Verdi Sings Erminia Frezzolini." *Verdi Forum* 21 (1997): 13–22.

———. *Waiting for Verdi: Opera and Political Opinion in Nineteenth-Century Italy, 1815–1848*. Oakland: University of California Press, 2018.

Solis, Gabriel, and Bruno Nettl. *Musical Improvisation: Art, Education, Society*. Urbana and Chicago: University of Illinois Press, 2009.

Staël, Germaine de. *Corinne, or Italy*. Translated and edited by Sylvia Raphael. Introduction by John Isbell. New York: Oxford University Press, 1998.

Stendhal (Henri Beyle). *Life of Rossini*. Translated by Richard Coe. Seattle: University of Washington Press, 1972.

———. *Oeuvres Complet de Stendhal: Vie de Rossini*. Paris: Michel Lévy Frères, 1854. Accessed at https://archive.org/details/bub_gb_94IwOqYMPxwC/page/n3/mode/2up.

Stern, Kenneth A. "A Documentary Study of Giuditta Pasta on the Operatic Stage." PhD diss., City University of New York, 1983.

Toft, Robert. *Bel Canto: A Performer's Guide*. New York: Oxford University Press, 2013.

Trilling, James. *Ornament: A Modern Perspective*. Seattle: University of Washington Press, 2002.

Verri, Alessandro. *The Adventures of Sappho, Poetess of Mitylene. Translation from the Greek Original, Newly Discovered*, vol. 1. London: T. Cadell, 1789. Eighteenth-Century Collections Online. Gale. University of Rochester. Accessed 10 March 2020. http://find.gale.com.ezp.lib.rochester.edu/ecco/infomark.do?&source=gale&prodId=ECCO&userGroupName=nysl_ro_rochstru&tabID=T001&docID=CW116874743&type=multipage&contentSet=ECCO Articles&version=1.0&docLevel=FACSIMILE.

Vincent, Patrick H. *The Romantic Poetess: European Culture, Politics and Gender, 1820–1840*. Durham: University of New Hampshire Press, 2004.

Waddington, Patrick. "Pauline Viardot-Garcia as Berlioz's Counselor and Physician." *Musical Quarterly* 59 (1973): 382–98.

———. "Turgenev and Gounod: Rival Strangers in the Viardots' Country Nest (Part I)." *New Zealand Slavonic Journal* 2 (1976): 11–32.

Waiblinger, Wilhelm. "Rosa Taddei, unter den Arkadiern Licori Partenopea." In *Werke und Briefe*, edited by Hans Königer, vol. 3, 454–78. Stuttgart: Cotta, 1986.

Walton, Benjamin. " 'Quelque peu théâtral': The Operatic Coronation of Charles X." *Nineteenth Century Music* 26 (2002): 3–22.

Williams, Kate. *England's Mistress: The Infamous Life of Emma Hamilton*. New York: Ballantine, 2006.

Willson, Flora. "Classic Staging: Pauline Viardot and the 1859 *Orphée* Revival." *Cambridge Opera Journal* 22 (2010): 301–26.

Wood, Elizabeth. "Sapphonics." In *Queering the Pitch: The New Gay and Lesbian Musicology*, 2nd ed., edited by Philip Brett, Elizabeth Wood, and Gary C. Thomas, 27–66. New York: Routledge, 2006.

Yatromanolakis, Dimitrios. *Sappho in the Making: The Early Reception*. Hellenic Studies Series 28. Washington, DC: Center for Hellenic Studies, 2008. Accessed at https://chs.harvard.edu/CHS/article/display/6011.dimitrios-yatromanolakis-sappho-in-the-making-the-early-reception.

Zavadini, Guido. *Donizetti: Vita, Musiche, Epistolario*. Bergamo: Istituto Italiano d'Arti Grafiche, 1948.

Index